Meditative States in Tibetan Buddhism

MEDITATIVE STATES
in Tibetan Buddhism

Edited and annotated by
LEAH ZAHLER

Lati Rinbochay's Oral Presentation
of the Concentrations and Formless Absorptions
Translated by
JEFFREY HOPKINS

Paṇ-chen S̄ö-nam-drak-b̄a's "Explanation
of the Concentrations and Formless Absorptions"
Translated by
LEAH ZAHLER

Denma Lochö Rinbochay's Oral Commentary on
Paṇ-chen S̄ö-nam-drak-b̄a's "Explanation
of the Concentrations and Formless Absorptions"
Translated by
JEFFREY HOPKINS

Wisdom Publications • Boston

Wisdom Publications
199 Elm Street
Somerville, MA 02144 USA
www.wisdompubs.org

First published in 1983

Library of Congress Cataloging-in-Publication Data

Meditative States in Tibetan Buddhism / edited and annotated by Leah Zahler.
p. cm.
Includes bibliographical references and index
Contents: Lati Rinbochay's oral presentation / translated by Jeffrey Hopkins—Paṇ-chen Sö-nam-drak-ba's "Explanation of the concentrations and formless absorptions"/ translated by Leah Zahler—Denma Lo-chö Rinbochay's oral commentary / translated by Jeffrey Hopkins
ISBN 0-86171-119-X
1. Meditation—Dge-lugs-pa (Sect) 2. Dge-lugs-pa (Sect)—Doctrines I. Zahler, Leah II. Lati Rinbochay's oral presentation III. Bsod-nams-grags-pa, Paṇ-chen, 1478-1554. Phar phyin spyi don. IV. Denma Lochö Rinbochay's oral commentary.
BQ805.M43 1996
294.3'443—dc20

ISBN 0 86171-119-X

07 06 05 04 03
7 6 5 4 3

Cover art: *Cosmic Buddha Vairochana and Acolytes,* Central Tibet, 2nd half of 12th century, courtesy of the Cleveland Museum of Art, Mr. and Mrs. William H. Marlatt Fund.

Designed by: L·J·Sawlit

Typeset in the Garamond Font Family at Wisdom Publications

Wisdom Publications' books are printed on acid-free paper and meet the guidelines for permanence and durability of the Committee on Production Guidelines for Book Longevity of the Council on Library Resources.

Printed in Canada.

To my mother, Zella Zahler
and to the memory of my father, Carl Zahler,
with love, and with thanks
for their love and understanding.

May this work bring help to all sentient beings.

Contents

Acknowledgments

THIS WORK HAS BEEN made possible by the teaching and help of many people. I would like to thank Professor P. Jeffrey Hopkins of the University of Virginia Department of Religious Studies, my dissertation director and mentor throughout my graduate work at the University of Virginia, as well as Professor Paul Groner, also of the University of Virginia Department of Religious Studies, for his discerning questions as a member of both my master's and doctoral defense committees. I would also like to thank the late Richard B. Martin, former South Asia Bibliographer and Curator of the Tibetan Collection at Alderman Library, University of Virginia, as well as Paul G. Hackett, for helping me find Tibetan resources. My thanks go also to Wisdom's editors of both editions—Robina Courtin and Constance Miller, respectively—and to the copy editor of the present edition, Sara McClintock, for their many helpful suggestions.

For their help in the preparation of the first edition, I would like to thank Dr. Harvey B. Aronson, formerly of the University of Virginia Department of Religious Studies, for working with me on the Sanskrit texts of material quoted from Indian sources and for his encouragement, and Professor Joe B. Wilson, Jr., now of the University of North Carolina at Wilmington, who, as a graduate instructor at the University of Virginia, saw me through the initial steps of the translation. Thanks also go to Nancy Oettinger (now Gazelles), the typist of the original manuscript in the pre-Macintosh era, and to Bethany Preston, Elizabeth Napper, Jules Levinson, and Gareth Sparham for help in proofreading. Finally, I should like to thank all my teachers—above all, the late Ge-s̄hay Wangyal, whose kindness cannot be repaid.

—Leah Zahler

CHARTS

Technical Note

The transliteration of Tibetan in this work follows the system of Turrell Wylie (see "A Standard System of Tibetan Transcription," *Harvard Journal of Asiatic Studies* 22 [1959], 261–67). The phoneticization of Tibetan follows Jeffrey Hopkins' system of "essay phonetics" (see *Meditation on Emptiness* [London: Wisdom Publications, 1983], pp. 19–21), which represents current Lhasa (Hla-sa) pronunciation, including its tonal elements, in a form accessible to English-speaking readers. A macron (¯) over a letter indicates a high tone. Low tones are not indicated, since they are customary in English. Aspiration is also not indicated, since unvoiced consonants are usually aspirated in English.

The table below shows the difference between the Wylie transliteration and the Hopkins phoneticization. It includes only that part of Hopkins's phoneticization applicable to authors' names and the names of monasteries and monastic colleges and is not a complete guide to pronunciation.

Tibetan Phoneticization

W	H	W	H	W	H	W	H	
							unaffected by superscription or prefix	*affected by superscription or prefix*
ka	ḡa	kha	ka	ga	ga	nga	nga	n̄ga
ca	j̄a	cha	cha	ja	ja	nya	nya	n̄ya
ta	d̄a	tha	ta	da	da	na	na	n̄a
pa	b̄a	pha	pa	ba	ba	ma	ma	m̄a
tsa	d̄za	tsha	tsa	dza	dza	wa	wa	
zha	sha	za	sa	'a	a	ya	ya	
ra	ra	la	la	sha	s̄ha	sa	s̄a	

A subjoined *la* is pronounced *l̄a.*
The letters *ga* and *ba* are phoneticized as *k* and *p* in suffix position.
dbang is phoneticized as *w̄ang*; and *dbyang* as *ȳang.*

This table does not apply to transliterations from Sanskrit into Tibetan, such as the syllable *paṇ* in "Paṇ-chen"—representing a transliteration into

Tibetan of the first syllable of *paṇḍita*. In such cases, the original correspondence between the Tibetan and Sanskrit alphabets, indicated in Wylie's transliteration system from Tibetan into English, is retained. The table also does not apply to the names of contemporary Tibetans, such as Lati Rinbochay, who have developed other forms of their names for use in the West.

For Sanskrit, the standard transliteration is used throughout. Both *c* and *ch* are pronounced like the English *ch*. Both *ś* and *ṣ* are pronounced like the English *sh*.

Technical terms are listed in the Glossary along with their Tibetan and Sanskrit equivalents. An asterisk (*) is used to mark an unattested or hypothetical Sanskrit word. Tibetan and Sanskrit equivalents for technical terms are also provided in the body of the text to aid the reader. In such cases, the Tibetan term appears first, followed by the Sanskrit. This order is reversed in the case of titles of Indian textual sources.

In Paṇ-chen S̄ö-nam-drak-b̄a's text, as in Tibetan monastic textbooks in general, the sources of citations are identified only by a Tibetan short title. In the translation, these short titles are expanded to include the author's name, when it is known, and an English short title, without brackets.

Introduction
by Leah Zahler

THE GE-LUK PRESENTATION of the meditative states known as the four concentrations (*bsam gtan, dhyāna*) and the four formless absorptions (*gzugs med kyi snyoms 'jug, ārūpyasamāpatti*) acts as a point of intersection for many approaches to the study of meditation. Since the topic of the concentrations and formless absorptions includes a Buddhist perspective on Indian non-Buddhist systems of meditation and raises important issues concerning the meditator's motivation and goals, as well as the content of the various types of practice, one point of intersection is a comparison of Buddhist and Indian non-Buddhist systems of meditation. Another is an examination of three major types of Buddhist meditators—Hearers, Solitary Realizers, and Bodhisattvas—since the concentrations and formless absorptions are studied in the Ge-luk monastic curriculum in conjunction with the topic of Grounds and Paths (*sa lam, bhūmimārga*), and the latter topic provides a chronological overview of the development of Hearers, Solitary Realizers, and Bodhisattvas from their entrance into the path to their attainment of their respective goals.

The topic of the concentrations and formless absorptions also provides a point of intersection between the topic of the Perfections (*phar phyin, pāramitā*), of which it is a subtopic, and the Manifest Knowledge (*chos mngon pa, abhidharma*) sources that supply the details of the presentation. Within the study of Manifest Knowledge, it is a point of intersection for what Ge-luk-b̄a writers call the upper, or Mahāyāna (*theg chen*), and lower, or Hīnayāna (*theg dman*) Manifest Knowledges—represented respectively by Asaṅga's *Compendium of Manifest Knowledge* (*abhidharmasamuccaya, mngon pa kun btus*) and Vasubandhu's *Treasury of Manifest Knowledge* (*abhidharmakośa, chos mngon pa'i mdzod*).

More immediately, the topic of the concentrations and formless absorptions serves as a point of intersection between the Buddhist cosmology and the mental states that occur within it, and between scholarly and practical approaches to meditation. Thus, non-scholars approaching the topic for the first time can locate both their present mental state, on the one hand, and their aspirations and goals, on the other, in a comprehensive map of mental states, and they can also find, on that map, a layout of means for reaching their goals.

The Ge-luk presentation of the topic of the concentrations and formless absorptions is represented here in four forms—three of which are oral and one that is textual. The first, an extensive oral presentation of the topic drawing on various Tibetan and Indian sources, is an edited version of a series of lectures given by Lati Rinbochay at the University of Virginia in the fall of 1976 and translated by Jeffrey Hopkins. The second, a textual presentation, is a translation of a short text by Paṇ-chen Sö-nam-drak-b̄a (*paṇ chen bsod nams grags pa*, 1478–1554), textbook writer of Dre-b̄ung monastery's L̄o-s̄el-l̄ing College—the "Concentrations and Formless Absorptions" section of his *General Meaning of (Maitreya's) "Ornament for Clear Realization"* (*phar phyin spyi don*). The third presentation is Denma Lochö Rinbochay's oral commentary on that same text. The comments of a third contemporary Ge-luk-b̄a, the late Ge-s̄hay Gedün Lodrö, who gave a seminar on calm abiding at the University of Virginia in the spring semester of 1979, have been added in the notes for the sake of clarification or to indicate points of difference.[1] This, too, was an oral presentation.

The three lamas—Lati Rinbochay, Denma Lochö Rinbochay, and Ge-s̄hay Gedün Lodrö—were trained at different monastic colleges. Lati Rinbochay is from S̄har-d̄zay College of Gan-den monastic university and Denma Lochö Rinbochay is from L̄o-s̄el-l̄ing College of Dre-b̄ung monastic university, both of which use Paṇ-chen S̄ö-nam-drak-b̄a's text. Ge-s̄hay Gedün Lodrö was from Go-mang College of Dre-b̄ung, which uses the *Great Exposition of the Concentrations and Formless Absorptions* of Jam-ȳang-shay-b̄a (*'jam dbyangs bzhad pa*, 1648–1721) as its textbook. Thus, the three scholars represent diverse traditions of interpretation within the Ge-luk system. Yet, although they differ, often strongly, in their understandings of several points, all agree on the basic presentation, which is grounded in two works by D̄zong-ka-b̄a (*tsong kha pa blo bzang grags pa*, 1357–1419), the founder of the Ge-luk-b̄a order: D̄zong-ka-b̄a's early work on the Perfections, the *Golden Rosary of Good Explanation* (*legs bshad gser gyi phreng ba*) and a student's notes on lectures he gave late in his life, *Notes on the Concentrations and Formless Absorptions* (*bsam gzugs zin bris*).

D̄zong-ka-b̄a's presentations, and those of his followers, synthesize material from various Indian sources and reconcile differences among them. Although the concentrations and formless absorptions are studied as a subtopic in the topic of the Perfections, the details of the presentation, as was mentioned earlier, are filled in from Manifest Knowledge sources, especially Asaṅga's *Compendium of Manifest Knowledge* and Vasubandhu's *Treasury of Manifest Knowledge.*

To supplement the brief presentation of the concentrations and formless absorptions in Asaṅga's *Compendium of Manifest Knowledge*, Paṇ-chen S̄ö-nam-drak-b̄a, like D̄zong-ka-b̄a, quotes extensively from Asaṅga's *Grounds of Hearers* (*śrāvakabhūmi, nyan sa*) and, for certain points, also from Asaṅga's *Compendium of Ascertainments* (*viniścayasaṃgrahaṇī, gtan la dbab pa bsdu ba*). He also quotes from Maitreya's *Ornament for the Mahāyāna Sūtras* (*mahāyānasūtrālaṃkāra, mdo sde'i rgyan*) and from the *Sūtra Unraveling the Thought* (*saṃdhinirmocanasūtra, mdo sde dgongs 'grel*). Other sources for the

Ge-luk presentation, not quoted here, are Maitreya's *Differentiation of the Middle and the Extremes* (*madhyāntavibhaṅga, dbu mtha' rnam 'byed*); Bhāvaviveka's *Heart of the Middle* (*madhyamakahṛdaya, dbu ma snying po*) with the autocommentary on it, the *Blaze of Reasoning* (*tarkajvālā, rtog ge 'bar ba*); and Kamalaśīla's three texts called *Stages of Meditation* (*bhāvanākrama, sgom rim*).[2]

Like the topic of the Perfections as a whole, the subtopic of the concentrations and formless absorptions is taught in Ge-luk monastic universities from the point of view of the Yogācāra-Svātantrika-Mādhyamika school of tenets, considered to be the system of Maitreya's *Ornament for Clear Realization* (*abhisamayālaṃkāra, mngon rtogs rgyan*) and, according to Kensur Lekden, the general Mahāyāna position for presentations of the path.[3] Thus, for the most part, Paṇ-chen S̄ö-nam-drak-b̄a presents general Mahāyāna positions, as do Lati Rinbochay and Denma Lochö Rinbochay in their oral presentations. The latter two also refer at times to the positions of the Prāsaṅgika-Mādhyamika school of tenets when it is at variance with the general Mahāyāna position; Prāsaṅgika positions are presented more extensively by Gedün Lodrö, and by Jam-ȳang-shay-b̄a in the Go-mang College textbook literature he represents.

Much of this book consists of edited transcriptions of oral teachings. Lati Rinbochay gave original lectures drawing on many texts of different schools, whereas Denma Lochö Rinbochay was teaching and commenting on a specific text. In the introduction to *Path to the Middle*, an edited and annotated translation of Kensur Yeshey Tupden's oral teachings on Mādhyamika, Anne C. Klein observes that:

> Oral textual commentary is typically just as rigorous syntactically and conceptually as the text on which it is based. In giving it, the teacher draws on material from other texts which supplement, or are supplemented by, his own analyses developed over a lifetime. What chiefly distinguishes it from the explanations contained in texts are its responsiveness to questions asked, its reflection on a wider range of topics than any one text is likely to include, and the insertion of unique examples, often from the lives of teacher or student, to illustrate the teacher's points. In addition the Lama adds to the reading an aura of kindliness, humor, excitement, or severity, depending on his demeanor.[4]

Here, both Lati Rinbochay and Denma Lochö Rinbochay add background information assumed to be generally known in the traditional setting, such as Lati Rinbochay's detailed presentation of the afflictive emotions (*nyon mongs, kleśa*) and Denma Lochö Rinbochay's presentation of the four seals (*phyag rgya, mudrā*). They also have different personal styles of presentation.

Lati Rinbochay's exposition is tightly organized according to a systematic outline of the topics included, except when he chooses to depart from the outline for the sake of heightened dramatic effect. Although the general organization of Denma Lochö Rinbochay's presentation necessarily follows that of the text on which he is commenting, his personal style tends to be less formal and more associative than that of Lati Rinbochay.

According to Klein, both presentations in this book belong to the genre of oral commentary known as "textual commentary" (*gzhung khrid*), in which the text "serves as a basis for lectures by a teacher or, in more intimate circumstances, for a series of discussions between student and teacher." It is immediately obvious that Denma Lochö Rinbochay's contribution to this book belongs to that genre, since it is a commentary on Paṇ-chen S̄ö-nam-drak-b̄a's text; according to Klein, that text is a "meaning commentary" (*don 'grel*), which "does not comment on every word but expands on a text's central issues." She also identifies Lati Rinbochay's presentation as a "textual commentary," even though it draws on many texts.[5]

Lati Rinbochay's presentation, perhaps because it is not based on a specific text and was addressed to a general classroom audience, demonstrates the capacity of oral teaching to reach students of different levels. After a short general introduction to the Buddhist path, its teacher, and the range of Buddha's teachings, he states briefly that the presentation of the three realms and nine levels—the Buddhist cosmology—serves as a necessary background for an understanding of the concentrations and formless absorptions. That said, he works dramatically from the outside in and gives a moving description of cyclic existence (*'khor ba, saṃsāra*) starting at the bottom, so to speak, with graphic descriptions of the hells—the mental states farthest from meditative states. The nervous giggles of some of the undergraduates (those who did not temporarily absent themselves after the first lecture on the hells) testified to the vividness of the presentation. Continuing upward through the nine levels, he arrives finally at the rebirth states of the Form and Formless Realms that are the cosmological manifestation of the meditative states of the concentrations and formless absorptions, and from there he moves in toward the topic itself—the meditative states and their cultivation.

Similarly, in his presentation of those preparations for the concentrations and formless absorptions in which the meditator considers the grossness of the level to be surpassed and the peacefulness of the next-higher level, Lati Rinbochay collapses the strict categories of reasoning—the six investigations (*rtog pa, vitarka*)—for the sake of vividness in his description of the grossness of the Desire Realm, whereas Denma Lochö Rinbochay, commenting on a specific text to students of Tibetan, explains in detail the six investigations and how meditators use them to view the Desire Realm as gross.

Lati Rinbochay's oral presentation also allows him to weave into an exposition of a technical, scholarly topic related teachings suitable for beginning Buddhist practitioners. One such teaching is the extensive discussion of meditation on impermanence included in the presentation of the preparations having the aspect of the truths. Here, the vividness of the less formal presentation serves the deeper purpose of analytical meditation, which has not only an intellectual but also an emotional component.

Ge-luk presentations distinguish between two main types of meditation—stabilizing and analytical. Both are necessary for the complete development of the mind. In general, stabilizing meditation (*'jog sgom*) is the cultivation of calm abiding (*zhi gnas, śamatha*), and analytical meditation is the cultivation of special insight (*lhag mthong, vipaśyanā*). Stabilizing meditation—the focusing of the mind on a single object of observation (*dmigs pa, ālambana*)—is what Westerners commonly think of as meditation, but analytical meditation is less well known. The term covers various degrees of analysis. At the minimum, it involves following a specific line of thought without any obvious formal reasoning, as in the meditation on the importance of relying on a spiritual guide in the Fourth Paṇ-chen Lama's *Instructions on [Dzong-ka-ba's] "Three Principal Aspects of the Path"* (*lam gyi gtso bo rnam gsum gyi khrid yig*).[6] Individual analysis involves examining a topic point by point according to specific criteria, such as the six investigations mentioned earlier. In its full form, analytical meditation involves formal reasoning, which takes the form of an internal debate similar to the debates of Tibetan monks in the debating courtyards of their monastic colleges. The meditator uses syllogisms (*sbyor ba, prayoga*) to challenge his or her own previously unquestioned views or explores their absurd consequences (*thal 'gyur, prasaṅga*).

The term "analysis" in this context covers more than is commonly understood by that term in the West. Analytical meditation is not cerebral. Rather, it uses intellectual means to develop deep-seated conviction, which itself may have emotional elements. Of the meditation on the importance of relying on a spiritual guide, the Fourth Paṇ-chen Lama says, "Meditate thus until the hairs of the body rise and tears well from the eyes."[7] In the second of the preparations, the mental contemplation of individual knowledge of the character (*mtshan nyid so sor rig pa'i yid byed, lakṣaṇapratisaṃvedīmanaskāra*), the meditator develops a conviction that the levels being examined really are as he or she has determined by analysis; that is why the next preparation is called the mental contemplation arisen from belief (*mos pa las byung ba'i yid byed, adhimokṣikamanaskāra*).[8] In a meditation involving syllogistic reasoning, the goal is an inferential consciousness (*rjes dpag, anumāna*). Such a consciousness is not the process of reasoning but the result of that process. Although it is a conceptual consciousness (*rtog pa, kalpanā*), it is clear—so clear that someone unfamiliar with it could easily mistake it for direct perception (*mngon sum, pratyakṣa*). It is an incontrovertible (*mi slu ba, avisaṃvādin*) cognition. When one arrives at an inferential consciousness, the steps of the reasoning process that preceded it are no longer needed; one can let them go. This inferential consciousness is the actual inference; a spoken proof statement—and by extension, the use of such a proof statement in meditation—is called an inference only by a figure of speech designating the cause with the name of the effect.[9]

Thus, mere intellectual assent is not the goal of analytical meditation. Rather, analytical meditation assumes particular importance when there is a discrepancy between our intellectual position and our deeper assumptions. In such cases, intellectual assent comes easily, but conviction comes only with difficulty. For example, we all agree that we will die and that the things around us—compositional phenomena (*'dus byas, saṃskṛta*): products, things that are made, ourselves—are impermanent, but we act as though they will last forever. If we agree to meet a friend for lunch at a certain restaurant next Tuesday, we assume that we, the friend, and the restaurant will be there at that time. We do not consider that either person may die before Tuesday and would be surprised if either had to cancel the appointment or if the restaurant burned down. Making appointments is a worldly convention and can be accepted as such, but ordinarily we make appointments without the slightest shade of mental reservation concerning that convention.

This is the question to which Lati Rinbochay addresses himself in his discussion of meditation on impermanence. He presents the meditation at length because, although it can be used in the cultivation of special insight and in the preparations for the concentrations having the aspect of the truths, it is also an analytical meditation generally recommended for beginners. His presentation does not at first seem to be part of a process of formal reasoning because he does not state the underlying syllogism, "The subject, ____________, is impermanent because of being a conditioned phenomenon." (The subject can be any conditioned phenomenon, or product—for example, a light bulb; we are always surprised when they blow out. Sound is a traditional subject. This syllogism, with sound as the subject, was often used in debate with Indian non-Buddhist opponents who held that the sound of the Vedas is eternal.)

In the full proof, the meditator would have to establish both the presence of the reason, or sign (*rtags, liṅga*), in the subject (*chos can, dharmin*)—namely, that a light bulb, or sound, is a conditioned phenomenon—and the pervasion (*khyab pa, vyāpti*): "Whatever is a conditioned phenomenon is necessarily impermanent." What Lati Rinbochay is trying to establish is the pervasion. He does so by multiplying examples—citing various conditioned phenomena and showing that they are impermanent. If he could find a counterexample, there would be no pervasion (in other words, if there were a counterexample, then whatever was a conditioned phenomenon would not necessarily be impermanent). Thus, what appears in his presentation is a series of examples grouped under various headings. Although no human being can examine all the possible examples in the universe, a wide range of examples derived from common experience is considered sufficient, and if the examples are strong enough to carry conviction, so much the better. The development of the ability to do such analytical meditation, in conjunction with stabilizing meditation, is at the heart of Lati Rinbochay's teaching. Thus, Lati Rinbochay and Denma Lochö Rinbochay's oral teachings, as well as those of many other Tibetan teachers, provide an additional point of intersection: between the formal textual presentation of the monastic colleges and the active mental process, emotional as well as rational, that the listener and meditator needs for transforming that presentation into lived experience.

Part One

Lati Rinbochay's Oral Presentation of the Concentrations and Formless Absorptions

Edited by
Leah Zahler

Translated by
Jeffrey Hopkins

1

Opening Remarks

Today we are going to talk about how to live our lives. How should we live our lives? There are some people who mainly seek happiness and comfort in this life only and do not think at all about future lives. Among them, there are many types. There are those who are engaged in the means of achieving happiness and comfort in this lifetime and who succeed in achieving them. No matter how many houses they want, they are able to buy them; if they want to go somewhere, they are able to arrange the necessary transportation—plane, train, car, or whatever. They are able to obtain a mate and children according to their wish and are able, also according to their wish, to bring together the food, clothing, and important circumstances for living. There are indeed people who spend their lives in seeking only the happiness and comfort of this lifetime and who actually live in happiness and comfort, except for the unavoidable sufferings of aging, sickness, and death.

Then, too, among the people who seek happiness in this lifetime, there are also those who do not succeed and who live only in hardship, whether it be from the point of view of their house, their car, their food and clothing, or other circumstances. There are others who do not experience difficulty with these external concordant circumstances, such as house and car, but who suffer from sickness and thereby are caused to live in hardship. There are also people who do not have prosperity with respect to these external concordant circumstances but who nevertheless have an adequate amount.

Indeed, we could not explain all the many and different ways in which people choose to spend their lives, but among them, the most vast in thought is that of people who do not mainly seek happiness and comfort in this lifetime but are instead concerned with future lifetimes. The best among them are those who not only are concerned with future lifetimes but who give up most of their concern with this lifetime as well. Beneath them are those people who, even though they cannot entirely give up concern for happiness and comfort in this lifetime, are nonetheless primarily concerned with the future. Just below those two levels are people who are concerned equally with happiness and comfort in this and future lifetimes.

Those who are concerned only with happiness and comfort in this lifetime have the most limited thinking. From the point of view of religious practice, their thought is like that of a child. Nevertheless, among those who pay attention only to the happiness and comfort of this lifetime, those who succeed in the means of achieving happiness and comfort are better than those who do not. Even though, in terms of their not having any consideration for the future, their thought is limited, from the point of view of their succeeding within this lifetime, they are better. Those who not only do not consider future lifetimes but put all their attention on the happiness and comfort of this lifetime without achieving them have happiness and comfort in neither the future nor the present lifetime. Within this world, however, there are many people who do consider future lifetimes and who have determined that the achievement of happiness and comfort within this lifetime does not help the future.

The methods for achieving help in the future are called religious practice or religion—*dharma* in Sanskrit. There are many different religious systems in the world. All of them are good; all of them involve a vast thought that is directed toward the future. We could say that so-called religious systems that involve harming other sentient beings are not religious systems because a religious system must be a method for achieving health and happiness for oneself and others. Therefore, if the system involves techniques that harm oneself or others and it is called a religious system, then that is an incorrect identification; whereas any system involving techniques that help oneself and others now and in the future is a religious system. Such a system is to be valued even if it is not vast in the sense of being thoroughly altruistic.

Among the many religious systems in the world, I am today beginning an explanation of the Buddhist system. What is the Buddhist system? It was set forth by its teacher, its speaker—Buddha. What is the status of Buddha? Who is Buddha? He is not a being who was always a Buddha; he is not a being who independently from the beginning was a Buddha, who did not become a Buddha through causes (*rgyu, hetu*) and conditions (*rkyen, pratyaya*). First of all, he was, like us, a sentient being (*sems can, sattva*), a being with a mind,[1] possessed of faults, wandering in cyclic existence (*'khor ba, saṃsāra*).[2] Then he met with excellent teachers and gave up seeking happiness and comfort in his present lifetime.

What does renunciation of happiness and comfort in this lifetime mean? It means renouncing the type of thought that worldly beings have. What is the worldly mode of thought? Who is this worldly being? One who likes happiness and dislikes suffering; who likes material goods and dislikes not obtaining them; who likes to be praised and does not like to be blamed; who likes great fame and does not like disgrace.[3] The worldly being is one who thinks of nothing deeper than his own purposes until death.

Now, when Buddha met with excellent teachers, he gave up this type of thought. He came to discard his own welfare (*don, artha*) and to have concern for the welfare of others; and he cultivated love (*byams pa, maitri*) and compassion (*snying rje, karuṇā*), which served as the root for the special mind, the Bodhisattva attitude. Bodhisattva (*byang chub sems dpa'*) means "hero with respect to contemplating enlightenment (*byang chub, bodhi*)." Thus, he changed his original attitude of cherishing himself and discarding others to that of cherishing others and discarding his own welfare. He also meditated on emptiness (*stong pa nyid, śūnyatā*). Through cultivating in union the wisdom realizing emptiness and the special Bodhisattva attitude, the altruistic mind of enlightenment, and through accompanying these practices with the six perfections (*phar phyin, pāramitā*)—giving (*sbyin pa, dāna*), ethics (*tshul khrims, śīla*), patience (*bzod pa, kṣānti*), effort (*brtson grus, vīrya*), concentration (*bsam gtan, dhyāna*), and wisdom (*shes rab, prajñā*)—he ascended the five paths (*lam, mārga*)—the paths of accumulation (*tshogs lam, saṃbhāramārga*), preparation (*prayogamārga, sbyor lam*), seeing (*mthong lam, darśanamārga*), meditation (*sgom lam, bhāvanāmārga*), and no more learning (*mi slob lam, aśaikṣamārga*)—and the ten grounds (*sa, bhūmi*) and completed the collections of merit (*bsod nams, puṇya*) and exalted wisdom (*ye shes, jñāna*).[4] He was able to extinguish all faults in his own mental continuum (*rgyud, saṃtāna*) and to accomplish all auspicious attributes. He was able to achieve the wisdom that knows phenomena (*chos, dharma*) and their status, and when he did this, he became a Buddha. Thus, a Buddha is not someone who is produced causelessly; he is produced in dependence on causes.

Once he achieved enlightenment and became a Buddha, what did he do? He taught doctrines from his great sense of mercy toward his students. He set these forth not only from his own point of view but also in accordance with the types of people he was talking to, in accordance with their faculties (*dbang po, indriya*), powers, interests, and predispositions (*bag chags, vāsanā*). He set forth many different doctrines. For persons who were able to achieve enlightenment in one short lifetime, he set forth one type of doctrine.[5] For those who were not able to achieve enlightenment in our usual short lifetime, he set forth the means for extending the lifetime so that enlightenment could be achieved over one very long lifetime. And for those who were not able to achieve enlightenment in one lifetime, short or long, he set forth the means for achieving enlightenment over many aeons (*bskal pa, kalpa*).[6] For those who were not able to engage in the means of achieving Buddhahood itself, who were temporarily unable to aim for such a high attainment, he set forth the path of a Solitary Realizer (*rang sangs rgyas, pratyekabuddha*), and for those who were duller than Solitary Realizers, he set forth the path of a Hearer (*nyan thos, śrāvaka*).[7] Thus, for these two, he set forth a path for achieving liberation (*thar pa, vimokṣa*) from cyclic existence, and within this system, he set forth one type of teaching for those who were able to achieve liberation from cyclic existence in one lifetime. For those who were not, he set forth a path whereby they could achieve liberation from cyclic existence in several lifetimes. For those who could not achieve liberation from cyclic existence at all, he set forth the means for rebirth in a pure place.[8] And for those who were not able to do even that, he set forth a path that involves techniques whereby one would not be reborn in a bad lifetime.

Bad lifetimes—what are called bad transmigrations (*ngan 'gro, durgati*)—

are of three types. The lowest is that of hell beings (*dmyal ba, nāraka*). Above it, but still a bad transmigration, is that of hungry ghosts (*yi dvags, preta*). Above that, but still a bad transmigration, is that of animals (*dud 'gro, tiryañc*). We divide animals into two kinds, those that are scattered about the surface of the earth and those that are in the ocean. All of us have experienced with our own eyes the bad conditions and the suffering and pain of animals. Even worse are the bad conditions and sufferings of hungry ghosts. Not only can they not find food and drink; they cannot even hear the words "food" and "drink." People do not usually see hungry ghosts, but there are a few who do. Worse than hungry ghosts are the hell beings—one group of hell beings suffers mainly from heat and another suffers mainly from cold. People like us cannot see them; but those who, through meditation, develop the ability to create magical emanations can go to those places and observe them. There are other types of hells also—neighboring (*nye 'khor ba, utsada*) and trifling (*nyi tshe ba, prādeśika*) hells. In the past, there were many people who saw these.

One is born in all the levels of the Desire Realm through actions (*las, karma*). As a fruition of a great non-virtue (*mi dge ba, akuśala*), one is reborn in the hells. Through a middling non-virtue, one is reborn as a hungry ghost, and through a small non-virtue, one is reborn as an animal. Within these types, however, there are special causes.[9]

On this lowest type of path, Buddha set forth a means of overcoming the tendency to be reborn in these states, a path for being reborn in high status, or happy transmigrations (*bde 'gro, sugati*). These are the transmigrations of gods (*lha, deva*—these are temporary gods), demigods (*lha ma yin, asura*), and humans (*mi, manuṣya*). Why are these called high status? What does it mean to be high? It means to be higher than the three bad transmigrations. Through engaging in a small virtuous (*dge ba, kuśala*) action—maintaining ethics and, say, performing an act of giving—one can attain rebirth as a human. Through a middling type of virtue, one can attain rebirth as a demigod; and through a great virtue, one can attain rebirth as a god.

Furthermore, there are many divisions within the small virtuous actions through which one can be reborn as a human. Through the greatest of the smaller virtuous actions that one can perform, one can be reborn in a continent called Unpleasant Sound (*sgra mi nyan, kuru*) where humans live; through a little less virtue than that, one is reborn in a continent called Using Oxen (*ba lang spyod, godānīya*); through still less virtue, one is born in a continent called Great Body (*lus 'phags po, videha*); and below that, one is born in what is called Jambudvīpa (*'dzam bu gling*), our own world. (Jambudvīpa means "the Land of Jambu.") There are also eight subcontinents in which humans can take rebirth.

From the performance of the middling virtues, one is born as one of the four types of demigods. Through the greater virtues, one can be reborn as a god, and, again, there are many divisions. One group consists of the six types of gods of the Desire Realm (*'dod khams, kāmadhātu*). Through a higher type of virtuous practice—through cultivating the meditative absorptions (*snyoms 'jug, samāpatti*) that correspond to those realms—one can be reborn in the Form Realm (*gzugs khams, rūpadhātu*) or in the Formless Realm (*gzugs med khams, ārūpyadhātu*). Later, I will explain the various states within the Form Realm and Formless Realm in which one can be reborn through engaging in these meditative absorptions. Thus, there are three types of happy transmigration, three types of high status, possessing the physical life support of humans, demigods, or gods—and Buddha set forth a path for achieving such lifetimes.

Buddha also set forth means by which one would undergo less suffering even if one were reborn in any of the three bad transmigrations—means of purifying the non-virtuous actions that bring about great suffering. In brief, Buddha set forth many different techniques of paths for the achievement of virtue in accordance with the ability of a great variety of sentient beings. For the lowest, he set forth even the circumambulation of a temple or an image; and he taught the repetition of mantras and bowing down to images. These are very easy to achieve; anyone can do them. Thus, except for the fact that people may not wish to practice them, he set forth many and various means that accord with the many and various dispositions and abilities of people.

Among the limitless number of techniques that Buddha taught, I am here going to explain the meditative absorptions of the Form and Formless Realms. The reason for explaining them is that this presentation includes many types of meditation, among them the cultivation of calm abiding (*zhi gnas, śamatha*) and of special insight (*lhag mthong, vipaśyanā*). In Europe, and especially in America, there are many people nowadays who are paying attention to religious practice. Among them, there are many who are greatly interested in meditation. Thus, I thought that if this system were explained, you would understand many facets of the topic of meditation and that this would be helpful.

2

Cyclic Existence

The four concentrations (*bsam gtan, dhyāna*)—that is, the four meditative absorptions (*snyoms 'jug, samāpatti*) of the Form Realm—and the four formless absorptions (*gzugs med, ārūpya*) of the Formless Realm cannot be explained out of context. Just as to drive a car or a train one needs an appropriate place to drive it—the road or the railroad tracks have to be laid—and just as to engage in a sport one needs a smooth playing field, similarly, to explain the form and formless meditative absorptions, we must first explain the three realms and the nine levels. If we know the presentation of the three realms and the nine levels, we can easily understand the presentation of the form and formless meditative absorptions.

From another point of view also, since we are people who are going to die and be reborn and since there may be some who want to know the various ways in which we can be reborn, this presentation will identify those conditions. What are the good ways in which we can be reborn? What are the bad ways? What are the causes of being reborn in these ways? Through this presentation, we can understand that information clearly. Also, those who do not believe that there is any rebirth will understand the many different types of lives other than our own. Thus, there is great virtue in presenting this topic, and although I touched on it earlier, I will speak on it somewhat more extensively now.

The three realms (*khams gsum, tridhātu*) are the Desire Realm, the Form Realm, and the Formless Realm.

The Desire Realm

What are the levels within the Desire Realm? They are those of hell beings, hungry ghosts, animals, humans, demigods, and the gods of the Desire Realm. These are the six different types of beings in the Desire Realm. They are called beings of the Desire Realm because they have desire for the five types of objects of desire—visible forms (*gzugs, rūpa*), sounds (*sgra, śabda*), odors (*dri, gandha*), tastes (*ro, rasa*), and tangible objects (*reg bya, spraṣṭavya*). We are attracted to pleasant visible forms—pleasant colors (*kha dog, varṇa*) and shapes (*dbyibs, saṃsthāna*); and we dislike unpleasant visible forms—unpleasant colors and shapes. Once we are attracted to pleasant forms, we seek them. The same is true of sounds; they can also be divided into pleasant and unpleasant. Once we are attracted to pleasant sounds, we seek them. Odors can also be classified as pleasant and unpleasant, and once we are attached to pleasant odors, we seek them. The same is true of tastes. We can divide them into the delicious and the not delicious, or the pleasant and the unpleasant, and, being attached to the delicious, we seek it. In a similar way, even though there are many types of tangible objects—smooth, rough, and so forth—we can divide them into the pleasant and unpleasant, and because of attachment to the pleasant, we seek pleasant tangible objects.

We cannot say that specific forms are necessarily pleasant; it is within our own thought that we make them pleasant, and, once we do that, we become attached to them. For example, with regard to the form of someone's body, one person may find it pleasant, whereas another person may find it unpleasant. We engage in desire or attachment based on our own individual estimation of what is pleasant; we cannot say definitively that certain things are pleasant and that others are unpleasant. The same is true of pleasant and unpleasant sounds, and of fragrant and unfragrant odors: some find certain odors fragrant that others find unfragrant. The same is true of tastes: if we prepare a meal, some will find it delicious, whereas others will not. There are some who like sweet things and some who like sour. Some people like hot tastes, such as the taste of hot pepper. Some people like smooth tangible objects; some like rough tangible objects. These preferences accord with one's own wish and interest. For example, with respect to colors, some prefer white, some red, and others blue, and we choose clothing accordingly.

Another explanation of the term Desire Realm is on the basis of union, that is, of how one is satisfied. There are four types of satisfaction. The first is the union of the male and female organs. Hell beings, hungry ghosts, animals, humans, demigods, and the first two of the six types of gods of the Desire Realm gain satisfaction in this way. The next type of satisfaction is through embracing or holding hands. Among the gods of the Desire Realm, the third type is satisfied merely through embracing; the fourth is satisfied merely through holding hands. The fifth type of Desire Realm god is satisfied merely through smiling at another god and through laughing; and the sixth type is satisfied merely through looking at another god: through merely a mutual gaze, bliss is generated in each person's mind, and it is satisfying. For humans, however, all of these methods are needed. We have to look at each other, laugh, hold hands and embrace, and copulate. If we do not have them all, we are not satisfied. Beings who have desire for any of these four types of union are called beings of the Desire Realm.

Hell Beings

Within the three realms and within the Desire Realm itself, hell beings have the greatest suffering. There are some hells in which the beings suffer from heat and others in which they suffer from cold. There are also neighboring (*nye 'khor ba, utsada*) and trifling (*nyi tshe ba, prādeśika*) hells.

A human who is about to be reborn in one of the hot hells knows that he or she will be reborn there. As such a human is about to die, he or she experiences great cold, and, because of the power of former actions, at the time of death desire for heat acts as a cause for rebirth in a hot hell. The reverse is true for rebirth in the cold hells.

The hot hells. In the hot hells, the land itself is composed of burning iron. There are eight different areas within the hot hells, but all of them are the same in that the land itself is composed of burning iron.

The first of the hot hells is called the Reviving (*yang sros, saṃjīva*). If you are born in the Reviving Hell, you are harmed only by the other beings born there. These hell beings all have weapons in their hands and are attacking and wounding one another. After being wounded, you swoon; it is as though you were killed, but then a voice from the sky says, "Revive!" and all the beings begin attacking and wounding one another once again.

How many years does a being stay in such a place? If fifty human years were a day, and thirty of these were a month, and twelve of those were a year, five hundred of those years would be one day in this hell, and one would live there five hundred years of such days. This is the general type of lifespan in this hell, but there are beings who die before their time; sometimes, if his or her former family and friends engage in a great deal of virtue, it is possible for the lifespan of a person who has been reborn there to be shortened.

Below the Reviving Hell is the hot hell called Black Line (*thig nag, kālasūtra*). There, there are workers who harm you, but these workers are produced by your own former actions. Just as a carpenter has a ruler with which he measures boards, so the workers there have a measuring stick that makes a black line on your body. Having drawn their lines, they take a saw and cut your body with it. Because the measuring stick itself is made of burning iron, it makes a wound, and the saw, too, is made of burning iron. (Factories, it seems, are like the Black Line Hell, but in a factory what is being cut up is steel or wood, whereas in this hell it is the bodies of the hell beings themselves.)

In the Black Line Hell, one hundred human years are a day, thirty of those are a month, and twelve of those are a year. A thousand such years are one day in the Black Line Hell, and a being lives there for one thousand years of such days.

The hell below that is called the Crushed Together (*'dus 'joms, saṃghāta*). Again, the land and the mountains are made of burning iron. The mountains come together like the heads of two goats or two sheep and crush the beings. Then, according to your own past actions, the mountains separate; when they separate, you again revive. The main cause of rebirth in this hell is murder. Someone who kills sheep is crushed between mountains the shape of sheep heads; someone who kills goats is crushed between mountains the shape of goat heads; someone who kills humans is crushed between mountains the shape of human heads.

In the Crushed Together Hell, two hundred human years are a day, thirty of those are a month, and twelve of those a year. Two thousand such years are one day in the Crushed Together Hell, and the lifespan is two thousand years of such days. But, again, there are cases of dying before one's time.

The fourth hell is the Crying (*ngu 'bod, raurava*). If you are reborn there, you find yourself alone in a land of burning iron, without family or friends. Arriving there, you are in great fear and seek to escape. Then you see a house in the distance; you run up to and into it, and the doors close of themselves. The house is made of burning iron. There is no way of getting out; you are stuck inside that house of burning iron. Therefore, you start to cry, and you stay there crying, calling the names of your father, mother, friends. Because the beings in this hell are crying, it is called the Crying Hell.

Here, four hundred human years equal a day, thirty of those are a month, twelve of those equal a year. Four thousand such years are one day in the Crying Hell, and the lifespan is four thousand years of such days. Again, there are cases of dying before one's time. In general, it takes a great non-virtue to be born there, but the special cause is to drink or serve a great deal of alcohol.

Below the Crying Hell is the hell called the Great Crying (*ngu 'bod chen po, mahāraurava*). There, too, the entire area is made of burning iron. Those who are reborn in this hell have the same type of fear as those in the Crying Hell. They are all alone and want to escape. Then, in the distance, they see a pleasant house and run into it. The door closes behind them, as in the Crying Hell, and when they have entered the house, it bursts into flame. It is a double house, one inside the other, whereas the house in the Crying Hell is only a single structure. Thus, with two sets of walls burning, it is all the hotter. Since they are suffering greatly, they are crying greatly; therefore, this hell is called the Great Crying.

What is the lifespan in this hell? Here, eight hundred human years equal a day, thirty of those are a month, and twelve of those equal a year. Eight thousand such years are one day in the Great Crying Hell, and eight thousand years of such days are the lifespan. Again, there are cases of dying before one's time.

The hell below that is called the Hot (*tsha ba, tāpana*). There, there is a big kettle, the size of the University of Virginia, containing boiling molten metal. The workers in this hell pick up the beings and cast them into the pot, much as we might fry meat. When they are boiled until there is only bone left, the workers take them out of the pot again. At that time, there is a cool breeze, and the beings revive. Then they are thrown back into the molten iron.

In this hell, sixteen hundred years equal a day, thirty such days are a month, and twelve such months equal a year. Sixteen thousand such years are one day in the Hot Hell, and one lives there for sixteen thousand years of such days. Again, there are cases of dying before one's time.

Below that is the hell called the Very Hot (*rab tu tsha ba, pratāpana*). The name is an understatement. Here, the kettle is even larger than in the Hot Hell; the molten metal and the fire below it are even hotter, and, as before, you are thrown into the fire and boiled. You are boiled again and again. What, then, is the difference between this hell and the Hot Hell? The difference is that here there are burning rods of iron wrapped around your body and pitchforks that run up through your heels and anus. These are just a few of the many different types of suffering here; I am explaining only the main types.

The lifespan of the Very Hot Hell is said to be half an intermediate aeon (*bar bskal, antaḥkalpa*). It would be too complicated to fully explain how long half an intermediate aeon is. If you dug a ditch that measured five hundred cubits on each side, and if you cut hair into fine pieces, and if, every hundred years, you took a little of the hair and threw it into the ditch, one intermediate aeon would be the length of time it would take to fill the ditch. Half of that time is half an intermediate aeon.

Below the Very Hot Hell is the last of the hot hells, which is called the Most Torturous (*mnar med, avīci*). It is so called because there is no time when you are not being tortured; you are being tortured continuously. Again, the area is made of burning iron. When you are born there, a fire begins immediately in the distance, on all sides, and comes together in the middle, where you yourself are. Except for your voice in the fire, no one would know that there is any sentient being in it. You become like fire, but there is a voice in the fire.

This is the worst type of physical suffering in cyclic existence. The lifespan of a being in the Most Torturous Hell is one intermediate aeon.

The neighboring hells. The eight hot hells are arranged on top of each other, and each of them, in each of its corners, has four neighboring hells, making sixteen times eight. Each group of four is the same, and all four groups are the same for each hell. Thus, if one understands the neighboring hells with respect to one hell, one understands them with respect to the others. Take, for example, someone who has been born in the Most Torturous Hell. The action that caused you to be reborn in that hell is about to be exhausted. You have the impression that you are leaving and feel relieved, but, no matter which direction you leave from, you have to pass through the four neighboring hells.

The first neighboring hell is called Burning Ashes (*me ma mur, kukūla*). You swoon and stay in the burning ashes as long as the power of the action that caused you to be there remains.

When the force of that action begins to be exhausted, you again revive and think you are leaving, but find yourself in the area called the Mud of Corpses (*ro myags, kuṇapa*)—mud with a great many rotten corpses in it. You sink into this corpse-mud up to your throat. There is a strong stench because of the filth. You swoon in the mud, and bugs with iron teeth gnaw on your body. You can stay there in such a condition for, say, a hundred thousand human years—as long as the force of the action that impelled you into such a situation remains.

Upon revival, you again think you are leaving, but then you arrive at a plain called the Plain of Razors (*spu gri gtams pa'i lam po che, kṣuramārga*). Just as, in the area around us today, there are fields of grass, so there is grass there also, but the grass in that plain is made of razor blades. You run on it, and the grass cuts as you put your foot down; but as you lift your foot, it is healed. You run for a long time but cannot get out; you stay there, running, hoping to get out but staying, perhaps for a hundred thousand human years—as long as the force of the action that impelled you into that place remains.

Next you arrive at a place called the Grove of Swords (*ral gri lo ma'i nags tshal, asipattravana*). In this grove, there are weapons instead of leaves, and they fall on your body as you enter and cut it into pieces. Just as in America there are dogs with sharp teeth, so there, in addition to the falling weapons, there are dogs that attack and bite, and you stay there until the force of the action that impelled you into that situation is consumed.

Then you arrive at the Iron Grater (*lcags kyi shing shal ma li, ayaḥśālmalī-vana*), which is like a tree trunk or pedestal made of iron. On top of this iron structure are your parents or a good friend. As you climb toward them, your body is grated, and when you arrive at the top, no one is there. Then a bird with an iron beak pecks out your brain. Suffering there, you look down and see a friend at the bottom saying, "Come down here!" You climb down, through the same kind of suffering, again. You climb up and down as long as the force of your own past action remains.

Afterward, you again seek to escape. Then you arrive at a river called the Extremely Hot River (*chu bo rab med, nadī vaitaraṇī*). Just as vegetables are thrown into boiling water, so you are thrown into this boiling river, and you stay there, swimming, until the force of your action is consumed. This river, the Iron Grater, and the Grove of Swords are counted together as the fourth neighboring hell.

The cold hells. The cold hells themselves are snowy mountains, and the lands around them are all made of ice. There is no illumination, as from sun or moon, and it is so dark that you cannot see your hand. There is no way to become warm. There is no such thing as fire; there are no such things as a bed or clothing or hot food. Snow is falling, and there are snow storms.

In the cold wind, without clothes, you get very chilled, and blisters form on your body. Thus, the first cold hell is called Blistering (*chu bur can, arbuda*). How long do you live there? In India there is a city called Magadha where they use a certain measure the size of three or four pecks. If twenty of these were a bushel, and if you had a storeroom that was able to hold eighty bushels, and if, every hundred years, you took a single sesame seed and began to fill the storeroom, the time it would take to fill the storeroom would be the lifespan of the Blistering Hell. (For the other cold hells, the lifespan in each is twenty times that in the hell above it.)

Below the Blistering Hell is the second cold hell, called Bursting Blisters (*chu bur rdol ba can, nirarbuda*). It is colder than the first, and the blisters that were produced before are now breaking open. Then horrible mosquitoes attack you, and blood and pus ooze from the wounds. There are also plagues in this hell. Thus, you suffer from cold, from the horrible mosquitoes, and from plague.

The next cold hell is called the Groaning or the Hahava Hell (*a chu zer ba, hahava*) because you are so cold that you make a sound like *ha ha va.* (In America you probably make a different sound when you get very cold.) This hell is colder than the first two and has mosquitoes and plagues as well.

The next hell is called Moaning (*kyi hud zer ba, huhuva*). It is even colder than the last, and you want to say ha ha va, as before, but you cannot; there is just the voice coming up from the middle of your throat.

The next hell is called Chattering (*so tham tham pa, aṭaṭa*).[1] It is so cold that your teeth are chattering. They are as though held together; you cannot open your mouth. Something similar happened to some Tibetans who went to India a while ago to do some trading. They arrived with their mules at a broad plain where it was snowing and very cold. People were dying standing up. One of them seemed to be grinning. His friend said, "Stop laughing and hurry up," but he was not laughing; he was dying.

The next hell is even colder, and your body begins to split from the cold. This hell is called Split like an Utpala (*utpala ltar gas pa, utpala*). (The utpala is a blue lotus.) As your body splits, it makes a noise like screaming. Just as, when wood splits in the heat of the sun, it makes a noise, so your body makes a noise. The split-off pieces are about the size of an utpala petal.

Below that is the hell called Split like a Lotus (*padma ltar gas pa, padma*). There, the split-off pieces are even finer. It, too, is cold, and there are mosquitoes and plague.

The last level is the coldest. It is called Split like a Great Lotus (*padma chen po ltar gas pa, mahāpadma*). This is the worst suffering in the cold hells.

In general, rebirth in one of these cold hells is the result of a great nonvirtue. The special cause of one's being reborn in such a place is to remove the offerings of cloth around holy images or clothing from one's parents or from someone who is undergoing suffering. In Tibet and India, there are thieves who steal clothing from travelers along the highway; if you have performed such an action, it serves as a cause for being reborn in a cold hell. (There do not appear to be such thieves in this country.) If you have carried off your parents or other people to a cold place and left them there, or if you were an official and left the people over whom you had power in a cold place, such actions would serve as a cause of rebirth in a cold hell. Putting lice or other insects in cold water or in another cold place would also serve as a cause of rebirth in a cold hell.

The trifling hells. There are trifling hells in the ocean. It is sometimes very difficult to distinguish between a being in a trifling hell and an animal. There are also trifling hells in which humans live. These are cases of people who have engaged in non-virtuous deeds only during the day and then suffer for them during the day in a trifling hell but are comfortable at night, or of people who have engaged in non-virtues during the night and therefore undergo great suffering at night but not during the day. For example, there was a group of monks with the previous Buddha, whose name was Kāśyapa. These monks had fought during their noon meal. In the Buddhist cosmology, the ocean extends on all sides, and then there are empty places; these monks were reborn in one of the empty places. They had a good assembly hall and appeared to be good monks. At night they were comfortable. In the morning they were comfortable. At noon, their mealtime, they were suddenly in the Reviving Hell; they had weapons in their hands and they began to attack one another. Then, in the afternoon, they were comfortable again.

In order for the hells to appear to your minds, I have explained them as if they were beneath the earth, one on top of the other. However, for someone who commits a great non-virtue, a hot hell or a cold hell appears right in the place of death in accordance with the action that was committed; at that very point, the whole realm is produced. We should not consider the hot and cold hells to be places like Europe, to which one would have to travel.

Hungry Ghosts

It is said that the abode of the hungry ghosts is to the south, within our own world. They are born in a place called the Yellowish. There are three different types of hungry ghosts; all three have obstructions. The first type has external obstructions; the second has internal obstructions; and the third has obstructions with regard to food and drink.

In what kind of environment do hungry ghosts live, and what kind of beings are they? Unlike our human world, their world has no green grass, no trees, no water; it is just sand. The plains and mountains are all made of

Place
Stamp
Here

WISDOM
PUBLICATIONS

199 Elm Street • Somerville MA 02144 USA

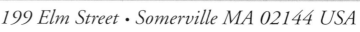

sand. The beings themselves have very large stomachs and weak, thin arms and legs. Their shape is displeasing. Because they have difficulty finding any kind of drink, their bodies have no blood or lymph. Thus, their bodies are like dry trees over which dry skin has been stretched. When their thin, emaciated legs bump against each other, they make a dry, percussive sound, and when their legs rub against each other, they give off sparks.

Those that have external obstructions. When hungry ghosts that have external obstructions look in the distance, they see such things as groves of fruit trees and large lakes. Thinking that there is food and drink in the distance, they run toward the trees and lakes, but they have great difficulty running. When they arrive, the fruit trees become dry and barren, and the lakes turn into beaches. Even if the trees do not become dry and barren, they are guarded by fierce protectors. Thus, when the hungry ghosts reach these various types of food and drink, they cannot partake of them. They are afraid of the protectors. Because they have come a long distance and have weak bodies, they are very tired, and there are no resources they can make use of once they arrive. Thus, physically and mentally, they have great suffering.

Those that have internal obstructions. Hungry ghosts that have internal obstructions often have knots tied in their necks; some even have three knots. Some have mouths that are only the size of the eye of a needle. Some have throats that are only the size of the eye of a needle. Some have huge goiters on their necks. Some have fire burning in their mouths. Thus, because of their internal obstructions, even if they arrive at a place that has food and drink, they cannot eat or drink anything.

Those that have obstructions with regard to food and drink. For some hungry ghosts that have obstructions with regard to food and drink, any food or drink they obtain changes in their mouths into husks of wheat or filth. Others, when they bring food or drink to their mouths, find themselves eating their own flesh. For still others, food or drink changes in their mouths into pellets of burning iron or into molten bronze. Thus, even when they manage to find resources, they not only do not have physical happiness; they have great physical suffering. When the sun shines on them in winter, they become very cold, and when moonlight touches them in summer they become even hotter; thus, they must undergo limitless suffering of heat and cold. Not only can they not find food and drink; sometimes they can spend a hundred years without even hearing the words "food" and "drink," and they spend all their time thinking about food and drink. When we get very hungry and thirsty, we, too, think about food and drink; humans usually remain hungry or thirsty for a few hours, but hungry ghosts remain hungry or thirsty for hundreds of years.

One human month is a day for a hungry ghost, thirty of those are a month, twelve of those are a year. Five hundred such years are the lifespan of a hungry ghost.

Because there are many ways in which we engage in actions and thereby accumulate predispositions, there are many types of hungry ghosts. Mainly, we are reborn as hungry ghosts through engaging in middling non-virtues. Moreover, one of the main causes of rebirth as a hungry ghost is miserliness. If we spend our lives not using our resources for either others' benefit or our own, this miserliness acts as a cause of rebirth as a hungry ghost.

Animals

Animals are of two types—those that live in the depths of the oceans and those that are scattered about the surface of the earth.

Those that live in the depths. Animals of the first type live at the depths of the ocean, where there are no humans. At the depths of the ocean, it is very dark and gloomy, without even the appearance of sun and moon. It is also very cold—there is no way for the animals that live there to become warm. They are piled up like rice inside a storeroom; those on the bottom can hardly breathe. Because they are piled up in this way, they have to eat the being closest to them; they have no chance to seek food elsewhere or to have any other type of food. Thus, they undergo various kinds of suffering—the suffering of cold, and sometimes as a result of previous actions, the suffering of heat, as well as the great difficulty of the way in which they live, crushed one on top of the other.

Those that are scattered about the surface. Animals of the second type are those that we see scattered about the lands in which humans live. They undergo several types of suffering. One type is ignorance or obscuration; a sheep, for example, does not know whether a person is leading it to pasture or to slaughter. Most of the animals that live among humans also undergo the suffering of being used for human purposes. In the United States, dogs are treated well, but most animals have great suffering; for example, consider how horses are used. Indeed, the animals that undergo the worst suffering are those of my own land, Tibet. We use oxen, horses, and yaks. When they are able to work, people work them hard, and when they are no longer able to work, people kill them. Because there are good farm machines in the United States, I doubt whether there is that much suffering for farm animals. Insects undergo still another type of suffering; the reason that they are always flying or crawling around and do not stay still is that they are always looking for food.

The lifespan of animals is indefinite. The longest would be one intermediate aeon. The lesser animals may have lifespans of ten years or even a few days.

Humans

The four continents and eight subcontinents. Among humans there are twelve different types—those of the four continents (*gling, dvīpa*) and those of the eight subcontinents (*gling phran*). Though this system is set forth, it is not clear whether it describes something that existed previously and can no longer be seen or whether the four continents and eight subcontinents cannot be seen with the ordinary eye at all.

The four continents are set around a central mountain, Mount Meru, which is said to be north of our own continent. To the east of Mount Meru is the continent Great Body (*lus 'phags po, videha*); to the south, our own continent—Jambudvīpa (*'dzam bu gling*), the Land of Jambu; to the west, the continent called Using Oxen (*ba lang spyod, godānīya*); and to the north, Unpleasant Sound (*sgra mi nyan, kuru*).

The eastern continent is called Great Body for several reasons. One is that the land itself is higher than that of the other three continents. In India there is a tree called tāla; the land of the eastern continent is seven times as high as a tāla tree. Another reason is that the bodies of the people in the eastern continent are twice as large as those of the people in our own. Furthermore, the people of the eastern continent live for two hundred and fifty years; thus, they also exceed those of our own continent from the point of view of their lifespan.

Our own continent is called the Land of Jambu because of Lake Mānasarovara (*yid kyi mtsho*) near India. On the shore of that lake is a large jambu tree; when its fruit falls into the lake, it makes a noise like *jam, jam.* A particular kind of dragon lives in that lake. Most of the fruit that falls into the lake is eaten by the dragons, and that which is not eaten turns into a type of gold called the watery gold of Jambu, which is not found anywhere else.

The height of an average human being in the Land of Jambu is four cubits. There is no certainty with regard to lifespan; originally, however, it was inestimable. ("Inestimable" is a specific length of time.) Then the lifespan began to shrink; nowadays, the lifespan is usually a hundred years at most, and it will decrease until the average lifespan is ten years. The special feature of our continent is a wish-granting tree; it is such that if we make any sort of wish to it we will receive whatever we wish.

The western continent is called Using Oxen. Its people are, on the average, sixteen cubits tall, and their average lifespan is five hundred years. The special feature of this continent is the wish-granting cow, which gives people whatever they want.

To the north of Mount Meru is the continent called Unpleasant Sound. The people have an average height of thirty-two cubits and live for a thousand years. It is said that their lifespan is definite; there is no untimely death in that land. This continent is called Unpleasant Sound because the people speak a language like that of evil spirits—a very rough language. From another point of view, it is called Unpleasant Sound because, seven days before they die, the people hear an unpleasant sound, a sound that informs them of their death.

Each of these continents has subcontinents, like islands, on either side. They are called the eight subcontinents.

Division from the point of view of sex. If humans are divided from another point of view, there are males (*skyes pa, puruṣa*), females (*bud med, strī*), the neuter (*za ma, ṣaṇḍha*), the impotent, and the androgynous (*mtshan gnyis pa, ubhayavyañjana*).[2] In general, there is no point in talking about these, but they are relevant to our subject of the eight meditative absorptions. Everyone knows what males and females are. Neuter human beings have neither male nor female organs. Either they are born without such organs or they lose their organs through sickness, through the application of medicine, or through the organs' being cut off by a weapon. There are two types of impotent humans—male and female. Someone who has the signs, the organs, of a male but does not have the capacity of a male is called an impotent male. There are some types of impotent males who are not necessarily without the capacity at all times; sometimes they have the capacity. An impotent female externally looks like a female; she has the organs but not the capacity of a female. There are also impotent females who sometimes have the capacity and sometimes do not. Androgynous human beings have both male and female organs.

Demigods

The demigods live at the base of Mount Meru. They have four different lands. The first is called Having Light. The second is called Moonlight. The third is called Good Land. The fourth is called Unmoving.[3] The central mountain comes down into the ocean, and the demigods live under the ocean, on the mountain. They are called demigods because they are similar to gods. There are two ways of presenting them; some people include them among gods, whereas others include them among animals. Those who include them among gods do so because the appearance and behavior of demigods is similar to those of gods. From the religious point of view, they can be included among animals, although they are not actually animals.

Gods

Above the demigods are the six types of gods of the Desire Realm. They are called the Four Great Royal Lineages (*rgyal chen rigs bzhi, cāturmahārājakāyika*), the Thirty-three (*sum cu rtsa gsum, trayastriṃśa*), Without Combat (*'thab bral, yāma*), the Joyous (*dga' ldan, tuṣita*), Enjoying Emanation (*'phrul dga', nirmāṇarati*), and Controlling Others' Emanations (*gzhan phrul dbang byed, paranirmitavaśavartin*).

The Land of the Four Great Royal Lineages. The Land of the Four Great Royal Lineages is the abode of the Four Great Kings, from which the land gets its name. The gods of this land have a height of one hundred and twenty-five fathoms. In this land, fifty human years are a day, thirty of those are a month, and twelve of those are a year. Five hundred such years are the lifespan of a being in the Four Great Royal Lineages. Thus, the lifespan is equivalent to one day in the life of the Reviving Hell.

The Land of the Thirty-three. Above them on Mount Meru is the Land of the Thirty-three. In the middle is the king of the gods, Indra, and around him, like cabinet ministers, are thirty-three main beings. Therefore, the land is called the Land of the Thirty-three. Two hundred and fifty fathoms is the height of the beings there. A hundred human years are a day in that land, thirty of those are a month, and twelve of those are a year. The beings there live for a thousand such years. Thus, their lifespan is like one day in the lifespan of a being in the Black Line Hell. As we have said, they engage in the deeds of desire just as humans do. However, unlike humans, they do not have any semen, only an energy that is transmitted.

The Land Without Combat. The third land is called Without Combat because the gods there do not have to fight the demigods. Below it, however, in the Land of the Four Great Royal Lineages and the Land of the Thirty-three, the gods engage in a great deal of fighting because the demigods are jealous of the gods' great prosperity and of the ambrosia of which the gods partake. They also fight over a wish-granting tree that has its roots in the land of the demigods but bears fruit in the lands of the gods. Furthermore, the female demigods are beautiful, and the gods take them away. Thus, in the lands of the Four Great Royal Lineages and of the Thirty-three, the gods have to engage in battle with the demigods, but in the Land Without Combat they do not.

The first two lands are on Mount Meru, above the demigods, but the Land Without Combat and those above it float in space, above the mountain.

In the Land Without Combat, the gods are three hundred and seventy-five fathoms tall. Two hundred human years are one day, thirty of those are a month, and twelve of those equal a year. The lifespan of the beings there is two thousand such years. Thus, the lifespan is like one day in the Crushed Together Hell.

The Joyous Land. The fourth land is called the Joyous because Maitreya, the next Buddha, lives there and continually sets forth the teaching of the Mahāyāna, the Great Vehicle.[4] Thus, this place has the joy of religious doctrine. It is also called the Undaunted. The gods of that land are five hundred fathoms tall. Four hundred human years are one day in their life, thirty of those are a month, and twelve of those equal a year. The beings there live for four thousand such years. Thus, their lifespan is one day of the lifespan of a person in the Crying Hell.

The Land of Enjoying Emanation. The next land is called Enjoying Emanation because the gods there have control over their own magical emanations. Their height is six hundred and twenty-five fathoms. Eight hundred human years equal a day, thirty of those days is a month, and twelve such months is a year. The beings there live for eight thousand such years. Thus, their lifespan is equal to one day of the lifespan of a being in the Great Crying Hell.

The Land of Controlling Others' Emanations. The sixth and last of these lands is called Controlling Others' Emanations because the beings there control not only their own magical emanations but also those of others. Their height is seven hundred and fifty fathoms. For them, sixteen hundred human years are a day, thirty of those are a month, and twelve of those are a year. Sixteen thousand such years make up their lifespan. Thus, their lifespan is equal to one day in the Hot Hell.

The Form Realm

Above the six types of beings in the Desire Realm are the seventeen divisions within the Form Realm. The beings of the Form Realm are also gods, but they are different from the gods of the Desire Realm. The Form Realm is so called because the gods of the Form Realm are free of the type of desire that beings have in the Desire Realm, but they still have desire for, or attachment to, visible form—that is, color and shape—as well as sounds and objects of touch. However, there are no odors or tastes in the Form Realm.

There are four main areas in the Form Realm, which correspond to the meditations that cause rebirth there. The first is called the First Concentration *(bsam gtan dang po, prathamadhyāna)*; the others, then, are the Second, Third, and Fourth Concentrations (*bsam gtan gnyis pa, dvitīyadhyāna; bsam gtan gsum pa, tritīyadhyāna; bsam gtan bzhi pa, caturthadhyāna*). Each of these four areas has three divisions within it, making a total of twelve divisions. In addition, there are five remaining areas within the Fourth Concentration, called the Five Pure Places (*gnas gtsang, śuddhāvāsakāyika*), where only Superiors can be born. Thus, there is a total of seventeen divisions within the Form Realm.

The First Concentration

The First Concentration has three lands. The first is called Brahmā Type (*tshangs ris, brahmakāyika*); the second, In Front of Brahmā (*tshangs mdun, brahmapurohita*); and the third, Great Brahmā (*tshangs chen, mahābrahmāṇa*). Brahmā, the main figure in the lands of the First Concentration, is one of the great gods. The first land is called Brahmā Type because it is included within the Brahmā group or collection, as New York and Virginia are included in the United States. If the White House were the abode of Brahmā, the rest of Washington would be in the vicinity or presence of Brahmā, or In Front of Brahmā, and Great Brahmā would be the White House itself. The example shows the relationship between the lower and higher deities in this realm.

In order to be reborn as one of these three types of beings, we would have to engage in the meditative absorption of the first concentration in lesser, middling, or greater form. In general, meditative absorptions may be cultivated in three ways—lesser, middling, and greater. These are posited from the point of view of the meditator's mode of application, or effort, and are combinations of intensity and continuity. The lesser form of meditative absorption is that of a person whose meditation is neither intense nor continual. The middling form is that of a person who meditates either intensely but not continually or continually but not intensely. The greater is that of a person who meditates both intensely and continually.

Although it is said that through cultivating the greater meditative absorption of the first concentration, we can be reborn as a Great Brahmā, it is also said that we can be reborn as a Great Brahmā through cultivating the four immeasurables (*tshad med bzhi, catvāryapramāṇāni*)—love (*byams pa, maitri*), compassion (*snying rje, karuṇā*), joy (*dga' ba, muditā*), and equanimity (*btang snyoms, upekṣā*). The latter statement probably means that the meritorious power that one gains through cultivating the four immeasurables is equal to that which it takes to be reborn as a Great Brahmā, since, to attain the four immeasurables, one has to attain the first concentration. But I doubt that there is any special need to cultivate the four immeasurables in order to be reborn as a Great Brahmā.

The Second Concentration

The Second Concentration also has three levels. They are called Little Light (*'od chung, parīttābhā*), Limitless Light (*tshad med 'od, apramāṇābhā*), and Bright Light (*'od gsal, ābhāsvara*). In Little Light, the bodies of the beings emit little light. In Limitless Light, the bodies of the beings emit a middling amount of light. In Bright Light, the bodies emit great light. As was true of the First Concentration, the causes for being reborn in these lands are three types of meditative absorption—lesser, middling, and greater—but this time they are meditative absorptions of the second concentration. As before, they are posited from the point of view of the meditator's effort. Through the lesser meditative absorption of the second concentration, one is reborn in the land called Little Light; through the middling meditative absorption, in Limitless Light; and through the greater meditative absorption, in Bright Light.

The Third Concentration

The Third Concentration also has three levels. They are called Little Bliss (*bde chung, parīttaśubha*), Limitless Bliss (*tshad med bde, apramāṇaśubha*), and Vast Bliss (*bde rgyas, śubhakṛtsna*).[5] In the first level, the beings experience a smaller degree of bliss; in the second, they experience a middling degree of bliss; and in the third, they experience a very great bliss.

In order to be reborn in these lands, beings have to cultivate the meditative absorption of the third concentration in lesser, middling, or greater form, as explained earlier. Through the lesser meditative absorption of the third concentration, they are reborn in the land called Little Bliss; through the middling meditative absorption, in Limitless Bliss, and through the greater, in Vast Bliss.

The Fourth Concentration

In general, there are eight divisions of the Fourth Concentration. First, however, I will explain the usual three. The first is called Cloudless (*sprin med, anabhraka*); the second is called Born from Merit (*bsod nams skyes, puṇyaprasava*), and the third is called Great Fruit (*'bras bu che, bṛhatphala*). The first is called Cloudless because its parts are scattered, like clouds that do not meet. Born from Merit is so called because beings are reborn there as a result of great merit. Great Fruit is the greatest result among the lands that are included within the levels of the concentrations.

One type of god within the Great Fruit Land is called a god of no discrimination (*'du shes med pa'i sems can, asaṃjñisattva*). Beings are reborn in this region as a result of cultivating a meditative absorption lacking discrimination (*'du shes med pa'i snyoms 'jug, asaṃjñisamāpatti*). At the beginning of their lifetime, those who are born in this place of non-discrimination have a slight discrimination that they have been born there, and when they are about to die they have the discrimination that they are about to die. However, they spend the rest of their very long lives in a meditative absorption of non-discrimination, which is much like dreamless sleep for us.

These twelve lands are lands in which common beings (*so so'i skye bo, pṛthagjana*) are born; therefore, they are called Lands of Common Beings, though Superiors (*'phags pa, ārya*), too, can be born there.[6]

The Five Pure Places. The five remaining areas are called the Five Pure Places (*gnas gtsang, śuddhāvāsakāyika*). In these five areas, only Superiors are born. The names of the five are Not Great (*mi che ba, abṛha*), Without Pain (*mi gdung ba, atapas*), Auspicious Appearance (*sudṛśa, gya nom snang ba*), Great Perception (*shin tu mthong ba, sudarśana*), and Not Low (*'og min, akaniṣṭha*). The first is called Not Great because it is the lowest of the five.

The second is called Without Pain because the beings there do not suffer the pains of the afflictive emotions. The third is called Auspicious Appearance because the beings there meet with auspicious religious doctrine. The fourth is called Great Perception because, mentally, the beings there have a correct view. The highest is called Not Low because there is no area of the Form Realm above it.

Superiors are born in these five areas through cultivating alternating concentrations. Among concentrations, there are two types, uncontaminated (*zag med, anāsrava*) and contaminated (*zag bcas, sāsrava*).[7] In the first moment, a yogi who is practicing alternating concentrations cultivates an uncontaminated fourth concentration; in the second moment, the yogi cultivates a contaminated type, and in the third moment, an uncontaminated type. It is very difficult to alternate concentrations in this way. Therefore, a person who can do only these three has to leave the meditation after three moments.

This cultivation serves as a cause of rebirth in Not Great. A series of six alternating concentrations causes a person to be reborn in Without Pain. Cultivation of alternating concentrations for nine moments causes rebirth in Auspicious Appearance; cultivation for twelve moments causes rebirth in Great Perception, and cultivation for fifteen moments causes rebirth in Not Low.

Only Superiors are able to cultivate these meditations; common beings are not. For those people who have not attained freedom from cyclic existence, the usual reason for cultivating these alternating concentrations is to be reborn in these lands, and for people who have overcome the afflictive emotions and attained freedom from cyclic existence, the reason is to increase still further their distance from the afflictive emotions in order to experience bliss in this very lifetime.

The remaining topics with regard to the Form Realm are the size of body and length of life. In the first of the seventeen areas, the beings are two thousand fathoms tall and live for twenty intermediate aeons. In the second area, the beings are four thousand fathoms tall and live for forty intermediate aeons. In the third area, the body size and lifespan are six thousand fathoms and sixty intermediate aeons, respectively; in the fourth, eight thousand fathoms and eighty intermediate aeons, and so on through the remaining areas of the Form Realm.

The Formless Realm

Above the Form Realm is the Formless Realm. It is so called because the beings there have separated from attachment to both the Desire Realm and the Form Realm. There are four levels in the Formless Realm, which correspond to four kinds of meditative absorption. The first is called Limitless

Space (*nam mkha' mtha' yas, ākāśānantya*); the second is called Limitless Consciousness (*rnam shes mtha' yas, vijñānānantya*); the third is called Nothingness (*ci yang med, akiṃcanya*); and the fourth, the highest, is called the Peak of Cyclic Existence (*srid rtse, bhavāgra*).

To be reborn in the level of Limitless Space, we would have to cultivate a meditative absorption in which we view form itself as gross and imagine that there is only space everywhere. To be reborn in the level of Limitless Consciousness, we would have to cultivate a meditative absorption that views limitless space as gross and seeks only limitless consciousness; on this level, we would cultivate a meditative absorption in which we would discriminate that there is only consciousness, that consciousness is limitless. To be reborn in the level of Nothingness, we would view limitless consciousness as gross and abide in a state of no discrimination at all. Then, in order to cultivate the meditative absorption of the Peak of Cyclic Existence, we would view this state of no discrimination as gross and seek a state that is without coarse discrimination but has subtle discrimination (*'du shes med 'du shes med min skye mched, naivasaṃjñānāsaṃjñāyatana*).

In the Formless Realm, there is no size to the body because, since there is no form, the beings do not have bodies. They abide in these areas for twenty, forty, sixty, or eighty great aeons (*bskal pa chen po, mahākalpa*).

Cyclic Existence: The Three Realms and Nine Levels

Read from bottom to top

Formless Realm	9. Peak of Cyclic Existence 8. Nothingness 7. Limitless Consciousness 6. Limitless Space
Form Realm	5. Fourth Concentration 4. Third Concentration 3. Second Concentration 2. First Concentration
Desire Realm gods demigods humans animals hungry ghosts hell beings	1. First Level

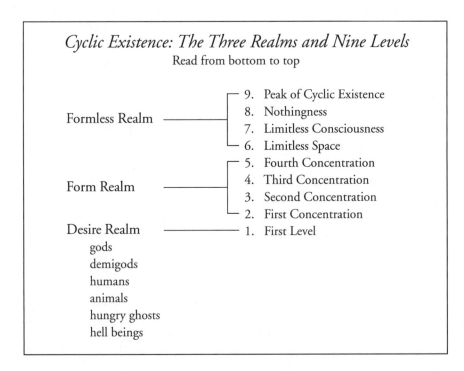

The Nine Levels

In the division of cyclic existence into nine levels, the Desire Realm is the first level. The First Concentration is the second level, the Second Concentration is the third level, the Third Concentration is the fourth level, and the Fourth Concentration is the fifth level. The four states of the Formless Realm are the sixth through the ninth levels. (See chart, page 46.)

In these four highest levels—that is, in the Formless Realm—there is no case of one being seeing another; there is no conversation. In the Form Realm, however, beings see and talk to each other. There are no day and night and no sleep in the Form Realm, but in the Desire Realm there are day and night and sleep. The lands of the four types of Desire Realm gods from Without Combat on up do not have day and night as we know them, but flowers open and close. There is the sound of birds. There are no sun and moon; the gods see each other by the light of their own bodies. From the Land of the Thirty-three on down, there are night and day, as well as sun and moon.

The three realms and the nine levels constitute cyclic existence; these are the states in which we wander. As was explained earlier, we are born in these states through actions (*las, karma*). Non-virtuous actions are called non-meritorious (*bsod nams ma yin pa, apuṇya*) actions; they cause us to be reborn in the bad transmigrations. Virtuous actions within the Desire Realm are called meritorious (*bsod nams, puṇya*) actions; they cause us to be reborn as humans or as gods of the Desire Realm. The virtuous actions that would cause us to be reborn in the Form and Formless Realms are called unfluctuating (*mi g.yo ba, āniñjya*) or invariable actions. Thus, from the point of view of taking rebirth in cyclic existence, these four concentrations and four formless absorptions are the best possible actions.

3

Background to the Concentrations and Formless Absorptions

ALTHOUGH THE CONCENTRATIONS and formless absorptions are called unfluctuating actions, "unfluctuating" does not mean that those who have cultivated these meditative absorptions are necessarily born in the Form or Formless Realms, for there are many Bodhisattvas who engage in these meditative absorptions not for the purpose of being born in these realms but for the sake of enhancing their minds. Many non-Buddhists also cultivate these eight absorptions; however, unlike Buddhists, they do not use them to gain other important minds and to progress on the path. In this context, the four concentrations and the four formless absorptions are extremely important.

Who can and who cannot generate the concentrations and formless absorptions?[1] Those who cannot generate them are the beings in the three bad transmigrations—hell beings, hungry ghosts, and animals. Even if they tried to cultivate them, they could not, because, as a fruition of their past deeds, they suffer a great deal and have no opportunity to develop these concentrations and absorptions. Because demigods are strongly afflicted by jealousy, they, too, cannot generate these concentrations and absorptions. The three higher types of gods of the Desire Realm,[2] gods of no discrimination in the Great Fruit Land of the Fourth Concentration, and humans who live in the northern continent, Unpleasant Sound, are also unable to generate the concentrations and formless absorptions. Gods of no discrimination do not have the capacity to analyze; without the power to analyze, it is impossible to generate the concentrations and formless absorptions. The three higher types of gods of the Desire Realm and the humans of the northern continent experience a continuous wonderful fruition of past actions. Thus, they do not have untimely death; things go well for them, and they experience the fruition of good past actions so strongly that they do not have much to think about and, therefore, do not have strong power of thought. Because they do not have the power of analysis, they cannot generate the concentrations and formless absorptions.

The three lower types of gods of the Desire Realm and humans of the three continents other than Unpleasant Sound can generate the concentrations and formless absorptions. Among these humans, however, the neuter, the impotent, and the androgynous cannot generate them. The reason is that such people have particularly strong afflictive emotions; their minds are continuously held by such afflictive emotions as desire, anger, and jealousy. Because there is no time at which they are free of these afflictive emotions, they have no opportunity to cultivate paths. Thus, there is no case of the new attainment of the concentrations and formless absorptions by the neuter, the impotent, and the androgynous.[3]

In general, males and females of the three continents can generate the concentrations and formless absorptions. However, not *all* males and females in the three continents can generate them. Those who have accumulated the actions of abandoning religious doctrine (*chos spong*) cannot, nor can those who have committed any of the heinous crimes (*mtshams med pa, ānantarya*), such as killing one's father or mother. Humans who have committed any of those particularly strong sinful actions have a very strong karmic obstruction (*las sgrib, karmāvaraṇa*). Until they have engaged in a means of purifying it, they cannot generate the concentrations and formless absorptions. Thus, those who can generate the concentrations and absorptions are the three lower types of gods of the Desire Realm and those males and females in the three continents who have not committed any of the heinous crimes or who have engaged in a means of purifying them if they have.[4]

What is the mode of cultivation of the concentrations and formless absorptions? To attain a concentration, it is necessary to attain a preparation for a concentration. (The means of attaining a concentration is called a preparation for a concentration; that which is attained is the actual [*dngos gzhi, maula*] concentration.) To attain a preparation for a concentration, one has to cultivate calm abiding (*zhi gnas, śamatha*) and special insight (*lhag mthong, vipaśyanā*).[5] All auspicious religious attainments arise from the cultivation of calm abiding and special insight—either from calm abiding and special insight themselves or from similitudes of calm abiding or special insight. This is said because these attainments come from engaging in stabilizing meditation (*'jog sgom*) and analytical meditation (*dpyad sgom*). Stabilizing meditation is the cultivation of calm abiding; analytical meditation is the cultivation of special insight.

What are the benefits of cultivating calm abiding? Calm abiding is a state in which the meditator sets his or her mind on an object of observation (*dmigs pa, ālambana*). Setting the mind on the object of observation is likened to tying an elephant to a post. The rope symbolizes mindfulness (*dran pa, smṛti*); the post symbolizes the object of observation; the elephant symbolizes the mind (*sems, citta*). It is said that if we tie the elephant of the mind to the post of an object of observation with the rope of mindfulness, we can achieve any good quality we want—for example, clairvoyance (*mngon shes, abhijñā*). Moreover, tying our minds to an internal object of observation is like tying up all possible external sources of harm, as well; external sources of harm will be unable to inflict damage. If we have not disciplined our own minds, we cannot succeed in subduing an external enemy; we will only have more enemies. Therefore, taming our own minds is explained as taming all external sources of harm.

What is the benefit of cultivating special insight? Buddha said that all the various practices he set forth, such as giving, were for the sake of developing wisdom. The great Indian paṇḍita Śāntideva also said that all other practices are for the sake of generating wisdom.[6] The reason is that, if we do not cultivate special insight, if we do not generate wisdom in our mental continua, it is impossible to uproot the afflictive emotions—desire, anger, jealousy, and so forth. However, when we have special insight in our mental continua, we can overcome our enemies, the afflictive emotions. Another Indian paṇḍita, Āryadeva, made this comparison: ignorance is to the afflictive emotions as the body sense power is to the other sense powers. Just as all the senses abide in the body and depend on the body sense power, all the afflictive emotions depend on ignorance; if we overcome ignorance, we overcome all afflictive emotions.[7]

It is necessary to generate both calm abiding and special insight. If we cultivate calm abiding but not special insight, we are like someone who has a strong body but no eyes; even if we develop stability through cultivating calm abiding, if we do not have special insight we do not have the wisdom to see. However, it would also be insufficient to cultivate special insight but not calm abiding. If we did so, we would be like someone who has strong eyesight but a weak body; because he staggers, he cannot see forms steadily. Thus, a person who has cultivated some special insight but does not have the stability factor of calm abiding cannot see reality clearly.

Since both calm abiding and special insight are necessary, which should we cultivate first? In general, it is said that we should cultivate calm abiding first and then, after that, cultivate special insight. This is said because, if we have not previously cultivated calm abiding, we have no opportunity to develop special insight. However, there are cases of cultivating a similitude of special insight before cultivating calm abiding. For example, to cultivate calm abiding itself, it may be necessary to suppress such afflictive emotions as desire and hatred. To suppress them somewhat, we first engage in the cultivation of special insight; we practice a type of analytical meditation and then cultivate calm abiding. This will be explained in greater detail later. (See pages 76–80.)

4

CALM ABIDING

CALM ABIDING (*zhi gnas, śamatha*) can be cultivated with regard to many types of objects of observation. Although calm abiding itself does not have different types, from the point of view of its objects of observation (*dmigs pa, ālambana*) there are many types. I will explain these in detail later. (See pages 74–83.) Now I will explain calm abiding in terms of a type of calm abiding that takes the body of a Buddha as its object of observation. First, however, we must set forth some terms.

TERMINOLOGY

The Five Faults

In order to develop calm abiding, one must overcome five faults (*nyes dmigs, ādīnava*).[1] The first is laziness (*le lo, kausīdya*). The second is forgetting the instruction (*gdams ngag brjed pa, avavādasammoṣa*)—that is, forgetfulness of the object of observation. The third is laxity (*bying ba, laya*) and excitement (*rgod pa, auddhatya*). The fourth is non-application (*'du mi byed pa, anabhisaṃskāra*)—that is, non-application of the antidotes to laxity and excitement. The last is [over]application (*'du byed pa, abhisaṃskāra*) of the antidotes to laxity and excitement.

The Eight Antidotes

To overcome these five faults, there are eight applications (*'du byed pa, abhisaṃskāra*)—that is, antidotes (*gnyen po, pratipakṣa*), or remedies. There are four antidotes to laziness: faith (*dad pa, śraddhā*), aspiration (*'dun pa, chanda*), exertion (*rtsol ba, vyāyāma*), and pliancy (*shin sbyangs, praśrabdhi*). The antidote to forgetting the instruction is mindfulness (*dran pa, smṛti*). The antidote to laxity and excitement is introspection (*shes bzhin, samprajanya*). The antidote to non-application is application (*'du byed pa, abhisaṃskāra*)—that is, application of the antidotes—and the antidote to overapplication is equanimity (*btang snyoms, upekṣā*)—that is, desisting from application. (See chart on following page.)

The Six Powers

When one engages in meditation, six powers (*stobs, bala*) are needed. The first is the power of hearing (*thos pa, śruta*). The second is that of thinking (*bsam pa, cintā*). The third is mindfulness. The fourth is introspection. The fifth is effort (*brtson 'grus, vīrya*). The sixth is familiarity (*yongs su 'dris pa, paricaya*).

Faults of Meditative Stabilization and Their Antidotes

Five Faults	*Eight Antidotes*
laziness	faith
	aspiration
	exertion
	pliancy
forgetting the instruction	mindfulness
[non-identification of] laxity and excitement	introspection
non-application	application
[over]application	equanimity

(Adapted from Jeffrey Hopkins, *Meditation on Emptiness*)

The Four Mental Engagements

The cultivation of calm abiding can also be seen in terms of four mental engagements (*yid la byed pa, manaskāra*). The first is called forcible engagement (*sgrim ste 'jug pa, balavāhana*)—that is, forcibly fixing the mind on its object of observation. The second is called interrupted engagement (*bar du chad cing 'jug pa, sacchidravāhana*)—interruptedly fixing the mind on its object of observation. The third is called uninterrupted engagement (*chad pa med par 'jug pa, niśchidravāhana*)—uninterruptedly fixing the mind on its object of observation. The fourth is called spontaneous engagement (*lhun grub tu 'jug pa, anābhogavāhana*)—spontaneously fixing the mind on its object of observation.

The Nine Mental Abidings

During the cultivation of calm abiding, a meditator passes through nine mental abidings (*sems gnas dgu, navākārā cittasthiti*)—nine states of mind. The first is called setting the mind (*sems 'jog pa, cittasthāpana*). The second is called continuous setting (*rgyun du 'jog pa, saṃsthāpana*). The third is called resetting (*slan te 'jog pa, avasthāpana*). The fourth is called close setting (*nye bar 'jog pa, upasthāpana*). The fifth is called disciplining (*dul bar byed pa, damana*). The sixth is called pacifying (*zhi bar byed pa, śamana*). The seventh is called thorough pacifying (*nye bar zhi bar byed pa, vyupaśamana*). The eighth is called making one-pointed (*rtse gcig tu byed pa, ekotīkaraṇa*). The ninth is called setting in equipoise (*mnyam par 'jog pa, samādhāna*). (See chart on following page.)

States and Factors in Achieving Calm Abiding

Read from bottom to top

Six Powers	*Nine Mental Abidings*	*Four Mental Engagements*
familiarity	9. setting in equipoise	spontaneous engagement
effort	8. making one-pointed	uninterrupted engagement
	7. thorough pacifying	interrupted engagement
introspection	6. pacifying	
	5. disciplining	
mindfulness	4. close setting	
	3. resetting	
thinking	2. continuous setting	forcible engagement
hearing	1. setting the mind	

(Adapted from Jeffrey Hopkins, *Meditation on Emptiness*)

Beginning to Meditate
Laziness

To achieve the first of the nine mental abidings, setting the mind, we must set the mind on the object of observation. To do so, we need aspiration, the wish to set it there; we must want to cultivate meditative stabilization (*ting nge 'dzin, samādhi*). Without that wish, there is laziness; even if we cultivated meditative stabilization a little, we would not want to cultivate it continually.

If such laziness arises before we have really begun to cultivate meditative stabilization, what should we do? The actual antidote to laziness is pliancy. This is a physical and mental serviceability that comes only later. Thus, it cannot help when we are just beginning to cultivate meditative stabilization. The initial technique for overcoming laziness is to cultivate faith. We have to contemplate the advantages of meditative stabilization; to do so, we first have to contemplate the faults of distraction (*rnam par g.yeng ba, vikṣepa*).

"From beginningless time until now," we think, "I have been lost in distraction. I have already undergone a limitless amount of suffering. If I still fall under the power of distraction, then I will have to undergo even more suffering." If distraction occurs, that is the first way of reflecting on its faults. The second is, "Even if I engage in repetition of mantra or meditate on a deity or cultivate a path, if I attempt to do these practices while distracted, I cannot achieve any fruit." Śāntideva himself said that.[2]

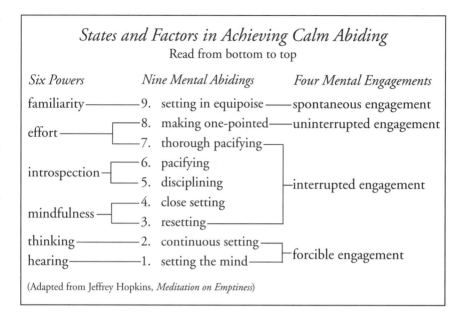

Then we contemplate the advantages of meditative stabilization. We think, "If I were able to set my mind one-pointedly, then, no matter what virtuous activity I wanted to do, I could do it. No matter what type of clairvoyance (*mngon shes, abhijñā*) or magical emanation (*sprul pa, nirmāṇa*) I wanted to achieve, I could achieve it based on meditative stabilization. Another advantage is that, if I had meditative stabilization, even my sleep would turn into meditative stabilization." Furthermore, we reflect, "If I had meditative stabilization, no matter what kind of religious path I wanted to cultivate, I could quickly go from the beginning to the end."

Thus, we reflect again and again on the disadvantages of distraction and the advantages of meditative stabilization. This reflection brings about faith in the value of meditative stabilization, and when we have such faith, aspiration for meditative stabilization will come. If we have aspiration, we will engage with exertion in the cultivation of meditative stabilization. Thus, even though pliancy is not applicable at the beginning of the practice of meditative stabilization, mental and physical pliancy will finally develop.

At the time of engaging in meditative stabilization, there are three types of laziness. The first is a sense of inferiority—the thought, "I could not possibly succeed at that." The second is the laziness that is an attachment to bad activities. The third is lack of impulse—the wish not to do it now.[3] Through contemplating the advantages of meditative stabilization, we overcome the three types of laziness, and when, within this state of having overcome these types of laziness, we first set the mind on the internal object of meditation, we have attained the first mental abiding, setting the mind.

Finding the Object of Observation

In order to set the mind on an internal object of meditation, we first have to search out that object. Indeed, there are many kinds of objects of observation, which will be discussed later. (See pages 74–83.) Now, however, I am going to present the meditation on the body of a Buddha.

First we have to look at a painting or statue of the body of a Buddha, and we have to put its appearance, its forms, its aspects, into our minds. We have to look again and again at the painting or statue and then, without looking at it, we have to cause the image of it to appear to the mind. In other words, we have to visualize it. We may look at a painting or a statue, as in this case, and cause it to appear to the mind; or our lama (*bla ma, guru*) may tell us what to meditate on, and through listening to the instructions again and again, we may put the appearance into our minds. Initially, when we first attempt to visualize it, the image of a Buddha's body does not appear to the mind; however, if we strain to see it, the meditation will get even worse. At the point at which even a portion of the object of observation—in this case, a Buddha's body—appears to the mind in a coarse way, one is said to have found the object of observation.[4]

When the object of observation has been found, we imagine the Buddha as sitting on top of the head. Then we imagine that from this Buddha a duplicate Buddha the size of the top joint of the thumb separates and sits about six feet in front of either the eyes or the navel. For someone who is experiencing excitement, it is better to move the image down; for someone experiencing laxity, it should be moved up to eye level. If possible, we should make the image smaller—even as small as a mustard seed. (Indeed, I find it very difficult, and I imagine that you would also find it difficult to make the image so small; however, there are some special people who are able to meditate on an extremely small object.)

Forgetting the Instruction

While we are setting the mind on the body of a Buddha, the object of observation may suddenly disappear. This is what is referred to as forgetting the instruction. Forgetting the instruction means that one loses the object of observation.

As soon as the object of observation is lost, we should immediately, with mindfulness, strongly and tightly bring it back. Therefore, it is said that mindfulness is the antidote to forgetting the instruction; this is because, when we forget and lose the object of observation, it is necessary, with tight mindfulness, to return to the object of observation. Tight mindfulness means holding the object of observation tightly, as we might hold a full mug tightly rather than loosely.

Among the six powers, the power that is operating at this point is the power of hearing, because we are applying the mind to what we have heard about the object of observation from the lama. If we did not hear about the object of observation from the lama, but became accustomed to it through looking at a painting or a statue, the reference of "hearing" would still be to that activity. Because the meditation is done based on the power of having sought out the object of observation earlier, of having trained in that object of observation, a meditator is said to achieve this state through the power of hearing.

Among the four mental engagements, in both the first and second mental abidings we are forcibly, or tightly, engaging the object of observation. We have to tighten the mind a great deal. Forcible engagement means that we have to take great care. At this point, there are many thoughts; sometimes the object of observation is there, sometimes not. We have to make great effort.[5]

We lose the object of observation because the mind is greatly distracted, and we may even feel that the distraction is increasing, that we are more distracted than usual. However, we are not more distracted; rather, because we are trying to fix the mind on an object of observation and using introspection to notice whether the mind is on the object of observation or not, we identify how much distraction we have. Similarly, someone who is going along the road usually does not notice how much traffic there is; sometimes, however, he or she stops and notices.

When we begin to feel that the meditation is becoming difficult, we should not switch to another object of observation that we think might be easier but we should stay with the original object of observation. Indeed, if we practice meditative stabilization well at all times aside from eating and going to the bathroom, we can develop the nine mental abidings one after another; but if we do not make effort, if we practice for a few days and then give up, we cannot develop meditative stabilization at all.

The Nine Mental Abidings

The First Mental Abiding

Now I am going to explain the five faults and the eight antidotes in terms of the first of the nine mental abidings, setting the mind. Then I will apply this discussion to the later mental abidings and distinguish which faults need to be eliminated and which antidotes need to be applied at those later mental abidings.[6]

Mindfulness. I have already talked about mindfulness, which is the antidote to forgetting the instruction, but I have not yet identified what mindfulness itself is. The Indian scholar and yogi Asaṅga said that mindfulness is a case of taking cognizance of a familiar object of observation, with the function of causing non-forgetfulness.[7] Mindfulness has three features. The first is that the object of observation must be an object with which the meditator is familiar—to which he or she has already become accustomed. It is impossible to be mindful of something that we have not previously seen. The second feature is the mode of apprehension, which must be continuous, without forgetfulness of the aspects of the object of observation. For example, at a time when we are particularly hungry, we have a continuous mindfulness of food. The third feature is the function, which is to cause non-distraction, non-scattering, to other objects.

If we now apply this explanation of mindfulness to the process of meditation itself, the object of observation in this particular meditation is the body of a Buddha visualized in front of the meditator, either straight out from eye level or straight out from the level of the navel. The meditator must hold on to that object of observation tightly, without distraction, and cause only that object to appear to the mind. That is the meaning, in easy form, of these three features of mindfulness.

Laxity and excitement. At the time of the session, when the meditator has mindfulness, the unfavorable circumstances to be overcome are non-identification of laxity and excitement, which together are the third of the five faults.

Laxity. To explain laxity, we have to distinguish between laxity (*bying ba, laya*) and lethargy (*rmugs pa, styāna*). Lethargy is a heaviness of mind and body. It is a state of being close to sleep (*gnyid, middha*). It causes an unserviceability of mind and body and is included within obscuration (*gti mug, moha*). The entity of lethargy can be either non-virtuous or neutral (*lung du ma bstan pa, avyākṛta*), but not virtuous, whereas the entity of laxity can be either virtuous or neutral. When lethargy arises during the cultivation of meditative stabilization, it is a contradictory circumstance. However, the reason that lethargy is not listed as a fault and that laxity is, is that lethargy is less frequent than laxity.[8] Moreover, when laxity is mentioned, lethargy is implied.

Laxity is of two types—coarse (*rags pa, audārika*) and subtle (*phra mo, sūkṣma*). Coarse laxity is a case of having stability—the ability to stay on the object of observation—but not clarity. Subtle laxity is a case of having stability and clarity but not intensity of clarity.

"Clarity" here refers not to the clarity of the object of observation but to the clarity of the mind apprehending the object.[9] When we do not have clarity, it is as if we have become dark, as if we are in a shadow. Not to have intensity of clarity means that, though we have stability and clarity, the mind's mode of apprehension has become loose with respect to the object of observation. If, within that looseness, we become even more stable, this state turns into subtle laxity. When we have intensity of clarity, we have not only stability and clarity but also a sense of tightness of mind with respect to the object of observation. The difference is like that between holding a mug loosely and holding it tightly.

Subtle laxity is the worst unfavorable circumstance with regard to generating meditative stabilization. Since subtle laxity, like meditative stabilization, has both stability and clarity, it is difficult to distinguish between subtle laxity and meditative stabilization. There is a time in the cultivation of meditative stabilization when the movement of breath stops; this also happens in subtle laxity, and the meditator is able to remain fixed on the object of observation even for a whole day. There were people in Tibet who mistook this for actual meditative stabilization and even tried to cultivate it; among their instructions, they said that when a meditator attains stability with respect to the object of observation and a subjective clarity, he or she should loosen the exertion involved in introspection, and that if the mind is loosened at that time, it is the best of meditations. Their wrong system was incorrectly based on the writings of an Indian scholar and yogi named Saraha. He said that the mind that is being held tightly is like a piece of leather rope being pulled through an iron device with a hole in it, and that, if a meditator loosens this mind that is being held tightly, there is no doubt that liberation will follow. Indeed, he said this, but this instruction applies to the eighth of the nine mental abidings and has nothing to do with the first, second, and third.

If we attempt to cultivate meditative stabilization but actually cultivate subtle laxity, it will not serve as a cause for generating any of the concentrations or formless absorptions. We will become forgetful in this lifetime, and our mindfulness and memory will become unclear; further, engaging in such meditation will cause rebirth as an animal. The famous Tibetan scholar and yogi S̄a-ḡya (*sa-skya*) Paṇḍita said that a stupid person who tries to cultivate the Great Seal (*phyag rgya chen po, mahāmudrā*) usually creates the causes for being reborn as an animal; what he is saying is that there are people who think they are cultivating the special technique called the Great Seal but are actually cultivating subtle laxity, and that this will cause them to be reborn as animals.[10]

Excitement. In general, in the discussion of excitement, there are two factors to be considered—scattering (*'phro ba*) and excitement. "Scattering" means the moving of the mind to external objects. Within scattering, there are many types, such as desirous scattering and hateful scattering. Almost all distractions are cases of the scattering of the mind. Indeed, at the time of cultivating meditative stabilization, if we think even about engaging in virtuous deeds, such as giving, that thought is a case of scattering.

Excitement itself is a case of scattering. However, in the discussion of how to cultivate meditative stabilization, excitement is posited as one of the five faults and scattering is not because in the cultivation of meditative stabilization, there are more cases of excitement than of scattering. Excitement occurs only with regard to objects of desire, whereas scattering occurs with regard to all objects. Excitement is a scattering of the mind to an object of desire; it is the remembering of a pleasant object while trying to meditate. It is included within desire; it prevents the mind from becoming calm and interrupts the development of calm abiding. When excitement is mentioned, scattering is implied.

Like laxity, excitement has two varieties: coarse and subtle. If we were meditating on the body of a Buddha and lost the object of observation—that is, if the body of a Buddha no longer appeared to the mind—and if we became mindful of an object of desire, that state would be coarse excitement. Subtle excitement is commonly explained through the example of water moving under ice; the meditator does not lose the object of observation, but a corner of the mind has come under the influence of discursiveness (*rnam rtog, vikalpa*),[11] and a pleasing object of desire is about to appear to the mind. Thus, there are two types of laxity and two types of excitement, coarse and subtle; using these as examples, we can apply this explanation to all other types of distraction and consider them to be faults.

Introspection. The sixth of the eight antidotes, introspection, has a nature of wisdom. It is posited as the antidote to laxity and excitement, although it is not the actual antidote, because its primary function is to identify laxity and excitement. Introspection is like a spy in wartime. Just as a spy is not an actual combatant but is included within the category of combatants, so introspection—which is like a spy in that it analyzes the mind to see whether laxity or excitement has arisen—is included among the antidotes. Not to rely on introspection when cultivating meditative stabilization is like not knowing that a burglar has entered the house and is carrying away all our goods; a fault would have arisen in our practice of meditative stabilization, and we would not have identified it.

Though we must rely on introspection, it should not be called up continuously. The reason is that if we engaged in this type of investigation continuously, there would be a danger of generating excitement. For example, when we hold a mug full of tea, we hold it tightly; this tightness symbolizes mindfulness. Like the hand holding the mug tightly, mindfulness holds on to the object of observation, and, like introspection, the eye also has to see from time to time whether the tea is about to spill or not. We have to sustain this mode of apprehension of the object of observation within occasional analysis to find out whether we have become lax or excited.

Non-application and application. The fourth of the five faults is non-application of the antidotes to laxity and excitement when laxity and excitement have arisen. At this point, we need the seventh of the eight antidotes, which is the mental factor (*sems byung, caitta*) of application. Not to apply the antidotes to laxity and excitement once the spy of introspection has discovered that laxity or excitement has set in would be like not sending out the troops once the spy had discovered the enemy's oncoming army. Therefore, once introspection has analyzed whether laxity or excitement has arisen and has determined that one or the other has, the meditator should engage in the appropriate antidote.

What are the antidotes? Let us say that we have generated subtle laxity and have stability and clarity but not intensity of clarity. Since the fault arises from weakness in the mode of apprehension of the object of observation, we should tighten the mode of apprehension. There is no need to change the object of observation or to give up the session. However, the mode of apprehension of the object of observation should not be tightened too much. Buddha set this forth with the example of the strings of a guitar; if one loosens or tightens the strings too much, the sound is unpleasant. Another example is that of holding a small bird in one's hands; if we held the bird tightly, we would kill it, and if we held it loosely, the bird would fly away. Therefore, it should be held with a moderation of tightness and looseness. If we reach the point of thinking, "If I continue in the same way, excitement will be generated," we should loosen a little; however, if we reach the point of thinking, "If I continue in the same way, laxity will be generated," we should tighten a little. Whatever the case may be, we need a moderation of looseness and tightness.

This, indeed, is very difficult to achieve. It can be achieved only in terms of one's own experience and with very clever introspection. The Indian scholar and yogi Candragomin wrote a piece in which he indicated his own fatigue with this process. He said, "When I apply great effort and hold on to the object of observation tightly, I become excited, and when I use less effort and relax a little, I generate laxity. It is very difficult to use moderate effort, to make it even. When I cultivate meditative stabilization, my mind becomes disturbed." The fact is, he was not fatigued at all; rather, he was giving us advice.

That is how it is in general. However, when there is an enemy in one's inner circle, it is extremely dangerous not to know it. Similarly, it is extremely dangerous when something appears in the mind that is like meditative stabilization but is actually an unfavorable circumstance for generating meditative stabilization. D̄zong-ka-b̄a (*tsong kha pa,* 1357–1419) said that therefore, in general, we should tend to err to the side of tightness. The reason is that if we put emphasis on tightening the mind, what will be generated will be excitement, and excitement is easier to overcome than laxity. If, however, when we loosen the mode of apprehension, subtle laxity is generated, it is difficult to distinguish from meditative stabilization; thus, it is very dangerous.

If we tighten the mode of apprehension of the object of observation but laxity is still being generated, if it seems as though the mind is falling apart, and if we also do not have clarity, we are at the point of generating coarse laxity. The reason is that the mind has become too withdrawn inside. Therefore, we have to enlarge the scope of the object of observation. One way of doing this is to make the object brighter, as though it were made of light. Or, instead of considering the body of a Buddha in general, we should consider the various features—the eyes, forehead, arms, and so forth.

If laxity persists, we should give up the original object of observation and engage in a means of invigorating the mind.[12] We may contemplate the difficulty of obtaining a human body, the type of human life we have now, which has the leisure (*dal ba, kṣaṇa*) and fortune (*'byor ba, sampad*) to accomplish religious practice (*chos, dharma*); or we may contemplate the qualities of Buddha, his Doctrine (*chos, dharma*), and the Spiritual Community (*dge 'dun, saṃgha*), or the benefits of the altruistic mind of enlightenment, or a bright object such as the sun or moon; or we may engage in meditative practices of giving. However, the main thought to engage in is the thought of the value of meditative stabilization, as was explained earlier. Such contemplations can be used, and if we have contemplated such topics before, they will quickly help. Contemplating such topics can be like splashing cold water on one's face.

However, because we are only beginners, it is difficult for such contemplations to help us, and it is necessary to rely on quintessential instructions for removing laxity forcefully—that is, for forcing it out of our mental continuum. We should visualize our own mind as a white light, the size of a white pea, at the heart. We can also visualize the mind in the shape of the Tibetan or Sanskrit letter *a* at the heart. Then we should say the syllable *phaṭ* loudly and visualize the mind exiting through the top of the head and dissolving in the sky. This is called a mixing of the expanse of space and the mind. It should be done again and again many times. There is no need to have qualms with regard to this practice, since there are many sources for it; Pa-dam-ba-sang-gyay (*pha dam pa sangs rgyas*, fl. 11th–12th c.)[13] said that this practice is the best means of refreshing the mind. If it does not help, we should stop the session.

The causes of laxity are lethargy, sleep, and those factors that cause the mind to become dark, like a darkened sky. In order to overcome these causes, we should go to a cool place or to a high place, a place with a wide view, or we should wash the face with cold water. If we need to rest, we should rest. Through these means, laxity can be overcome, and once it has been overcome, we can again enter into meditative stabilization.

In subtle excitement, we do not lose the object of observation, but part of the mind has come under the influence of discursiveness. It is caused by the mind's being a little too tight. Therefore, we should loosen the mode of apprehension a little. If loosening the mode of apprehension a little does not help, we know that coarse excitement is about to be generated. Excitement is caused by something that pleases the mind. An example is found in a story concerning the Buddha's father. After his enlightenment, Buddha met with his father and with others and explained the doctrine. Though the others realized the doctrine and the fruit of Buddha's teaching, Buddha's father did not because he was too happy to see his son. Therefore, Buddha set forth for his father a means of lessening this joy, and his father was able to attain the fruit of Stream Enterer (*rgyun zhugs, śrotāpanna*).[14]

In coarse excitement, we should reduce the mind's elation. We should leave the object of observation, which here is the body of a Buddha, but we should not leave the session. Rather, we should meditate on such topics as death and impermanence; and on the suffering of cyclic existence in general and of the bad transmigrations in particular—topics that cause the mind to be slightly sobered. Thoughts that would cause a wish to leave cyclic existence will help people who are familiar with such contemplation. However, if these contemplations do not clear away the fault of excitement, we should get rid of it forcefully. We should meditate on a black drop at the navel (that is, in the center of the body behind the navel), or we should concentrate on the inhalation and exhalation of the breath. We should not make noise when exhaling or inhaling but should breathe gently. When exhaling, we should think, "Exhaling," or, "Going out," and when inhaling, "Inhaling," or, "Coming in"; then, mentally (not aloud but mentally), we can count, "One has gone out," "Two have gone out," and so on. For those of sharp faculties, coarse excitement will be gone by the time they count to five. However, those of duller faculties will have to count to seven, fourteen, or twenty-one.

If engaging in this meditation does not overcome excitement, we should give up the session and rest. We should not force the process of meditation too much. For example, if two people are traveling together and having a good time, when they separate, they separate happily; therefore, they are happy when they come together again. In the same way, when we leave a meditation session, we should not leave it when the meditation is difficult. We should leave it at some point when it is going well, so that we will want to meditate again later on. If we make meditation into a kind of hardship, then later we will become tired and angry as soon as we see the meditation cushion.

Overapplication and equanimity. The fifth of the five faults is overapplication. This would be a case of applying the antidotes to laxity and excitement when laxity and excitement have not occurred or have been eliminated. As an antidote to this fault, one desists from application. This antidote is called desisting from application, or equanimity. Though overapplication occurs mainly in the eighth mental abiding, a similitude of it can occur earlier. If, in the earlier mental abidings, we are beginning to meditate well, we should not apply the antidotes to laxity and excitement. If the meditation is proceeding well, application of such antidotes would generate laxity or excitement.

Thus, in some sense, all five faults can arise in the first mental abiding. Although at some point we would indeed have to apply antidotes and, thus, would not desist from application altogether, there could be opportunities for using a similitude of equanimity; thus, we could say that, except for the fifth fault (overapplication) and the eighth antidote (equanimity) all the others pertain to the first mental abiding.

In the first mental abiding, we only occasionally set the mind on the object of observation; the mind does not stay on the object of observation continuously. The measure of having finished the first mental abiding is that the mind stays on the object of observation for as long as it would take to count twenty-one breaths; however, it is easier to count the breath to twenty-one than to stay on another object of observation for the same length of time. Thus, with another object of observation, it would take longer to progress from the first mental abiding to the second.

The Second Mental Abiding

When we are able to extend slightly the duration of the setting of the mind on its object of observation, we have arrived at the second of the nine mental abidings, continuous setting. It is said that at this point a meditator should be able to stay on the object of observation for as long as it takes to go around the rosary once reciting the mantra *oṃ maṇi padme hūṃ*;[15] at the correct speed, the recitation would take about a minute and a half. The difference between the first and second mental abidings is that, in the second, a meditator is able to stay on the object of observation longer than in the first. During the second mental abiding, thoughts sometimes appear to the mind and sometimes do not; thus, at that time, the meditator has a sense that thought is resting.

Among the five faults, laziness occurs during the second mental abiding, as during the first, in all three forms—not wishing to engage in the cultivation of meditative stabilization, becoming attached to bad activities, and developing a sense of inadequacy with respect to the task. As in the first mental abiding, we should overcome laziness by thinking about the advantages of meditative stabilization. The fault of forgetting the instruction—forgetting the object of observation—will also occur; as in the first mental abiding, we should hold on to the object of observation through mindfulness. Laxity and excitement, the third of the five faults, also arise and have to be identified through introspection. When, through introspection, we recognize that we have come under the influence of laxity or excitement, we must engage in application of the antidotes, not in non-application. If subtle laxity arises, we should engage in the means of overcoming subtle laxity; if coarse laxity arises, we should engage in the means of overcoming coarse laxity. If subtle excitement arises, we should engage in the means of overcoming subtle excitement; if coarse excitement arises, we should engage in the means of overcoming coarse excitement. The same antidotes that were explained with regard to the first mental abiding should be applied to the second. When laxity and excitement have not arisen, application of the antidotes to them would be a fault.

For the first two of the nine mental abidings, the mental engagement is the same; both are cases of forcible engagement—forcibly fixing the mind on its object of observation. However, the powers with which the two mental abidings are achieved are different; the second mental abiding is achieved by the power of thinking, because the meditator again and again contemplates the object of observation.

The Third Mental Abiding

In the third mental abiding, resetting, we are able not only to extend the duration of staying on the object of observation but, within that state, to increase our ability to abide on the object of observation and to shorten the periods of distraction. Moreover, when the mind is distracted, we immediately know that it is distracted and, as in mending fabric, immediately put the mind back on the object of observation.

Among the five faults, the fault of laziness may occur in the third mental abiding. At that time, as in the first two mental abidings, we need the antidotes to laziness, of which the first is the faith that sees the disadvantages of distraction and the advantages of meditative stabilization. The second fault, forgetting the instruction, may also occur, and the application of the antidote, mindfulness, is the same as in the first two mental abidings; we should immediately put the mind back on the object of observation and, with mindfulness, continuously keep the mind on that object. The third fault, laxity and excitement, could also occur; as in the earlier mental abidings, these are identified through introspection, which investigates whether laxity or excitement has arisen. When introspection identifies either of these, we have to rely on application of the antidotes to laxity and excitement, as explained earlier. When the meditation is proceeding well, there is no need to engage in techniques for overcoming laxity and excitement, and we should desist from application.

From the third mental abiding through the seventh, the mental engagement is that of interrupted engagement. Among the six powers, the power manifest in the third and fourth mental abidings is that of mindfulness. The reason that the power of mindfulness is posited for the third and fourth mental abidings is that, even though one had to apply great mindfulness during the first and second mental abidings in order to remain on the object of observation, in the third mental abiding, as an effect of one's previous mindfulness, one has the power of mindfulness.

The Fourth Mental Abiding

The fourth mental abiding is called close setting because the meditator has become more familiar with the object of observation—closer to it and better able to set the mind on it continuously. Through familiarization with strong mindfulness during the third mental abiding, the meditator reaches the point of not losing the object of observation at all; that is the difference between the third and fourth mental abidings. From the fourth mental abiding on up, the object of observation will never be lost.

Among the five faults, laziness can again occur; the way of relying on the antidotes is as before. However, the second fault, that of forgetting the instruction, no longer occurs. Introspection is still needed to find out whether we have come under the influence of laxity or excitement. However, coarse excitement does not occur because we no longer run after objects of desire, thereby losing the object of observation. Thus, we can still have subtle excitement, coarse laxity, and subtle laxity and must apply the appropriate antidotes. Again, there would be a similitude of desisting from application when we have overapplied the antidotes to laxity and excitement.

The mental engagement of the fourth mental abiding is still that of interrupted engagement, and at this point, the power of mindfulness has matured.

The Fifth Mental Abiding

During the fourth mental abiding, the meditator is able to stay on the object of observation continuously; therefore, the mind withdraws too much, until strong laxity develops. That point marks the beginning of the fifth mental abiding.

In this mental abiding, the meditator still needs to rely on the antidotes to laziness. The fault of forgetting the instruction, however, is absent. As before, introspection must analyze whether laxity or excitement has arisen. Although, as in the fourth mental abiding, there is no coarse excitement, the meditator needs to rely on the antidotes to coarse and subtle laxity and to subtle excitement. Since the fifth mental abiding is marked by strong laxity, it is especially necessary to heighten and revivify the mind by contemplating the advantages of meditative stabilization. Because, through doing so, the meditator overcomes dislike for meditative stabilization, the fifth mental abiding is called disciplining.

The mental engagement here is still that of interrupted engagement, and among the six powers, the meditator must rely on strong introspection.

The Sixth Mental Abiding

Because the mind has been revivified during the fifth mental abiding, there is danger of generating subtle excitement. At that point, the meditator has arrived at the sixth mental abiding, pacifying. In the earlier mental abidings, because of distraction, the meditator had felt a dislike for meditative stabilization; in the sixth mental abiding, however, any dislike for meditative stabilization has been completely overcome. Therefore, this mental abiding is called pacifying.

In the sixth mental abiding, the meditator still has to rely on the antidotes to laziness. As in the two preceding mental abidings, forgetting the instruction no longer occurs. The meditator still has to rely on introspection to investigate whether laxity or excitement has arisen, and upon the realization that either has arisen, must apply the appropriate antidotes. In the sixth mental abiding, coarse laxity and coarse excitement are not generated and, therefore, there is no need to rely on their antidotes. However, it is necessary to apply the antidotes to subtle laxity and subtle excitement. As before, the meditator should rely on a similitude of desisting from application when laxity and excitement have been successfully overcome.

Again, the mental engagement is that of interrupted engagement, and among the six powers, the power of introspection has matured.

The Seventh Mental Abiding

The seventh mental abiding is called thorough pacifying because, though it is possible for desire and for secondary afflictive emotions (*nye ba'i nyon mongs, upakleśa*) such as harmfulness (*rnam par 'tshe ba, vihiṃsa*) to arise between sessions, the meditator is able either to rely on an antidote or, through not getting involved in these afflictive emotions, to suppress them.

In the seventh mental abiding, laziness probably still occurs,[16] and the meditator must rely on the antidotes to it. However, the second fault, forgetting the instruction, does not occur. Since subtle laxity and subtle excitement occur in the seventh mental abiding, introspection still has to analyze whether subtle laxity and excitement have arisen. However, though they occur, they cannot harm the process of meditative stabilization. They are treated as a general would treat an enemy that had been weakened; he would still maintain his strength and send out spies but would not have to fight. Similarly, it is not necessary to rely on the antidotes to subtle laxity and subtle excitement set forth earlier; it is sufficient merely to stop them. Therefore, the meditator needs to rely on a similitude of desisting from application of the antidotes to laxity and excitement when the meditation has been successful.

Although actual interruption by laxity and excitement occurs only from the third mental abiding to the sixth, these unfavorable circumstances for the cultivation of meditative stabilization still exist in the seventh mental abiding. Therefore, it is said that the mental engagement in the seventh mental abiding is that of interrupted engagement. Among the six powers, the meditator must rely on effort.

The Eighth Mental Abiding

The difference between the seventh and eighth mental abidings is that between the presence and absence of laxity and excitement. At the beginning of the session, the meditator is able to rely on only a little effort with regard to them; then, during the rest of the session, he or she is entirely free of them and remains one-pointedly on the object of observation. Therefore, the eighth mental abiding is called making one-pointed.

Since laxity and excitement do not arise during the eighth mental abiding, it is probably not necessary to rely on the antidotes to laziness. As in all mental abidings beginning with the fourth, forgetting the instruction no longer occurs. Since laxity and excitement no longer arise, it is no longer necessary to rely on introspection; the meditator relies only on a little effort at the beginning of the session and is able to sustain the remainder of the session without further effort. Therefore, from the eighth mental abiding, the meditator is able to loosen the exertion involved in introspection; it is at this point that Saraha's quintessential instructions for loosening, mentioned earlier, become relevant. In the eighth mental abiding, application of the antidotes to laxity and excitement would be a fault; the antidote to overapplying those antidotes is equanimity—desisting from application.

The mental engagement here is that of uninterrupted engagement. Among the six powers, the power of effort has matured.

The Ninth Mental Abiding

There is a point at which the meditator is able, spontaneously and without any striving at all, to engage in meditative stabilization; at that point, he or she has reached the ninth mental abiding, called setting in equipoise.

In this mental abiding, none of the five faults occurs. The mental engagement is that of spontaneous engagement, and because, from the first mental abiding to the eighth, the meditator has become familiar with the object of observation, he or she now has the power of familiarity. With the attainment of the ninth mental abiding, the meditator is able to remain in meditative stabilization without effort but does not yet have actual calm abiding.

Calm Abiding

In addition to the effortless meditative stabilization of the ninth mental abiding, pliancy is necessary for calm abiding. There are two types of pliancy—mental pliancy and physical pliancy. There are also the bliss of mental pliancy and the bliss of physical pliancy. Among the two types of pliancy, mental pliancy is achieved before physical pliancy, and among the two types of bliss, the bliss of physical pliancy is achieved before the bliss of mental pliancy.

How are these achieved? Through increased familiarity with meditative stabilization, the meditator overcomes bad physical states, which are physical currents of energy, or winds (*rlung, prāṇa*). Having overcome these, the meditator has a sense of bliss, and the top of the head tingles. This tingling, which is very pleasant, occurs because the winds, or energy currents, of the bad physical states are leaving the body through the top of the head. Immediately afterward, the meditator overcomes bad mental states and attains mental pliancy. These bad mental states are an unserviceability of mind with respect to virtuous objects. With mental pliancy, one attains serviceability of mind, the ability to set the mind on whatever virtuous purpose one wishes. Then, through the power of the achievement of mental pliancy, a wind of physical pliancy pervades the whole body, and with the overcoming of bad physical states, the meditator attains physical pliancy. Physical pliancy is a serviceability of the body such that the body can be used for whatever virtuous purpose one wishes, without any sense of hardship, and is an absence of the bad physical states of roughness and coarseness, which are objects of touch. The body is now light, like cotton; with physical pliancy, there is a sense of softness and lightness, leading to the bliss of physical pliancy. The bliss of physical pliancy is a very blissful object of touch.

As the meditator remains in meditative stabilization, he or she has a sense that the body has melted into the object of observation, and there is no sense of other objects. At this point, the meditator has the special bliss of mental pliancy. The mind is very joyous, almost as though it can no longer stay on the object of observation. When this sense of almost feverish joy diminishes, an immovable mental pliancy is attained; this immovable mental pliancy accords with meditative stabilization and involves complete stability with respect to the object of observation. At that point, the meditator has attained calm abiding.

Calm abiding is stabilizing meditation brought to fulfillment. It is called calm abiding because the meditator has calmed the distraction of the mind to external objects and the mind abides stably on an internal object of observation. At the same time, the meditator attains the preparation (*nyer bsdogs, sāmantaka*) called the not-unable (*mi lcog med, anāgamya*), which is a mind not of the Desire Realm, but of the Form Realm.

Signs of Calm Abiding

There are many signs of having attained calm abiding. The attainment of pliancy is one sign. Another is that, during meditative equipoise (*mnyam bzhag, samāhita*), there is a sense of appearances vanishing and of the mind fusing with space itself. The mind is like a mountain, able to abide firmly and steadily on its object of observation. A sound produced near such a meditator, whether of a train going by or of a cannon, would not affect him or her at all. The meditator has great clarity and feels as though he or she could count the particles in a wall. Further, having risen from meditative stabilization, the meditator retains some portion of pliancy, or mental and physical serviceability. Pliancy and meditative stabilization enhance each other, so that sleep can be mixed with meditative stabilization. Upon rising from meditative equipoise, the meditator has a sense of achieving a new body. Afflictive emotions are generated to a lesser degree, are weaker, and disappear of their own accord. The meditator is free of the five obstructions (*sgrib pa, āvaraṇa*) that we ordinarily have—aspiration to attributes of the Desire Realm (*'dod pa la 'dun pa, kāmacchanda*); harmfulness (*gnod sems, vyāpāda*); lethargy and sleep (*rmugs pa dang gnyid, styānamiddha*); excitement and contrition (*rgod pa dang 'gyod pa, auddhatyakaukṛtya*); and doubt (*the tshom, vicikitsā*).

Prerequisites of Calm Abiding

To generate such meditative stabilization, a practitioner needs its prerequisites, or causal collections, at the beginning, middle, and end. There are six main prerequisites. The first is to abide in a favorable area. The second is to have few desires. The third is to know satisfaction. The fourth is to have pure ethics. The fifth is to forsake commotion. The sixth is to forsake desire, as for example, thoughts of copulation.

What does "to abide in a favorable area" mean? Maitreya said that the area in which one is going to meditate should be a place free of war, starvation, and so forth; it should be a place in which people have independence. The United States has all those qualities; there is peace, not war; there is a great deal of food; and there is freedom. It also appears to have good laws. Buddha set forth certain laws for countries; these were gathered together by Nāgārjuna in his *Precious Garland.*[17] The United States has many customs that accord with Nāgārjuna's recommendations for altruistically helping others. Is it not true that there is help for the aged, help for the young, help for the poor? Is this not good?[18] Nāgārjuna said that a country should have good roads, and the United States has them. He said, further, that the roads should have places of rest along them, places where there is water, and indeed, the roads have them. Since the customs I have seen accord with religious practice, I think that this is a very favorable area.

In such an area, a practitioner must be able to obtain food and clothing easily, and to obtain it, must not engage in wrong livelihood—that is, must not obtain money or food and clothing through negative activity. The practitioner also needs an auspicious place, a place in which some adept has meditated and which has that person's blessing. If such a place cannot be found, the practitioner should find a place that he or she likes and that is free of harm from animals or non-human sources and far from loud noises that would interfere with meditative stabilization; it should be a place in which there are not many cars, trucks, planes, or trains passing by, or people yelling. An auspicious ground is also needed—that is, an area in which the ground itself does not generate sickness but is conducive to good health. The practitioner also needs good friends, helpers suitable for people seeking to achieve religious practice, as well as all the necessary articles for achieving meditative stabilization, especially books; we need to ascertain the process of meditative stabilization—what the faults are, how to overcome them, how to rely on the antidotes, and so forth—and if we need books, we should have them.

The sixth prerequisite is to abandon thoughts of desire, and so forth—that is, to abandon attachment to the attributes of the Desire Realm, the chief of which is the desire for copulation. If we retain the desire to engage in copulation, we have to rely on a partner; men and women consort with each other, and afterward there may be children, and there are many things to do after that. If we do not give up thoughts of desire, the strength of our thought will go into them, and they will harm the process of meditative stabilization.

Of these six prerequisites, the first two (to abide in a favorable area and to have few desires) refer to the period before the beginning of cultivation, and the others, to the period during cultivation.

These prerequisites are specifically for a person who is seeking to achieve calm abiding within six months. It would not be suitable for such a person to take a day off—say, Saturday or Sunday. In the beginning, such a practitioner should divide the day into many portions, even eighteen different meditation sessions during the day. Then, when the factor of stability increases, the session can be gradually lengthened and the number of sessions decreased.[19] If a practitioner is able to cultivate meditative stabilization in long sessions, it is sufficient to divide the day into four parts and meditate in four sessions. Thus, if a practitioner is actually meditating in this way, he or she should spend the entire time, except for eating, sleeping, and so forth, in meditation. However, people like us who meditate only in short sessions—for ten minutes or a half-hour—should try to have as many of these prerequisites as possible, but it is not necessary to have them all. For example, with regard to having few desires and knowing satisfaction, we should do whatever we can; with regard to having great desire, and so forth, we should have less, and with regard to the other prerequisites, we should also do whatever we can. There are many levels of engagement in the practice. Thus, we should not think that we necessarily have to have all six prerequisites in order to cultivate calm abiding; if we thought that, we might give up the practice altogether because we could not get all the prerequisites together.

The Beginning of the Session

When we are going to begin to meditate, we need a good place to sit. We should first sweep the area where we will be sitting.

The Cushion

What we put under the cushion is important. It is said that Buddha's cushion was above crossed vajras.[20] This would be unsuitable for us because we are common beings who have not attained such potency of mind. Instead of vajras, people like us can sit on top of a swastika drawn clockwise.[21] (The counterclockwise swastika is that of the pre-Buddhist Tibetan religion called Bon.) The purpose of the clockwise swastika is to make mindfulness more steady; it also keeps out obstructions, or obstructors, that might cause the mind to fluctuate.

On top of the swastika, we put kuśa grass (*Poa cynosuroides*) or quitch grass (*Agropyron repens*). There does not seem to be any in this area; however, if we are actually going to accomplish the cultivation of meditative stabilization, putting these grasses underneath the cushion makes a difference. Quitch grass is used for the sake of increasing the lifespan, and kuśa grass is used for increasing wisdom and for the sake of the mind's remaining clear.

On top of this, we put the cushion. The cushion should be square. It should be large enough for us to sit entirely on it. The back should be higher than the front, for two reasons. One reason is to prevent the buttocks from aching when we meditate for a long time. The other is that sitting with the buttocks higher than the knees causes the body to straighten; when we straighten the body, the channels (*rtsa, nāḍi*) in it are straightened. When the channels are straightened, the currents of energy, or winds, that travel in them are enabled to travel easily and well. This causes the mind to remain steady.

Posture

It is best to sit in the vajra, or adamantine, cross-legged posture (*rdo rje skyil krung, vajrāsana*).[22] First, we place the left foot on the right thigh and then, the right foot on the left thigh. Then we put the left hand in front of the navel, palm up, and the right hand on top of it, palm up; the hands are held close to the body, with the thumbs lightly touching. The shoulders should be level. We should not sit with raised shoulders, as though we had wings; this would become uncomfortable after a while. The backbone should be as straight as an arrow. We should bend the head slightly, as if pressing the Adam's apple just a little, and the neck should be like the neck of a peacock. The lips and teeth should be left in a natural manner. However, the tip of the tongue should be placed at the ridge just behind the upper teeth. The reason is that if we meditate for a long time, this placement of the tongue will keep the saliva from flowing too much and it will also keep us from being thirsty. The eyes should be aimed at the nose; though non-Buddhists generally meditate with their eyes closed, we should leave the eyes slightly open, looking at the sides of the nose. Breathing should be quiet and gentle.

This is the posture of the Buddha Vairocana, and these seven features are called the seven features of Vairocana's way of sitting. If we are able to stay in this posture well, its imprint will eventually produce the Form Body (*gzugs sku, rūpakāya*) of a Buddha. Buddha Vairocana is the symbol of the purification of the form aggregate (*gzugs kyi phung po, rūpaskandha*); since he is the Buddha who, symbolically, is mainly concerned with the body, it is his posture that we use for sitting.

If, when we meditate, we are able to sit in this manner, the mere posture establishes auspicious predispositions. Therefore, the great Tibetan yogi Mar-ba (*mar pa*)[23] once said that if all the great meditators of Tibet competed with him they could not match even his way of sitting; by this statement Mar-ba was indicating that how one sits is extremely important. For people with minds like ours, it is less important; however, for one who is cultivating the stage of completion (*rdzogs rim, niṣpannakrama*) of Highest Yoga Tantra (*rnal 'byor bla med kyi rgyud, anuttarayogatantra*), it is unsuitable not to be in this posture.

When we cultivate calm abiding, it is good to stay in this position, but if we cannot, it is best to sit in whatever way is comfortable. Because of our familiarity with different positions, we may find a certain position uncomfortable and another comfortable. There was a Foe Destroyer (*dgra bcom pa, arhan*) who could not at all cultivate meditative stabilization in the position just described. He asked his teacher what was wrong. The teacher, who was clairvoyant, saw that the student had been an ox in his previous life. Therefore, he had the student cultivate meditative stabilization lying down, and he was able to do so. Thus, when we cultivate calm abiding, we may use whatever position is most conducive to meditation. Tibetans often sit with the left foot on the right thigh and the right foot underneath. If that is not comfortable, we may sit in the manner of the goddess Tārā,[24] with the left foot against the inside of the right thigh and the bent right leg extended.

Motivation

Once seated in a good posture, we have to consider our motivation. If the mind is under the influence of anger, desire, or another afflictive emotion, we should first concentrate on the inhalation (*dbugs rngub pa, āna*) and exhalation (*dbugs 'byung ba, apāna*) of the breath, breathing in and out through the nose, not harshly and not extremely slowly, and counting the inhalations and exhalations. Count to three, five, seven, nine, or twenty-one. When the mind, less influenced by desire or hatred, becomes somewhat neutral, establish the motivation. If you are able to set up the motivation in vast detail, reflect on the altruistic mind of enlightenment (*byang chub kyi sems, bodhicitta*), but more briefly the motivation should at least be to establish all sentient beings in happiness and in freedom from suffering. Then switch to the regular object of observation.

Objects of Observation

The Body of a Buddha

As I have already explained, we can imagine a Buddha sitting on top of our heads, after which a duplicate the size of the top joint of the thumb separates from that Buddha, and we imagine that second Buddha at whatever place is most comfortable—at eye level or navel level, about six feet in front of us; or inside the throat, inside the heart, or inside the solar plexus. Or, alternatively, we can meditate on ourselves as Buddhas.

Meditating on the body of a Buddha is not a case of looking at an image with the eye but of imagining or visualizing it. We have to hold the mind to this object of observation with tight mindfulness and cause the mind not to be distracted. Holding the mind tightly with mindfulness in itself eliminates laxity and, by preventing distraction, eliminates excitement as well. Through reliance on the eight antidotes to the five faults and through using the four mental engagements and the six powers, meditative stabilization is achieved, as explained earlier. If stability increases, we should guard against excitement. Proceeding, we will be able to cultivate meditative stabilization faultlessly.

Choosing the body of a Buddha as the object of observation brings great benefit. It hastens the collection of meritorious power and serves as a basis for cleansing sins; for a trainee in the Mantra Vehicle (*sngags kyi theg pa, mantrayāna*), it gives familiarity with meditating on oneself as a deity. Furthermore, it involves recollection of a Buddha's qualities and aids the quick generation of meditative stabilization.

One's Own Mind

Instead of meditating on the body of a Buddha, we can meditate on our own minds; in the beginning, this is more difficult. Here, the object of observation is the mind itself, which has three features: it is clear (*gsal ba*); it is a knower (*rig pa, saṃvedana*); and it is empty (*stong pa, śūnya*). The mode of meditation is the same.

With the achievement of calm abiding using the mind itself as the object of observation, there is a possibility of error because, with that achievement, one attains a state similar to a realization of emptiness. Many Tibetan meditators in the past achieved calm abiding using the mind itself as the object of observation but thought that they had gained the view of emptiness (*stong pa nyid, śūnyatā*) when they had not. Furthermore, when they achieved the bliss of pliancy, they mistakenly believed that they had achieved the innate bliss; thus, when they achieved calm abiding using the mind itself as the object of observation, they thought that they had achieved the primordial, innate wisdom-consciousness when they had not. They felt that they had achieved Buddhahood and explained their experience as the primordial, innate wisdom-consciousness, whereas they were actually describing the mind of calm abiding. This would be like explaining the qualities of a lion by explaining the qualities of a Tibetan Lhasa Apso.[25]

It is possible to generate meditative stabilization using either the body of a Buddha or one's own mind as the object of observation; however, they do not have the special features of other objects of observation, and, thus, it may be more difficult to generate meditative stabilization using them.

Categories of Objects of Observation

Buddha set forth four categories of objects of observation to be used in the achievement of calm abiding—pervasive objects of observation (*khyab pa'i dmigs pa, vyāpyālambana*), objects of observation for purifying behavior (*spyad pa rnam sbyong gi dmigs pa, caritaviśodanālambana*), skillful objects of observation (*mkhas pa'i dmigs pa, mkhas par byed pa'i dmigs pa, kauśalyālambana*), and objects of observation for purifying afflictive emotions (*nyon mongs rnam sbyong gi dmigs pa, kleśaviśodanālambana*).

Pervasive Objects of Observation

Pervasive objects of observation are of four types. The first is called an analytical image (*rnam par rtog pa dang bcas pa'i gzugs brnyan, savikalpakapratibimba*). The second is called a non-analytical image (*rnam par mi rtog pa'i gzugs brnyan, nirvikalpakapratibimba*).[26] The third is called observing the limits of phenomena (*dngos po'i mtha' la dmigs pa, vastvantālambana*). The fourth is called thorough achievement of the purpose (*dgos pa yongs su grub pa, kṛtyānuṣṭāna*). "Limits of phenomena" refers to the two types, the varieties (*ji snyed pa*) and the mode (*ji lta ba*). The varieties are conventional phenomena, and the mode is their emptiness. "Thorough achievement of the purpose" refers not to the object of observation but to the purpose for which one is meditating; this class includes all the fruits of meditative stabilization from liberation up to the omniscience of a Buddha.

Objects of Observation for Purifying Behavior

I have already explained how to achieve calm abiding using certain objects of observation. However, it is necessary to mention other objects of observation, since for people who are dominated by certain afflictive emotions, it is helpful to use objects of observation for purifying behavior rather than those I have already talked about.

A person who is dominated by desire (*'dod chags, rāga*) should meditate on ugliness (*mi sdug pa, aśubha*). For someone who is dominated by hatred (*zhe sdang, dveṣa*), the object of observation is love (*byams pa, maitrī*). Someone who is dominated by obscuration (*gti mug, moha*) should meditate on dependent-arising (*rten cing 'brel bar 'byung ba, pratītyasamutpāda*). Someone who is dominated by pride (*nga rgyal, māna*) should meditate on the division of constituents (*khams, dhātu*). Someone who is dominated by discursiveness (*rnam rtog, vikalpa*) should meditate on the inhalation and exhalation of the breath (*dbugs 'byung rngub, ānāpāna*).

A meditator knows whether or not a particular afflictive emotion is predominant.[27] However, for someone who is not dominated by one of these afflictive emotions but has all of them equally, it is suitable to meditate on a Buddha's body, the mind itself, or any of these objects of observation.

Objects of observation for purifying desire. If we recognize that we are dominated by the afflictive emotion of desire, we should meditate on ugliness. There are many different meditations on ugliness, among which are those on internal ugliness and external ugliness.

The meditation on internal ugliness is on the thirty-six impure substances. With regard to the generation of desire, we could be attached to or desirous of our own bodies or someone else's body. If we are attached to our own bodies, we should meditate on the thirty-six impure substances in our own bodies, and if we are desirous of someone else's body, we should meditate on the thirty-six impure substances in that person's body. How do we meditate on this? We should consider how the body abides, from the soles of the feet to the hair on the head, and inside the skin. When we consider this, we see that it is filled with the thirty-six impure substances: hair, nails, teeth, sweat and body odor, skin, flesh, bones, channels, arteries, ducts, veins, the kidneys, the heart, the liver, the lungs, the small intestine, the large intestine, the stomach, the upper part of the stomach, the urinary bladder, the spleen, the rectum, saliva, snot, oily connective tissue, lymph, marrow, fat, bile, phlegm, pus, blood, the brain, the membrane covering the brain, urine, and old-age spots. Whatever the source of our desire, be it our own body or another's, we meditate on it as composed of these thirty-six impure substances. We should analyze these one by one and engage in analytical meditation until desire has lessened. When it has, we can remain in stabilizing meditation on just the thought that the body is composed of these thirty-six impure substances and thereby achieve calm abiding.

There are nine facets to the meditation on external ugliness. There are four antidotes to attachment to color. They are the four colors of rotting corpses—putrid blue, putrid black, pus color, and putrid red. If you want to know what these colors are, buy a piece of meat in summer and hang it in your room. If you examine it each day, you will understand. First it becomes a dull bluish color; then it becomes a putrid black; then blood and lymph rise to the surface, ready to roll off, and when the blood rolls off, it is putrid red. When we are desirous of someone else's body, we should consider the body as being like these.

There are two antidotes to attachment to shape. If we are attached to the shape of someone's face, for example, we can meditate on that face as though a dog or cat had chewed part of it. Then we could meditate on it as though a dog or a cat had ripped off pieces, such as the ears and the nose, and scattered them about.

As an antidote to attachment to touch there are two meditations, one on the flesh as eaten by worms but with the bone and skin still intact, and another on the skeleton held together by ligaments. In the first, worms or organisms under the skin have eaten away the flesh, leaving only skin and bone, and even the skin is partly eaten away. The second is just the skeleton and ligaments.

There is a single antidote to attachment to copulation (*bsnyen bkur, upacāra*). A man who has desire for a woman or a woman who has desire for a man is to meditate on the other as a dead body that does not move.[28]

As with meditation on internal ugliness, engage in analytical meditation until desire is overcome and then remain in stabilizing meditation.

Objects of observation for purifying hatred. If dominated by hatred, we should cultivate love. Love is cultivated with respect to friends, persons toward whom we are neutral, and enemies; a practitioner cultivates love using these three as the objects of observation. Of the many ways of cultivating love within Buddhism, there are two that may be used in this context. The first is to take cognizance of friends—father, mother, mate, and other friends—and to cultivate the belief that they have attained happiness free of suffering and then to see them that way. Similarly, the practitioner concentrates on persons toward whom he or she is neutral and on enemies. This is called a mental engagement of belief.

The second type is called taking to mind. It has three aspects. The first is the thought, with respect to friends, persons toward whom the practitioner is neutral, and enemies, "How nice it would be if they possessed happiness free of suffering!" The second aspect is, "May they possess happiness free of suffering!" The third is, "I will cause them to possess happiness free of suffering." In the first type of meditation, the mental engagement of belief, the practitioner believes or pretends that they have attained a meditative equipoise in which they have this type of happiness. This second type is directed toward the future.[29]

There is great benefit in cultivating love. Nāgārjuna said in his *Precious Garland* that if one put into a vessel three hundred different kinds of food and fed all the sentient beings in the area three times a day, great meritorious power would be generated by this act of charity; but one moment of cultivating love would be stronger.[30] It is said that by cultivating immeasurable love, a practitioner can be reborn in the Great Brahmā area of the First Concentration, and if we generate great love toward all sentient beings, we can eventually attain Buddhahood. In the meantime, as Nāgārjuna said, there are eight benefits:

> Gods and humans will be friendly,
> Even [non-humans] will protect you,
>
> You will have pleasures of the mind and many
> [Of the body], poison and weapons will not harm you,
> Effortlessly will you attain your aims
> And be reborn in the world of Brahmā.[31]

When Buddha was meditating under the tree of enlightenment, he was attacked by a great many demons. He had no weapons to fight them; he had only love. It is said that in a place in which there are many harmful beings, such as demons, the most helpful protection is the meditative stabilization of love.

Objects of observation for purifying obscuration. If we are dominated by obscuration, we should meditate on dependent-arising. This is a meditation on phenomena (*chos, dharma*) as not being created by a permanent (*rtag pa, nitya*) agent or creator but as having their own function—that of creating their own specific effect. In this context, we should meditate on phenomena of the past, present, and future as having a specific relationship of cause (*rgyu, hetu*) and effect (*'bras bu, phala*); we should meditate on the fact that phenomena have their own causes and conditions (*rkyen, pratyaya*), and that effects arisen from causes and conditions act as causes and conditions of other effects.[32] It is said that by meditating in this way, we will refute the existence of a permanent self (*bdag, ātman*); thus, this is one of the best meditations for eventually generating special insight. Until a sharper mind develops, do analytical meditation; then remain in stabilizing meditation until calm abiding is achieved.

Objects of observation for purifying pride. If dominated by pride, we should meditate on the division of our own constituents. There are six constituents—earth (*sa, pṛthivī*), water (*chu, āp*), fire (*me, tejas*), wind (*rlung, vāyu*), space (*nam mkha', ākāśa*), and consciousness (*rnam shes, vijñāna*). "Persons" (*gang zag, pudgala*) are designated based on a composite of these six constituents. How do we identify these in our own continuum? The earth constituent is identified as flesh, skin, bone—that which is hard. Water is blood, lymph, and so forth. Fire refers to the heat in one's own continuum. Wind is the factor of movement. Space refers to the empty places within the body. Consciousness, in this context, refers to the mind that is connected with this body.

In this meditation, we analyze and identify these constituents in our own continuum. In time, a sense of unpleasantness develops with regard to the body; this overcomes pride. Once pride has been overcome, concentrate on just this sense of the many divisions of constituents with respect to your own continuum and achieve calm abiding with that as the object of observation.[33]

Objects of observation for purifying discursiveness. If dominated by discursiveness—that is, if we think too much—we should meditate on the inhalation and exhalation of the breath. Meditation on the breath is done differently by those with sharp faculties and by those with duller faculties. Those with duller faculties have to count the breath, whereas those with sharper faculties pay attention to the breath without counting. Those who have to count should count mentally, not aloud.

There are two ways of counting. The first is to count the exhalation as one and the inhalation again as one; the meditator counts up to ten and then down to one. The second is to count the series as one—that is, to count only the exhalations; here, too, the meditator counts up to ten and then down to one. If you have great discursiveness, count the breath in this manner until discursiveness is overcome. Then concentrate solely on the breath, using this as the object of observation to achieve calm abiding.

We can imagine discursiveness as a dark color being expelled with the breath; then, with inhalation, we imagine the blessings of the Three Jewels being drawn into us in the form of bright light. This way of expelling discursiveness and drawing in blessings is done only at the beginning of this practice. Once discursiveness has been overcome, concentrate on the breath without the visualization. Since this technique of visualization is not mentioned in the Indian texts, it is not necessary to use it, but it is helpful.

Skillful Objects of Observation

Skillful objects of observation are of five types—the aggregates (*phung po, skandha*), constituents (*khams, dhātu*), spheres (*skye mched, āyatana*), dependent-arising (*rten cing 'brel bar 'byung ba, pratītyasamutpāda*), and the appropriate and the inappropriate (*gnas dang gnas ma yin pa, sthānāsthāna*). They are called skillful because, by taking them as objects of observation, we can become skilled with respect to them. I will discuss them only briefly.

The aggregates. How do we meditate on the aggregates? The aggregates are the basis of the designation "person." They are not an amorphous whole; when they are divided, there are five—the aggregates of form (*gzugs, rūpa*—that is, the body), feelings (*tshor ba, vedanā*), discriminations (*'du shes, saṃjñā*), compositional factors (*'du byed, saṃskāra*), and consciousness (*rnam shes, vijñāna*). Further, if form is divided, there are ten different forms. These are not hard to understand; five of them are the five sense powers (*bdang po, indriya*)—the eye sense power (*mig gi dbang po, cakṣurindriya*), ear sense power (*rna ba'i dbang po, śrotrendriya*), nose sense power (*sna'i dbang po, ghrāṇendriya*), tongue sense power (*lce'i dbang po, jihvendriya*), body sense power (*lus kyi dbang po, kāyendriya*)—and the other five are the objects of the five sense consciousness—forms (*gzugs, rūpa*), sounds (*sgra, śabda*), odors (*dri, gandha*), tastes (*ro, rasa*), and tangible objects (*reg bya, spraṣṭavya*). We could even divide feelings into many types; if we did, everyone would fall asleep. In brief, there are three types—the feeling of pain (*sdug bsngal, duḥkha*), the feeling of pleasure (*bde ba, sukha*), and neutral feeling (*sdug bsngal ma yin bde ba ma yin, aduḥkhāsukha*). There is no feeling that cannot be included within these three.

There are also many types of discrimination, but all of them can be included within two types—non-conceptual (*rtog med, nirvikalpaka*) and conceptual (*rtog pa, kalpaka*); the former does not involve words, whereas the latter involves conceptual determination (*zhen pa, adhyavasāna*). There is also a limitless number of compositional factors, but they can be included within two types—associated compositional factors (*ldan pa yin pa'i 'du byed, saṃprayuktasaṃskāra*) and non-associated compositional factors (*ldan min 'du byed, viprayuktasaṃskāra*). There are six types of consciousness—eye consciousness (*mig gi rnam shes, cakṣurvijñāna*), ear consciousness (*rna ba'i rnam shes, śrotravijñāna*), nose consciousness (*sna'i rnam shes, ghrāṇavijñāna*), tongue consciousness (*lce'i rnam shes, jihvāvijñāna*), body consciousness (*lus kyi rnam shes, kāyavijñāna*), and mental consciousness (*yid kyi rnam shes, manovijñāna*).

The aggregates are these many parts piled up, or brought together. When we understand this presentation of the aggregates, we understand that there is no partless, independent person apart from these aggregates; this is called skill in the aggregates. When this is understood well, set the mind in meditative stabilization just on this and achieve calm abiding.

The constituents. The next type of skillful object of observation is the constituents. There are eighteen constituents. (There is also a presentation of sixty-two constituents, which I will not describe here.) The eighteen constituents are very easy because they are with us all the time. First, there are the six sense powers—eye, ear, nose, tongue, body, and mental sense powers (*yid kyi dbang po, mana-indriya*). Then there are the six consciousness—eye, ear, nose, tongue, body, and mental consciousness. Then there are the six objects of these consciousness—forms, sounds, odors, tastes, tangible objects, and a sixth category called phenomena. Each of these has the potentiality of its function—the function of producing its own later moments. The function of the six sense powers is to produce the six consciousness. The eye sense power produces the eye consciousness; the ear sense power produces the ear consciousness, and so forth. The six objects serve as the objects apprehended by the six consciousness, and the six consciousness have the function of apprehending their six objects. When we understand this, we understand that there is no separate creator of these, such as a substantially existent (*rdzas su yod pa, dravyasat*) self; therefore, this is called skill in the constituents. When this is understood through analysis, set the mind in stabilizing meditation just on this and achieve calm abiding.

The spheres. The next type of skillful object of observation is the spheres. There are twelve spheres. They are the six objects and the six sense powers, which were also included within the eighteen constituents; through the rearrangement of these, all phenomena can be included in the twelve spheres. The six objects are the objects of use, and the six sense powers are the users. When we understand that the six powers use the six objects and that pleasurable, painful, and neutral feelings are produced as a result of this use, we understand that there is no substantially existent person separate from these. This is called skill in the spheres. When this is understood well, set the mind in stabilizing meditation on it and achieve calm abiding.

Dependent-arising. The next type of skillful object of observation is dependent-arising. Dependent-arising refers to the fact that all internal and external phenomena depend on causes and conditions for their arising. The arising of a lifetime in cyclic existence depends on its root cause, ignorance (*ma rig pa, avidyā*). The process of producing such a lifetime is spelled out in the twelve links of dependent-arising. The first is ignorance; the second is actions (*las, karma*); the third is consciousness (*rnam shes, vijñāna*); the fourth is name and form (*ming gzugs, nāmarūpa*); the fifth is the six spheres (*skye mched drug, ṣaḍāyatana*); the sixth is contact (*reg pa, sparśa*); the seventh is feeling (*tshor ba, vedanā*); the eighth is attachment (*sred pa, tṛṣṇā*); the ninth is grasping (*len pa, upādāna*); the tenth is existence (*srid pa, bhava*); the eleventh is birth (*skye ba, jāti*); and the twelfth is aging and death (*rga shi, jarāmarana*). For each of these, those that precede it act as causes for those that follow; similarly, in the external world, a sprout is produced from a seed when all the contributing causes are present and cannot be produced when the contributing causes are not present. When we examine in this way and understand the situation well, we know that a lifetime in cyclic existence is not produced causelessly and is not produced from discordant causes, such as a permanent deity. This is called skill in dependent-arising. Understanding this, concentrate on what has been understood, and, using it as the object of observation, achieve calm abiding.

The appropriate and the inappropriate. The last skillful object of observation is called the appropriate and the inappropriate. It involves an understanding of what effects arise, and what effects do not arise, from what causes. The appropriate and the inappropriate is a vast topic; though I am explaining it only briefly, we can thoroughly understand actions and their effects through it. In turn, it is one factor of the topic of dependent-arising, but, because of its importance, it is considered separately.

"The appropriate and the inappropriate" means the possible and the impossible. It would be impossible for the performance of a sinful action to cause rebirth in a happy transmigration; for example, a deed of hatred is a cause of rebirth in a bad transmigration. Though no one wishes to be reborn in a bad transmigration, every such birth is preceded by a bad action we ourselves have performed. We are not reborn there through our own wish. Similarly, through the power of accumulating a virtuous action, we are reborn in a happy transmigration; a virtuous action is not a cause of rebirth in a bad transmigration. Again, we cannot merely choose to be reborn in a happy transmigration. When we understand well that births in bad transmigrations and in happy transmigrations depend on specific actions, we understand that these births are not created by a permanent deity and do not result from the activity of a substantially existent person. This is called skill in the appropriate and the inappropriate. When this is understood well, concentrate on it in stabilizing meditation and achieve calm abiding.

Objects of Observation for Purifying Afflictive Emotions

Objects of observation for purifying afflictive emotions are of two types—those having the aspect of grossness/peacefulness (*zhi rags, *śāntaudārika*) and those having the aspect of the truths (*bden pa, satya*). To avoid repetition, I will explain them extensively in relation to the preparations for the concentrations. (See pages 86–102, 117–125.)

These are the four types of objects of observation for the cultivation of calm abiding, as set forth in Buddha's sūtras. They are said to be the best objects of observation for diminishing desire and facilitating the development of meditative stabilization. Thus, although the choice of the object of observation may be determined by the factor of ease or difficulty, our own disposition is also a factor. There is a story of an Indian meditator who had difficulty achieving calm abiding; he tried many objects of observation and finally achieved it with respect to the horn of an ox. Thus, the main thing is to see what is most suitable to oneself. Any of these can be used as the object of observation.

5

The Four Concentrations

After achieving calm abiding, we can cultivate the concentrations and formless absorptions; I will now explain how to develop them. At this point, it is also customary to insert an explanation of the cultivation of special insight. However, since the mode of cultivating the preparations (*nyer bsdogs, sāmantaka*) for the concentrations and the mode of cultivating special insight are similar, I will discuss them together.

The Seven Preparations

There are four concentrations—the first, second, third, and fourth. Each of the concentrations has seven preparations—the mental contemplations (*yid la byed pa, manaskāra*) that are the means of attaining it. The first is called the mental contemplation of a mere beginner (*las dang po pa tsam kyi yid byed*).[1] The second is called the mental contemplation of individual knowledge of the character (*mtshan nyid so sor rig pa'i yid byed, lakṣaṇapratisaṃvedīmanaskāra*). The third is called the mental contemplation arisen from belief (*mos pa las byung ba'i yid byed, adhimokṣikamanaskāra*). The fourth is called the mental contemplation of thorough isolation (*rab tu dben pa'i yid byed, prāvivekyamanaskāra*). The fifth is called the mental contemplation of joy-withdrawal (*dga' ba sdud pa'i yid byed, ratisaṃgrāhakamanaskāra*). The sixth is called the mental contemplation of analysis (*dpyod pa yid byed, mīmāṃsāmanaskāra*). The seventh is called the mental contemplation of final training (*sbyor mtha'i yid byed, prayoganiṣṭhamanaskāra*).

Preparations for the First Concentration

The first preparation, the mental contemplation of a mere beginner, is calm abiding itself. (See pages 69–70.) The second through the seventh are of two types; each of them could have either the aspect of grossness/peacefulness (*zhi rags, *śāntaudārika*) or the aspect of the truths (*bden pa, satya*).[2] At present, I will discuss the mode of cultivation having the aspect of grossness/peacefulness.

The Mental Contemplation of Individual Knowledge of the Character

"Individual knowledge of the character" means reflection on the individual character of these two levels—one level being gross and the other peaceful—or on the general character (*spyi'i mtshan nyid, sāmānyalakṣaṇa*) and the specific character (*rang gi mtshan nyid, svalakṣana*) of these levels. At this point, the meditator is mainly analyzing through mental states arisen from hearing (*thos byung, śrutamayī*) and arisen from thinking (*bsam byung, cintāmayī*).[3]

The mode of cultivating the mental contemplation of individual knowledge of the character is the same as the mode of cultivating special insight. To cultivate either special insight or the mental contemplation of individual knowledge of the character, it is necessary to pass through nine states exactly like the nine mental abidings that lead to calm abiding. Here, however, there are two objects of observation—the Desire Realm and the First Concentration. The meditator observes the Desire Realm and views it as gross and then observes the First Concentration and views it as peaceful.

The mode of cultivation having the aspect of grossness/peacefulness. How do we view the Desire Realm as gross? To contemplate the Desire Realm as gross is to contemplate the faults of the beings and environments of the Desire Realm. The beings of the Desire Realm are the sentient beings (*sems can, sattva*), or persons (*gang zag, pudgala*), who abide in it—ourselves, animals, and so forth. The sentient beings of the Desire Realm have a bad nature; the sign of their having a bad nature is that they quarrel with one another and make war. They are also ugly in color and shape. When we look at one another, we tend to think that some of us are attractive and others are not; however, compared to the beings of the First Concentration, we are all ugly; those of us who are considered beautiful would look like monkeys next to a being of the First Concentration. Further, the beings of the Desire Realm are filled with the afflictive emotions (*nyon mongs, kleśa*)—hatred (*zhe sdang, dveṣa*), ignorance (*ma rig pa, avidyā*), resentment (*'khon 'dzin, upanāha*), dissimulation (*g.yo, śāṭhya*), jealousy (*phrag dog, irṣyā*), miserliness (*ser sna, mātsarya*), and so forth. Thus, the beings of the Desire Realm are of a very coarse mental disposition in which the afflictive emotions are not pacified. We also have ill behavior of body, speech, and mind; we commit all ten of the non-virtues.

Not only do the beings of the Desire Realm engage in these bad activities; they also have great suffering. At the time of birth, they undergo the suffering of birth; then they undergo the sufferings of aging, sickness, and death. They also undergo the sufferings of separation from the pleasant and meeting with the unpleasant. They lack what they want and must seek it with great exertion and fatigue; they have to engage in many types of work—road building, the manufacture of iron, carpentry—and once they have achieved what they want, they have to maintain it; as soon as we leave the house, we have to lock the door. There is also the suffering of not knowing satisfaction with what we have. Further, there is the suffering of lacking independence; though we achieve what we want and maintain it, we cannot use it as we wish. Sometimes, even when we can use something as we wish, it causes trouble, as when we cannot digest food. There are many cases of not being able to enjoy what we use—for example, having a thick coat but getting too warm in it, or getting cold from wearing a thin garment. There is also the suffering of losing friends and mates: boyfriends lose girlfriends and girlfriends lose boyfriends. Even these sufferings would be bearable, but the beings of the Desire Realm also have the suffering of a short lifespan, as well as the suffering of sleep, which is a fault. As for resources in the Desire Realm, the beings use impure substances for nourishment; moreover, there are impure substances such as urine and feces that do not exist in the First Concentration. This is how we contemplate the faults of Desire Realm beings.

When we have considered the faults of the beings in the Desire Realm, we consider the faults of the environment—the lumpy landscape we have, with its mountains and valleys; it is a land of ordinary stones and earth, of thorns, cesspools, and harmful places.

Then, having considered the faults of the Desire Realm, we view the First Concentration as peaceful in the sense of not having these faults. The nature of the beings of the First Concentration is peaceful in that they do not fight or quarrel. They also have a better mental disposition than beings in the Desire Realm; afflictive emotions such as hatred, resentment, belligerence (*khro ba, krodha*), jealousy, miserliness, non-shame (*ngo tsha med pa, āhrīkya*)—the many afflictive emotions that exist in the mental continua of the beings of the Desire Realm—do not exist in the continua of the beings in the First Concentration. From the point of view of behavior, the beings of the First Concentration are peaceful in that they do not engage in the ten non-virtues: they do not engage at all in killing (*srog gcod pa, prāṇātighāta*), stealing (*ma byin len, adattādāna*), sexual misconduct (*'dod pas log par g.yem pa, kāmamithyācārā*), lying (*rdzun du smra ba, mṛṣāvāda*), divisive talk (*phra ma, paiśunya*), harsh speech (*tshig rtsub, pāruṣya*), and foolish talk (*ngag bkyal, saṃbhinnapralāpa*), and they do not engage in covetousness (*brnab sems, abhidhyā*), harmfulness (*gnod sems, vyāpāda*), and wrong views (*log lta, mithyādṛṣṭi*) the way beings in the Desire Realm engage in them.

The beings of the First Concentration also have less suffering than the beings of the Desire Realm. They do not have the suffering of birth or aging or the type of sickness that exists in the Desire Realm. They do not meet with the unwanted or lose the wanted. They do not lack what they want; they do not have to acquire food and drink with great hardship. Since there is no case of not knowing satisfaction, they do not have to work hard to fulfill their desires, and when they go outside, they do not have to lock the door. Moreover, unlike the beings of the Desire Realm, the beings of the First Concentration have a long lifespan. They also have pure resources.

The First Concentration is also peaceful from the point of view of environment. Our ordinary environment does not exist in the First Concentration. The houses of the First Concentration are called inestimable mansions (*gzhal med khang, *amātragṛha*) because their value cannot be measured. It is said that they are made of precious substances and that the land itself is made of precious substances; impure substances do not exist there. Therefore, relative to the Desire Realm, the First Concentration is peaceful, just as, if we are living in a time without war or disturbance, we call it a time of peace.

The mode of procedure. The mode of meditation of the second preparation, the mental contemplation of individual knowledge of the character, is similar to that set forth for achieving calm abiding. As before, the meditator sits on a soft and comfortable cushion, and if thoughts of desire or hatred arise, concentrates on the breath. When the mind becomes neutral, the meditator establishes his or her motivation, as explained earlier.

Since calm abiding has already been attained, it is on the basis of this mind of calm abiding that one meditates. Within one-pointed meditative equipoise one takes the Desire Realm as the object of observation, as already explained. At this point, the meditator begins to analyze it. In the more extensive form of this meditation, there are six investigations according to which the Desire Realm is analyzed; however, I have combined them in order to make them easier to comprehend.[4]

Because the meditator is analyzing, he or she cannot remain in calm abiding but has to cultivate the nine mental abidings within analytical meditation, in dependence upon the calm abiding already achieved. With this stability of mind, he or she views the Desire Realm as gross. At the beginning of this type of analysis, it is difficult to maintain the analysis for very long. This experience is equivalent to the first of the nine mental abidings. Thus, because the meditator is again cultivating the first mental abiding, it is necessary to rely on the antidotes, the powers, and the mental engagements explained earlier with regard to calm abiding.

Because the meditator is mixing the mind of calm abiding with analysis, it is difficult to analyze. Therefore, it is easy to become lazy again. At this point, it is necessary to contemplate the advantages of meditative stabilization, as explained earlier, and to take joy in it and thereby develop faith. When, through reflection on the advantages of meditative stabilization, faith in it arises, aspiration for it arises automatically. With the aspiration to meditative stabilization, exertion also arises, and indeed, as happens after the ninth mental abiding leading to calm abiding, pliancy also arises. Thus, pliancy, the actual antidote to laziness, is now the way of overcoming laziness.

If forgetting the instruction occurs—that is, if the meditator loses the object of observation—it is necessary to regain the object through mindfulness, as I have already explained.

Since laxity and excitement are also faults at this time, introspection has to investigate whether laxity or excitement has arisen. If, through introspection, the meditator recognizes that laxity or excitement has arisen but does not apply the appropriate antidote, then non-application would be a fault, and application would be necessary. However, the mode of applying the antidotes would be different. At this point, because the meditator is analyzing the object of observation and is engaged in many investigations concerning it, excitement can be generated and stability lost; he or she may become unable to stay on the object of observation. When, through introspection, the meditator realizes that excitement has set in, it is necessary to enter into stabilizing meditation and merely set the mind on the object of observation. Initially, however, with engagement in stabilizing meditation, it is possible for the object of observation and the aspect of consciousness analyzing it to become slightly unclear. If either coarse or subtle laxity begins to arise, the meditator should immediately begin to analyze again. Thus, it is necessary to alternate analytical meditation and stabilizing meditation; when one realizes that excitement is about to arise, one should engage in stabilizing meditation, and when one realizes that laxity is about to arise, one should engage in analytical meditation. Though it is difficult to analyze, it is less difficult than it would have been had calm abiding not been achieved. The meditator has a very stable mind. However, it is necessary to develop skill in alternating analytical meditation and stabilizing meditation.

If the antidotes are applied when laxity and excitement have not arisen, that application of the antidotes is a fault; that is the fifth of the five faults. At this time, one should desist from application of the antidotes. Although we posited that actual desisting from application, or equanimity, takes place only in the eighth mental abiding, there is a similitude of desisting from application in the earlier mental abidings. In this way, the meditator overcomes the five faults by engaging in the eight antidotes.

Here, as in the cultivation of calm abiding, the mental engagement is that of forcible engagement—forcibly fixing on the object of observation—and again, the first of the nine mental abidings is achieved by the power of hearing; the meditator analyzes the faults of the Desire Realm and the peacefulness of the First Concentration just as he or she heard it explained.

The ability to extend the continuum of this analysis a little marks the beginning of the second mental abiding. Here, reliance on the antidotes to laziness and to forgetting the instruction is as before. If, through introspection, the meditator notices that laxity or excitement has arisen, the appropriate antidote should be applied; if excitement has arisen, the meditator immediately enters into stabilizing meditation, whereas if laxity has arisen, he or she enters into analytical meditation. The alternation of analytical and stabilizing meditation is the same as for the first mental abiding. This, again, is a time of forcible engagement, and at this point the meditator has the power of thinking; because, during the first mental abiding, he or she thought again and again about the object, the second mental abiding has the power of thinking with respect to the object.

When the periods of distraction lessen somewhat, one has arrived at the third mental abiding. At this point, the meditator recognizes distraction immediately and puts the mind back on the object of observation. Again, if laziness arises, it is necessary to rely on the antidotes; if forgetting the instruction occurs, it is necessary, through mindfulness, to put the mind back on the object of observation; it is also necessary, through introspection, to analyze whether laxity or excitement has arisen and, if either has, to rely on the appropriate antidote. From the third through the seventh mental abiding, the mental engagement is that of interrupted engagement. At the time of the third mental abiding, because of reliance on mindfulness in the previous mental abidings, mindfulness has become stronger; thus, the meditator has the power of mindfulness.

When the power of mindfulness developed in the third mental abiding has matured, one has arrived at the fourth mental abiding. From this time on, the meditator no longer loses the object of observation. Thus, coarse excitement is no longer generated. However, coarse laxity is still generated. Indeed, it is still necessary to rely on the antidotes to laziness, but the second fault, that of forgetting the instruction, no longer occurs, and there is no longer any need to rely on its antidote. It is no longer necessary, through introspection, to analyze whether coarse excitement has arisen, but the meditator still has to analyze whether subtle excitement or coarse or subtle laxity has arisen.

At the point at which coarse laxity is no longer generated, the meditator has arrived at the fifth mental abiding. Laziness can still arise, and the meditator still has to rely on its antidotes. As in the fourth mental abiding, forgetting the instruction no longer occurs, and its antidote is no longer needed. Introspection must analyze whether subtle laxity or excitement has arisen; if the meditator recognizes that either of them has arisen, he or she should rely on the antidote, the alternation of analytical and stabilizing meditation, as before. During the fifth mental abiding, there is great danger of developing subtle laxity, and the mind may have to be invigorated by reflection on the advantages and auspicious qualities of meditative stabilization; at this point, however, the main antidote to laxity is analytical meditation itself. The mental engagement is still that of interrupted engagement, and the power is that of introspection; through the full development of the power of mindfulness during the fourth mental abiding, one comes to have the power of introspection in the fifth.

When the meditator arrives at a point at which there is great danger of subtle excitement, he or she has passed to the sixth mental abiding. However, there is less danger of subtle laxity. As before, if laziness arises, it is necessary to rely on its antidote. The antidote to forgetting the instruction is not needed. Introspection must investigate whether subtle laxity or excitement has arisen. If, through introspection, the meditator recognizes that subtle laxity has arisen, analytical meditation should be done; if the meditator realizes that subtle excitement has arisen, stabilizing meditation should be done. In the sixth mental abiding, the power of introspection has matured.

When laxity and excitement can no longer harm the process of meditative stabilization, the meditator has reached the seventh mental abiding. As before, if laziness occurs, it is necessary to rely on the antidotes. Forgetting the instruction does not arise, and its antidote is not needed. However, it is still necessary to analyze with introspection to see whether laxity or excitement has arisen. Though subtle laxity and excitement can no longer harm the process of meditative stabilization, if the meditator recognizes that they have arisen, their antidotes—analytical or stabilizing meditation—must be applied. The seventh mental abiding is achieved through the power of effort.

When subtle laxity and excitement are no longer generated, the meditator has arrived at the eighth mental abiding. Probably laziness could no longer arise. The fault of forgetting the instruction does not occur. In the eighth mental abiding, at the very beginning of the session, it is necessary to analyze with introspection concerning laxity and excitement, but there is no need to analyze again for the rest of the session. However, the meditator still alternates analytical and stabilizing meditation. In the eighth mental abiding, the power of effort has matured. The mental engagement is that of uninterrupted engagement.

The meditator will arrive at a point at which there is no longer any need to rely on introspection; meditative stabilization operates effortlessly and spontaneously. At that point, one has arrived at the ninth mental abiding. Within this stabilized mind, the practitioner is able, through the power of familiarity, to engage in viewing the Desire Realm as gross and the First Concentration as peaceful. Nevertheless, one does not yet have a union of calm abiding and special insight.

Cultivation of this meditative stabilization again and again over a long period leads to the attainment of mental and physical pliancy. Previously, during stabilizing meditation, it was difficult to analyze, and during analytical meditation, it was difficult to stabilize; that was an unserviceability of mind. When this unserviceability of mind is overcome, the meditator has mental pliancy—the ability to direct the mind at will to any object. In dependence upon this mental pliancy, physical pliancy is attained. The meditator becomes free of bad physical states—physical unserviceability—and achieves a lightness of body like that of cotton, a physical pliancy exceeding that attained earlier, with the attainment of calm abiding. In dependence upon this physical pliancy, the meditator attains a bliss of physical pliancy. Then, after attaining the bliss of physical pliancy, the meditator again and again prolongs meditative stabilization and, through the power of that, attains a bliss of mental pliancy; this is a special mental pliancy even greater than that attained earlier, with the attainment of calm abiding. At this point, the meditator attains a meditative stabilization that is a union of calm abiding and special insight (*zhi lhag zung 'brel, śamathavipaśyanāyuganaddha*). One simultaneously attains special insight, the meditative stabilization that is a union of calm abiding and special insight, a bliss of mental pliancy (this time induced by analysis), and the third of the seven preparations for the first concentration—the mental contemplation arisen from belief.

The Mental Contemplation Arisen from Belief

The mental contemplation arisen from belief is so called because, during the mental contemplation of individual knowledge of the character, the meditator reflected on the grossness of the Desire Realm and the peacefulness of the First Concentration through mental abidings arisen from hearing and thinking and believed them to be that way. Since this state arises through the power of such belief, it is called the mental contemplation arisen from belief.

At this point, a practitioner has attained the capacity to abandon certain features of the Desire Realm. We have afflictive emotions pertaining to the Desire Realm—principally attachment, but also hatred and other afflictive emotions. These afflictive emotions are divided into nine types according to strength, and one overcomes them by degrees. There are three basic divisions—great (*chen po, adhimātra*), middling (*'bring, madhya*), and small (*chung ngu, mṛdu*)—each of which is then subdivided into three. Thus, there are the great of the great (*chen po'i chen po, adhimātrādhimātra*), the middling of the great (*chen po'i 'bring, adhimātramadhya*) and the small of the great (*chen po'i chung ngu, adhimātramṛdu*); the great of the middling (*'bring gi chen po, madhyādhimātra*), the middling of the middling (*'bring gi 'bring, madhyamadhya*), and the small of the middling (*'bring gi chung ngu, madhyamṛdu*); and finally, the great of the small (*chung ngu'i chen po, mṛdvadhimātra*), the middling of the small (*chung ngu'i bring, mṛdumadhya*), and the small of the small (*chung ngu'i chung ngu, mṛdumṛdu*).

The Mental Contemplation of Thorough Isolation

Through again and again cultivating the mental contemplation arisen from belief, the meditator is able to overcome the great of the great afflictive emotions pertaining to the Desire Realm and attains what is called an uninterrupted path (*bar chad med lam, ānantaryamārga*) that is an antidote to the great of the great afflictive emotions. This point marks the beginning of the mental contemplation of thorough isolation. This uninterrupted path and the mental contemplation of thorough isolation are attained together. It is called thorough isolation because it is the meditator's initial isolation from afflictive emotions pertaining to the Desire Realm. The mental contemplation of thorough isolation has three parts, which are path consciousnesses that act as antidotes. They are the small of the small, which acts as the antidote to the great of the great afflictive emotions; the middling of the small, which acts as the antidote to the middling of the great afflictive emotions;

and the great of the small, which acts as the antidote to the small of the great afflictive emotions.

The afflictive emotions. Just as, when we talk about big and small humans, we have to identify what a human is, so, when we set forth the convention of the nine levels of afflictive emotions, we have to identify the basis of this convention, the afflictive emotions. To make this series of nine appear more easily to your minds, I will explain the afflictive emotions of people like us in the Desire Realm.

The afflictive emotions are mental factors. The first is desire (*'dod chags, rāga*)—that is, the desire connected with the Desire Realm. We observe internal or external pleasant objects and are attracted to them. We wish to see them or to touch them. Not only do we wish to see them or to touch them, we wish to see them or to touch them again and again. If we divide pleasant external objects even further, there are pleasant visible forms, pleasant sounds, pleasant odors, pleasant tastes, and pleasant tangible objects. Whether these objects are actually pleasant or not, the mental factor of desire sees them as pleasant in their own right and is attached and attracted to them. Internal desires can be illustrated by the desire of male for female and of female for male; from these illustrations, one can understand many other types. If I described all the various types of desire, I would not be able to finish the subject under discussion. For example, there are many different visible forms; thus, there is a desire for each of them. The same is true of sounds, odors, tastes, and tangible objects.

The next afflictive emotion is anger (*khong khro, pratigha*). There are three types of objects of anger. The first is sentient beings who harm us; the second is suffering itself; and the third is sources or causes of suffering such as weapons or thorns. Anger is a wish to harm these—to harm these sentient beings, to harm suffering itself, or to harm phenomena that are sources of suffering. The main object is other persons, but there are also objects that are not persons. For example, we might get angry at our mug, or if we are carrying a heavy bag and become tired, we may get angry at the bag and throw it on the ground. Thus, anger is a wish to harm any of these three objects. We can generate anger toward any of the phenomena of the Desire Realm, but whether the object is actually pleasant or unpleasant, the mental factor of anger views the object as inherently unpleasant.

The next afflictive emotion is pride (*nga rgyal, māna*). Pride is generated as a result of viewing our own wealth, good qualities, youth, and so forth; in viewing these, we have a sense of being puffed up. For example, if we come from a particularly good family or class, or if we are well educated, or if we have great wealth and resources, or youth, or a good voice, or are particularly skilled in sports, any of these qualities can be taken as a reason for being puffed up. If we are particularly tall or handsome, we may think, "I am very tall and handsome." There are many types of pride. The rest can be understood through these illustrations.

The next afflictive emotion is ignorance (*ma rig pa, avidyā*). Ignorance is obscuration with respect to the nature of phenomena. Though this applies to the deep nature of phenomena, it applies to the more superficial nature of phenomena as well; for example, I have an ignorance which is obscuration with respect to the language of the United States. An ignorance can be posited with respect to any object. There are two types of ignorance; one is lack of knowledge with respect to an object, and the other is a misconception of the nature of objects. Both are ignorance. As an example of misconception, one could observe oneself and conceive that person to possess inherent existence (*rang bzhin gyis grub pa, svabhāvasiddhi*); this would be a case of an ignorance which is an obscuration with respect to the reality of the person. Through the power of this obscuration, we engage in contaminated actions (*zag bcas kyi las, sāsravakarma*), accumulate such predispositions (*bag chags, vāsanā*), and are forced into rebirth in cyclic existence (*'khor ba, saṃsāra*).

The next afflictive emotion is doubt (*the tshom, vicikitsā*). Afflicted doubt is an undecidedness of mind wondering, for example, whether the cause and effect of actions exist or not and thinking that they probably do not, or thinking that former and later lives may or may not exist or that engaging in religious practice may or may not help. There are many types of non-afflicted doubt that are not included here—for example, if we are going along the road, wondering whether it is the right road, or if we are composing a letter, wondering about the spelling of a word. Such doubt is not afflicted.

The next afflictive emotion is view (*lta ba, dṛṣṭi*)—that is, afflicted view. In general, there are two types of views, good and bad; "view," here, means bad views, afflicted knowledge. If afflicted views are divided, there are five types. The first is called the view of the transitory collection (*'jig tshogs la lta ba, satkāyadṛṣṭi*); the second is called the view holding to an extreme (*mthar 'dzin par lta ba, antagrāhadṛṣṭi*); the third is called perverse view (*log par lta ba, mithyādṛṣṭi*); the fourth is called the conception of a bad view as supreme (*lta ba mchog tu 'dzin pa, dṛṣṭiparāmarśa*); and the fifth is called the conception of bad ethics and modes of conduct as supreme (*tshul khrims dang brtul zhugs mchog tu 'dzin pa, śīlavrataparāmarśa*).

The view of the transitory collection is the observation of one's own mind and body, the physical aggregates, which are transitory and are a collection, as a real "I" or real "mine." The afflicted knowledge that views the mind and body in this fashion is called the view of the transitory collection.

The view holding to an extreme takes what is held to be a real I (that is, the transitory collection) as either existing forever—not disintegrating—or as being annihilated at death. These are the two extremes (*mtha', anta*). They are called the extreme of permanence (*rtag mtha', śaśvatānta*) and the extreme of annihilation (*chad mtha', ucchedānta*). Through them, we view a real I as not disintegrating moment by moment or as not connecting to a future lifetime.

Perverse view is so called because one is conceiving the opposite of the fact. In the case of afflicted doubt, we think, for example, that the cause and effect of action may or may not exist and even that they probably do not, but in the case of perverse view we hold the view that the cause and effect of actions in fact do not exist, that former and later rebirths in fact do not exist.

The conception of a bad view as supreme is a case of viewing any of the first three views—the view of the transitory collection, the view holding to an extreme, or perverse view—as the supreme view, that is, as one's own view and as the best.

Bad ethics and modes of conduct are bad systems of ethics and modes of conduct that are motivated by bad views. In India, for example, there are systems of conduct that propound the desirability of acting like a dog and that view such conduct as supreme. The advocacy of this doglike mode of conduct could be the result of a person's attaining the first concentration, achieving clairvoyance on the basis of that, and seeing that he has been a dog in his previous lifetime. Seeing through clairvoyance that he had been a dog before being reborn as a human, the person draws the mistaken conclusion that a doglike life leads to the life of a human. Therefore, the person behaves like a dog, walks like a dog on all fours, eats like a dog, sleeps and copulates like a dog. The conception of this as supreme would be the view that this is a mode of liberation. Thus, to view wrong systems of ethics or modes of conduct as paths of purification is the conception of bad ethics and modes of conduct as supreme.

These six afflictive emotions are called the six root afflictive emotions (*rtsa nyon, mūlakleśa*). They are afflictive emotions in and of themselves and do not have to depend on other states to be afflictive emotions. They are the roots of our wandering in cyclic existence, and they act as the roots of other, secondary, afflictive emotions.

The secondary afflictive emotions. The first of the secondary afflictive emotions (*nye nyon, upakleśa*) is belligerence (*khro ba, krodha*). Belligerence occurs when we are near any of the three causes of anger; it is an intention to harm another through striking, and so forth. There are nine sources of harm at which we get angry. The first three are accompanied by the thoughts, "This person has harmed me," "This person is harming me," or "This person will harm me." The next three are accompanied by the thoughts, "This person has harmed my friend," "This person is harming my friend," or "This person will harm my friend." The last three are accompanied by the thoughts, "This person has helped my enemy," "This person is helping my enemy," or "This person will help my enemy." When we experience any of these nine, our anger increases until we want to strike out at the other person; this is called the mental factor of belligerence.

The next secondary afflictive emotion is resentment (*'khon 'dzin, upanāha*). Resentment is a wish to return harm that was done in the past and involves maintaining the continuum of anger and remembering—for example, remembering, perhaps for many years, that such and such a person harmed us in a certain way, that such and such a person said a rough word to us.

The next afflictive emotion is concealment (*'chab pa, mrakṣa*). Concealment is a wish to hide a fault when another person points it out. The fault could be of any type. For example, someone may point out that we are breaking a vow, or in a worldly context, someone may point out that we are breaking the law or breaking the rules of a college. Concealment is the mental factor that wishes to hide that we had ever committed such a fault.

The next afflictive emotion, spite (*'tshig pa, pradāśa*), is a wish to speak harsh words to another person who has pointed out a fault. For example, if someone tells us that if we act in a certain way we will be committing a non-virtuous action and if we, through attachment to that action, speak harshly, this is a case of spite.

The next afflictive emotion is jealousy (*phrag dog, irṣyā*). Jealousy is a disturbance of the mind from the depths; it involves the inability to bear another's good fortune because of being attached to goods and services. In other words, if a person whom we dislike attains success, we cannot bear it. Among the greater forms of jealousy are jealousy between countries, jealousy between states, jealousy between cities, and jealousy between families. We can be jealous even of our own relatives; if our brother or sister attains some success that we do not have, we can become jealous. This inability to bear the superior fortune of someone else is called jealousy. Inability to bear a type of fortune equal to our own is called competitiveness, but competitiveness can be included within jealousy.

The next afflictive emotion, miserliness (*ser sna, mātsarya*) is the tight holding on to wealth through fear that it will decrease. There are many examples of miserliness, such as having a thousand dollars and being afraid that that thousand dollars would be reduced if we spent any of it and, therefore, not buying even the things we need; or not using our car because we are afraid that the paint on it may get scratched, or having a good coat and not wearing it even in very cold weather because it may get dirty.

The next afflictive emotion is deceit (*sgyu, māyā*). Deceit is the pretense of having good qualities we do not have, through strong attachment to goods and services. For example, we might pretend to know a language in order to be paid respect for knowing it. A deceitful religious practitioner is someone who is not disciplined but who pretends to be disciplined in order to get donations, and so forth, from others.

The next afflictive emotion, dissimulation (*g.yo, śāṭhya*), is similar to concealment. However, it differs in that it is a general wish to hide our faults, whereas concealment is a wish to hide our faults when someone else has identified them. Dissimulation is a wish not to make our faults manifest through fear of not receiving respect or offerings from others.

Though the next afflictive emotion, haughtiness (*rgyags pa, māda*), is similar to pride, haughtiness is included within the factor of desire. Haughtiness is a puffing up of the mind through enjoying comfort or our own good health, youth, beauty, power, and so forth. There are many examples of haughtiness, such as someone who is promoted to a higher position and pretends not to know people he or she knows, or someone who becomes rich and pretends not to notice even his or her own relatives.

The next afflictive emotion is harmfulness (*rnam par 'tshe ba, vihiṃsā*). Harmfulness is an unmerciful wish to harm other sentient beings. It is not merely lack of mercy but lack of mercy coupled with the wish to harm.

The next afflictive emotion is non-shame (*ngo tsha med pa, āhrīkya*), which is failure to avoid non-virtue from the point of view of our own disapproval. From our own point of view, we do not care. If we cared, we would think, "Now I am a human; I am a person who can engage in thought. Since I have been born in my present situation, I should not engage in this non-virtuous activity." Or we would think, "If I engage in this action, I will have to undergo suffering in the future as a result of it."

Non-embarrassment (*khrel med pa, anapatrāpya*), the next afflictive emotion, is failure to avoid faults from the point of view of another's disapproval. If we avoid faults from the point of view of another's disapproval, we would think, "If I do this, other people will dislike me," or, "If I engage in such a terrible action, many people will find fault with me."

The next afflictive emotion is lethargy (*rmugs pa, styāna*). Lethargy is dullness; it is an unserviceability, or heaviness, of mind and body; here "unserviceability" means heaviness. This has been discussed in relation to calm abiding.

The next afflictive emotion, excitement (*rgod pa, auddhatya*), has also been discussed in relation to calm abiding. It is a scattering of the mind to previously experienced attributes of the Desire Realm. It involves desire and is a case of the mind's scattering to a pleasant object.

The next afflictive emotion, non-faith (*ma dad pa, āśraddhya*), is the opposite of faith. It is a lack of respect for or belief in good qualities or those who possess good qualities. Thus, it is an absence of belief, of delight, and of wishing with respect to virtuous phenomena.

The next afflictive emotion is laziness (*le lo, kausīdya*). Laziness is a lack of enthusiasm for virtue due to attachment to the pleasures of lying down, and so forth. The three types of laziness were explained earlier.

The next afflictive emotion, non-conscientiousness (*bag med pa, pramāda*), is a case of not keeping the mind from faults—of allowing faulty mental, physical, and verbal actions without trying to avoid them.

The next afflictive emotion is forgetfulness (*brjed nges pa, muṣitasmṛtitā*). Forgetfulness is afflicted mindfulness, afflicted attention to an object. It involves taking to mind an object of the afflictive emotions and thereby forgetting a virtuous object.

The next afflictive emotion, non-introspection (*shes bzhin ma yin pa, asaṃprajanya*), is an unknowing engagement in physical, mental, and verbal deeds. Through non-introspection, one does not know what one is doing physically, verbally, or mentally.

The last afflictive emotion is distraction (*rnam par g.yeng ba, vikṣepa*). Distraction is a scattering of the mind from its object of observation. All bad conceptions are distractions.

These are the objects to be abandoned—the afflictive emotions pertaining to the Desire Realm. At this point, a practitioner cannot overcome them from the root, but he or she can temporarily cause them to become non-manifest, or suppressed. As was explained earlier, the manifest forms of these afflictive emotions can be divided into great, middling, and small, and each of these divisions can in turn be divided into three. They are suppressed by the path consciousnesses that act as their antidotes. The path consciousness at this point is called the mental contemplation of thorough isolation.

The mode of procedure. The mental contemplation of thorough isolation, the fourth of the seven preparations for the first concentration, is so called because the yogi's mental continuum is separated for the first time from the great afflictive emotions pertaining to the Desire Realm. When this mental contemplation is first generated, the Desire Realm is viewed as gross. The mode of viewing now becomes more condensed than that explained earlier; the Desire Realm is viewed as gross in nature and in number. Viewing the Desire Realm as gross in nature means viewing it as full of faults and as extremely miserable; this type of life is seen as very short and very low. Viewing the Desire Realm as gross in number means viewing the five aggregates of the Desire Realm as miserable in many ways; in dependence on these aggregates, there are many actions and afflictive emotions to be overcome.

When the first moment of the mental contemplation of thorough isolation views the Desire Realm as gross in nature and in number, it develops the capacity to overcome the great of the great afflictive emotions. It has two factors. First, it views the Desire Realm as gross and develops the capacity to overcome the great of the great afflictive emotions pertaining to the Desire Realm; then it views the First Concentration as peaceful. Thus, there are two periods. The first period is called an uninterrupted path (*bar chad med lam, ānantaryamārga*) and the second, a path of release (*rnam grol lam, vimuktimārga*). The first period of the mental contemplation of thorough isolation is called an uninterrupted path because it acts as the antidote to the great of the great afflictive emotions and is able to suppress them; afterward, there will be no interruption or interference by these great of the great afflictive emotions. The second period of the mental contemplation of thorough isolation is called a path of release because it is a path consciousness that is released from the great of the great afflictive emotions pertaining to the Desire Realm.

Because the mental contemplation of thorough isolation overcomes all the great afflictive emotions pertaining to the Desire Realm, two more steps are needed, each of which also has two periods. This process is merely a matter of continuing the meditation and attaining the power of mind to overcome the middling of the great afflictive emotions pertaining to the Desire Realm. The first period of this second division again views the Desire Realm as gross in nature and in number and is again called an uninterrupted path, and the second period again views the First Concentration as peaceful and is called a path of release. The first period suppresses the middling of the great afflictive emotions, and the second period is the state of release from the middling of the great afflictive emotions. In the third of the three divisions of the mental contemplation of thorough isolation, the Desire Realm is again analyzed and observed as gross in nature and in number. With the attainment of the capacity to overcome the small of the great afflictive emotions pertaining to the Desire Realm, the meditator attains the first period of the third division of the mental contemplation of thorough isolation—that is, an uninterrupted path. Then he or she attains a path of release that is the state of having been freed from the small of the great afflictive emotions pertaining to the Desire Realm. (See chart on following page.)

Thus, the mental contemplation of thorough isolation has three uninterrupted paths and three paths of release. They are the three uninterrupted paths that are the antidotes to the great of the great, the middling of the great, and the small of the great afflictive emotions and the three paths of release—that is, the three path consciousnesses that are the states of having been freed from the great of the great, the middling of the great, and the small of the great afflictive emotions pertaining to the Desire Realm.

There is a third type of mental contemplation of thorough isolation that occurs between the path of release and the next uninterrupted path. It occurs when a meditator has had a path of release and is trying to achieve the capacity to reach the next uninterrupted path and thus is neither of those two. Before the first uninterrupted path, a meditator would have the third of the seven preparations, the mental contemplation arisen from belief, but before the others, he or she would have the mental contemplation of thorough isolation that is neither a path of release nor an uninterrupted path; after overcoming the small of the great afflictive emotions and until attaining the capacity to overcome the great of the middling, a meditator would again have a mental contemplation of thorough isolation that was neither a path of release nor an uninterrupted path.

The Mental Contemplation of Thorough Isolation

Read from bottom to top

Great Afflictions of the Desire Realm	*Path*
small	path of release uninterrupted path
middling	path of release uninterrupted path
great	path of release uninterrupted path

The Mental Contemplation of Joy-Withdrawal

Read from bottom to top

Middling Afflictions of the Desire Realm	*Path*
small	path of release uninterrupted path
middling	path of release uninterrupted path
great	path of release uninterrupted path

The Mental Contemplation of Joy-Withdrawal

The fifth preparation is called the mental contemplation of joy-withdrawal. (In Tibetan, it is given as "joy-withdrawal" for reasons of euphony; however, "withdrawal-joy" is correct.[5]) "Withdrawal" refers to the uninterrupted paths and is so called because the practitioner is observing the Desire Realm and turning away from attachment to it; the mind becomes withdrawn from coarser objects of observation. The paths of release of this preparation are called "joy" because the practitioner has become freed from the middling afflictive emotions pertaining to the Desire Realm.[6]

As in the mental contemplation of thorough isolation, there are three uninterrupted paths and three paths of release. (See chart above.) Again, the meditator continues to view the Desire Realm as gross in nature and in number. With the attainment of the capacity to overcome the great of the middling afflictive emotions pertaining to the Desire Realm, the meditator attains the first uninterrupted path that is a mental contemplation of withdrawal. This is followed by a path of release that is called a mental contemplation of joy because of the delight of having become freed from the great of the middling afflictive emotions pertaining to the Desire Realm; this path of release views the First Concentration as peaceful. Through further cultivation of the view of the Desire Realm as gross, the meditator eventually attains the capacity to suppress the middling of the middling afflictive emotions and, at that point, attains the second uninterrupted path that is a mental contemplation of withdrawal. Again, it is followed by a path of release that is a mental contemplation of joy and that views the First Concentration as peaceful. Through continued familiarity with and cultivation of the view of the Desire Realm as gross, the meditator attains the capacity to suppress the small of the middling afflictive emotions pertaining to the Desire Realm and, at that point, attains the third uninterrupted path that is a mental contemplation of withdrawal. Again, a path of release is generated afterward that views the First Concentration as peaceful. These uninterrupted paths and paths of release, as well as those paths that are neither, are the various forms of the mental contemplation of joy-withdrawal. Thus, the first six of the nine afflictive emotions pertaining to the Desire Realm are overcome.

The Mental Contemplation of Analysis

Because the meditator has overcome the first six afflictive emotions pertaining to the Desire Realm and thinks that he or she has overcome all nine, it is necessary to investigate whether all afflictive emotions pertaining to the Desire Realm have actually been overcome or whether some still remain. Thus, a different factor of analysis is now needed. The meditator takes to mind—visualizes—some object that is an object of desire or hatred within the Desire Realm and in its presence analyzes whether any desire or hatred is left with respect to that object; the meditator knows from previous experience what objects aroused desire or hatred and tests himself or herself in that situation.

The path consciousness that engages in such investigation is called the mental contemplation of analysis and is the sixth of the seven preparations; this preparation has neither uninterrupted paths nor paths of release. Having investigated in this manner, the meditator understands that there are still afflictive emotions pertaining to the Desire Realm to be overcome and again engages in meditation.

The Mental Contemplation of Final Training

With the attainment of the capacity to overcome the great of the small afflictive emotions, which comes about through repeated familiarity with and cultivation of the view of the Desire Realm as gross in nature and in number, the meditator attains the uninterrupted path that is the antidote to the great of the small afflictive emotions. This is the first of the three uninterrupted paths of the mental contemplation of final training, after which the first of the paths of release is attained. Then the meditator again investigates whether there are afflictive emotions still to be abandoned. Seeing that there are afflictive emotions still to be abandoned, he or she again enters into contemplation of the Desire Realm as gross in nature and in number. With the attainment, through repeated familiarity, of the capacity to suppress the middling of the small afflictive emotions, the meditator attains the second uninterrupted path of the mental contemplation of final training. Afterward, when the middling of the small afflictive emotions pertaining to the Desire Realm have been suppressed, a path of release that views the First Concentration as peaceful is generated.

Again, a mental contemplation of analysis is needed; it is necessary to investigate whether any of the afflictive emotions pertaining to the Desire Realm remain. The mode of analysis is as before. Then, seeing that some afflictive emotions still remain, the meditator again enters into the contemplation of the Desire Realm as gross in nature and in number and, with the attainment, through repeated familiarity, of the capacity to suppress the small of the small afflictive emotions pertaining to the Desire Realm, he or she attains the third of the three uninterrupted paths of the mental contemplation of final training.

These three uninterrupted paths and the paths of release that follow the first two constitute the mental contemplation of final training. It is so called because it is the last of the preparations and because it is a training. (See chart below. For a complete layout of the preparations, see chart, page 104.)

The Mental Contemplation of Final Training and the First Concentration

Read from bottom to top

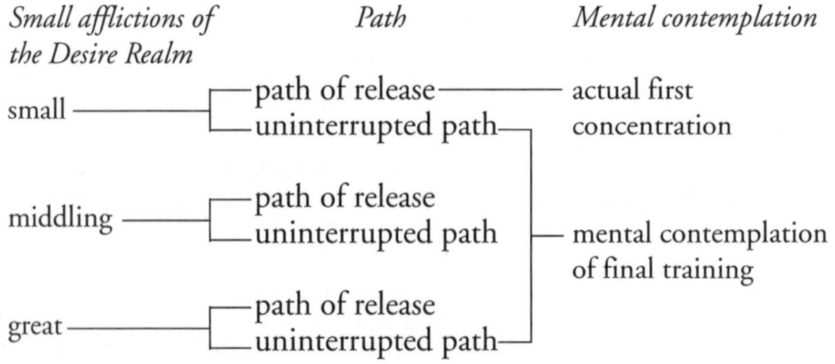
Small afflictions of the Desire Realm
Path
Mental contemplation
small
path of release
uninterrupted path
actual first concentration
middling
path of release
uninterrupted path
mental contemplation of final training
great
path of release
uninterrupted path

The First Concentration

After the last uninterrupted path, the meditator generates the last of the paths of release; it is the path of release that is a state of having overcome the small of the small afflictive emotions pertaining to the Desire Realm, and it views the First Concentration as peaceful and auspicious. That path itself is the actual first concentration.

There are various ways of referring to the first concentration. It is also called the meditative absorption (*snyoms 'jug, samāpatti*)—or the actual meditative absorption (*dngos gzhi'i snyoms 'jug, maulasamāpatti*)—of the first concentration. It is called an actual meditative absorption because it is not a preparation. It is called a meditative absorption (*snyoms 'jug, samāpatti*) because the mind and mental factors are all equally operating on the object of observation.[7] It is also called an absorption, or equalization, because the four elements—earth, water, fire, and wind—have become balanced. It is called a concentration (*bsam gtan, dhyāna*) because the yogi is holding the mind inside;[8] and because it is the first of the four actual meditative absorptions of the four concentrations, it is called the first concentration.

Branches of the First Concentration

The first concentration has five branches (*yan lag, aṅga*), which are considered in three groups—antidote (*gnyen po, pratipakṣa*), benefit (*phan yon, anuśaṃsa*), and basis (*gnas, āśraya*). In the category of antidote, there are two branches—investigation (*rtog pa, vitarka*) and analysis (*dpyod pa, vicāra*). In the category of benefit are joy (*dga' ba, prīti*) and bliss (*bde ba, sukha*). The basis is meditative stabilization (*ting nge 'dzin, samādhi*).

The antidotal branches. Investigation and analysis are the antidotal branches. They are called antidotal because they cause separation from the faults of the Desire Realm. Since, in the first concentration itself, the meditator is beyond attachment to the Desire Realm, these branches do not actually cause non-attachment with regard to the Desire Realm. However, they are the continuation of the investigation and analysis that took place during the preparations for the first concentration. Therefore, investigation and analysis within the composite of the factors included in the first concentration are posited as antidotes, and indeed, they are antidotes in the sense of causing the meditator to become more distant from attachment to the Desire Realm.

The mental factor of investigation engages its object in a slightly coarse way. It merely investigates roughly the entity of the object under consideration, whereas analysis is a more detailed investigation of the object. Analysis involves searching out and analyzing the attributes of the object rather than its general entity; it also involves searching out the reason.

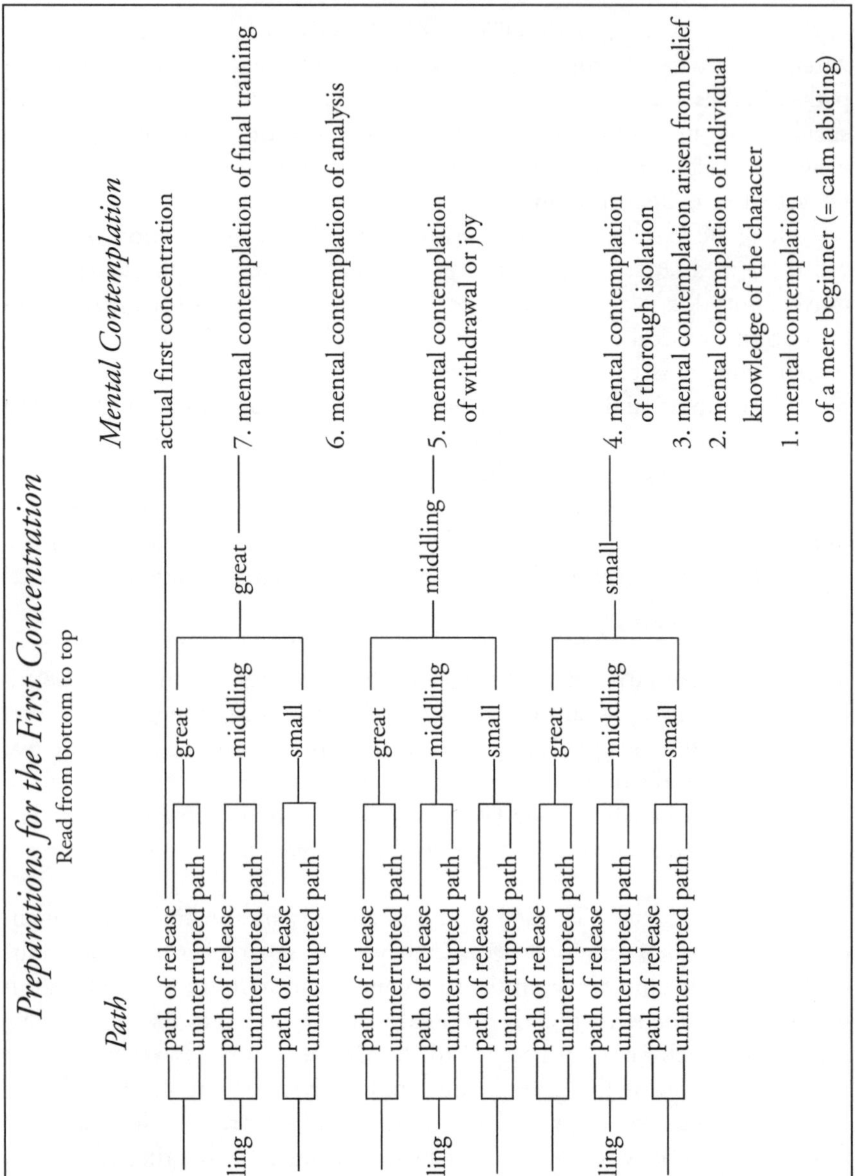
Preparations for the First Concentration
Read from bottom to top
Afflictive Emotions of the Desire Realm
Path
Mental Contemplation
small
9. small
8. middling
7. great
middling
6. small
5. middling
4. great
great
3. small
2. middling
1. great
path of release
uninterrupted path
path of release
uninterrupted path
path of release
uninterrupted path
path of release
uninterrupted path
path of release
uninterrupted path
path of release
uninterrupted path
path of release
uninterrupted path
path of release
uninterrupted path
path of release
uninterrupted path
great
middling
small
great
middling
small
great
middling
small
great
middling
small
actual first concentration
7. mental contemplation of final training
6. mental contemplation of analysis
5. mental contemplation of withdrawal or joy
4. mental contemplation of thorough isolation
3. mental contemplation arisen from belief
2. mental contemplation of individual knowledge of the character
1. mental contemplation of a mere beginner (= calm abiding)

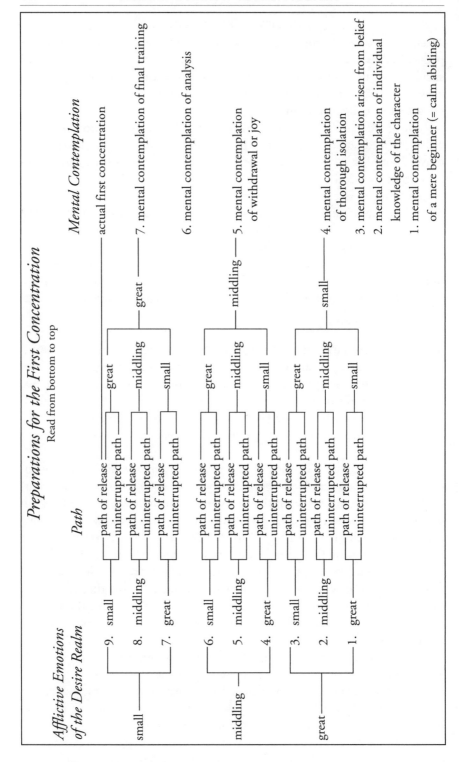

The benefit branches. There are two branches that are benefits—joy and bliss. Though they are counted as two, they are actually one thing—mental bliss (*yid bde, saumanasya*)—seen from two points of view. Because the mental bliss that accompanies the first concentration performs two functions, two benefits are enumerated. (For example, one person within a family may be both a husband and a father.) Bliss is so called because mental bliss helps the body and the sense organs; "help," in this context, means that mental bliss causes a sense of bliss in the body as well. The meditator becomes somewhat lighter. For example, if we are very happy, the body can sustain itself well even without much food, and if we have a great deal of mental suffering, we can become thin even when we eat a great deal; this is how mental bliss helps the body. Mental bliss also causes the other factors that accompany the mental consciousness to be joyful; that is its other function, and from that point of view the mental bliss is called joy. Thus, because mental bliss has these two functions, it is designated with the two names "joy" and "bliss."

The mental bliss of the first concentration is the mental feeling of bliss that accompanies the mental consciousness (*yid kyi rnam shes, manovijñāna*) of a being in the first concentration. Joy and bliss are called benefits because they are produced as a result of separation, by way of investigation and analysis, from attachment to the Desire Realm.

The basis branch. Meditative stabilization is the branch called basis; meditative stabilization means that the mind abides one-pointedly on an object of observation. It is posited as the branch called basis because the two antidotes and the two benefits exist in dependence on meditative stabilization; it is the basis, or source, of the antidotes and benefits.

The composite of these five branches is called the meditative absorption of the first concentration. There are many other factors present in this composite, but these five—investigation, analysis, joy, bliss, and meditative stabilization—are the main ones and are therefore cited.

Types of Meditative Absorption of the First Concentration

The meditative absorption of the first concentration has two types—causal (*rgyu, kāraṇa*) and resultant-birth (*'bras bu skye ba, kārya*). A meditative absorption of the first concentration cultivated during this lifetime would be causal; if, in dependence upon having cultivated the meditative absorption of the first concentration in this lifetime, a practitioner were born in the next lifetime in one of the lands of the First Concentration, he or she would have a resultant-birth meditative absorption of the first concentration. A causal meditative absorption of the first concentration is an actual first concentration; the yogi is not merely working on its causes. Rather, it is causal in the sense that it can cause a rebirth in the First Concentration. The mental and physical aggregates that are a fruition of that action—that is, of that causal meditative absorption—are a resultant meditative absorption of the first concentration—a resultant birth.

The factors posited as a resultant birth are the fruitional (*rnam smin, vipāka*) mental and physical aggregates—that is, mind and body—and causally concordant effects (*rgyu mthun gyi 'bras bu, niṣyandaphala*). Whereas the causal meditative absorption of the first concentration is mainly the five branches, the mind and body of a being born in the First Concentration are called a resultant-birth type of meditative absorption of the first concentration, though the five branches are also present in a resultant birth. The causally concordant effects are to have a soft mental continuum, to have fewer afflictive emotions than are present in the Desire Realm, and to have peacefulness, stability, and mindfulness. There are many types of causally concordant effects. For example, when a being is born in the First Concentration, a house and a land with groves and parks are produced along with that being's mind and body; these are also included in the resultant-birth type of meditative absorption of the first concentration. As was stated earlier, there are three areas in the First Concentration—Brahmā Type, In Front of Brahmā, and Great Brahmā; a resultant-birth type of meditative absorption of the first concentration can occur in any of these.

The causal meditative absorption of the first concentration has two more types—a mere first concentration (*bsam gtan dang po'i dngos gzhi'i snyoms 'jug tsam po ba*) and a special first concentration (*bsam gtan dang po'i dngos gzhi'i snyoms 'jug khyad par can*). Since investigation is slightly coarser than analysis, the first concentration of a person who has separated from investigation and has only the other four branches is a special first concentration. The first concentration of a person who has all five branches is called a mere first concentration.

It is only for the first concentration, not for the second, third, or fourth, that these two types are posited. The reason is that there is a difference in degree of coarseness and subtlety between investigation and analysis. Because investigation is coarser than the other branches, it is possible to separate from investigation and not from the others; a special first concentration is posited from this point of view. However, for the second, third, and fourth concentrations there is no such difference of coarseness and subtlety in the branches; therefore, mere and special concentrations are not posited.

The causal meditative absorption of the first concentration, and probably the resultant-birth type as well, has yet another division into three types.[9] The first is pure (*dag pa, śuddha*); the second is uncontaminated (*zag med, anāsrava*); and the third is afflicted (*nyon mongs can, kliṣṭa*). In the first concentration, the meditator is separated from the afflictive emotions (*nyon mongs, kleśa*) pertaining to the Desire Realm; if the meditator is also free of all the afflictive emotions pertaining to the First Concentration, he or she is said to have a pure meditative absorption of the first concentration. Pure meditative absorptions of the first concentration are contaminated (*zag bcas, sāsrava*). Uncontaminated meditative absorptions of the first concentration, in brief, are those used by Superiors (*'phags pa, ārya*) as a mental basis for their path consciousness. An afflicted meditative absorption of the first concentration is a meditative absorption that is polluted by the afflictive emotions pertaining to the First Concentration.[10]

How can a first concentration be polluted by afflictive emotions pertaining to the First Concentration itself? The First Concentration has five types of afflictive emotion. The first is attachment (*sred pa, tṛṣṇā*) with respect to the First Concentration; the second is view (*lta ba, dṛṣṭi*); the third is pride (*nga rgyal, māna*); the fourth is ignorance (*ma rig pa, avidyā*), and the fifth is doubt (*the tshom, vicikitsā*).

The first concentration can become polluted by attachment with respect to the First Concentration—that is, by attachment to the bliss of the first concentration. The meditator experiences its taste and becomes attached to it, and through that attachment the first concentration becomes afflicted.

How can view pollute the first concentration? In dependence upon the first concentration, clairvoyance can be achieved; upon attaining this clairvoyance, the meditator sees his or her past and future lifetimes and assumes that the self is permanent. This is a mistaken view, and through the generation of this mistaken view, the first concentration becomes afflicted.

The first concentration becomes polluted by pride if the meditator gets puffed up and thinks, "Who except me could have attained this meditative absorption?" Through the generation of this pride, the first concentration becomes afflicted.

Ignorance and doubt are explained together. Through the power of ignorance, the meditator generates doubt wondering whether the first concentration itself is a path of liberation. Since the first concentration is not a path of liberation, this doubt is mistaken and is a means by which the first concentration becomes afflicted.

Achievement of the Clairvoyances

As I said earlier, one can achieve many meditative absorptions and many clairvoyances on the basis of calm abiding. It is through the first concentration that the clairvoyances are actually achieved.

The Mundane Path

I have already explained that there are nine uninterrupted paths and nine paths of release and that the ninth path of release is the meditative absorption of the first concentration itself. This is the path of release that is the state of having abandoned the afflictive emotions pertaining to the Desire Realm. Here, abandonment of the afflictive emotions pertaining to the Desire Realm does not mean abandonment from the root. What, then, is the mode of abandonment? It is the suppression of the manifest form, not the seed form, of the coarse afflictive emotions, but not of the subtle afflictive emotions. This suppression is like the control of a chronic illness. Through misuse of food and drink and through inappropriate behavior, a chronic illness can develop. When we rely on a doctor, some of the pain of the disease will diminish, and if we do not encounter unfavorable circumstances, we can control the symptoms. However, we have not overcome the basic disease. The preparations for the first concentration overcome afflictive emotions in a similar way.

To generate an afflictive emotion, we first have to conceive of ourselves as substantially existing (*rdzas yod, dravyasat*). With that conception of substantial existence, there is a mental factor of desire. This conception that the person substantially exists and the desire that accompanies it are like a disease. When we meet with a pleasant object and good circumstances, we think about the various beautiful qualities of the object and, impelled by improper mental application, generate great desire. When we meet with an unpleasant object, we engage in and feed on many mistaken reasons for considering the object unpleasant; through improper mental application, we superimpose these reasons and generate great hatred. This form of great desire and great hatred is what is temporarily suppressed through the preparations. However, the basic disease remains. This process is called diminishing the coarse afflictive emotions or suppressing the manifest form of the coarse afflictive emotions.

The nine uninterrupted paths that overcome these afflictive emotions and the nine paths of release that are states of having overcome them are called mundane paths. They are so called because a mundane path of meditation acts as an antidote to these afflictive emotions. From another point of view, they are called mundane paths because the meditator is familiarizing himself or herself with a higher mundane consciousness. This explanation also applies to the remaining levels.

The Second Concentration

Preparations for the Second Concentration

Like the first concentration, the second concentration has seven preparations. The mental contemplation of individual knowledge of the character again has as its mental basis the mind of calm abiding—that is, the mental contemplation of a mere beginner.[11] In dependence upon this mental contemplation of a mere beginner, the meditator now views the First Concentration as gross and the Second Concentration as peaceful. The First Concentration is gross in nature because it is low and has a short lifespan; though the beings in the First Concentration have a long lifespan compared to ours, they have a short lifespan compared to that of the beings in the Second Concentration.

The beings in the First Concentration also have less light and a worse color than the beings in the Second Concentration. The First Concentration is gross in number because it has more faults than the Second Concentration; the First Concentration has investigation and analysis and can involve deceit and dissimulation. An example of deceit and dissimulation in the First Concentration is the false claim of Brahmā that he created the world. A Hearer (*nyan thos, śrāvaka*) asked him, "From what do the four elements originally arise? How do the four elements eventually cease?" Brahmā did not want to say he did not know and therefore answered, "I am the Great Brahmā." Thus, the First Concentration has more faults than the Second Concentration.

Through hearing and thinking, the meditator reflects on the grossness of the First Concentration, and, as in the preparations for the first concentration, passes through the nine mental abidings during the mental contemplation of individual knowledge of the character. It is necessary to pass through the nine mental abidings again in order to achieve the special insight included within the second concentration. However, it will be easier than it was in preparation for the first concentration. Again, the meditator alternates analytical meditation and stabilizing meditation. Gradually, he or she advances over the nine mental abidings and eventually is able to engage in analytical meditation, within a stabilized mind, spontaneously and without exertion. Through repeated familiarity with this process, the meditator attains mental and physical pliancy and, at that point, attains the special insight that is included within the level of the second concentration, though it is not the second concentration.

Simultaneously, the meditator also attains the mental contemplation arisen from belief. Through renewed familiarity with this union of calm abiding and special insight, he or she attains the capacity to overcome the great of the great afflictive emotions pertaining to the First Concentration and, at that point, attains the first of the three uninterrupted paths of the mental contemplation of thorough isolation. Then he or she attains a path of release that is the state of having become freed from the great of the great afflictive emotions pertaining to the First Concentration.

The process of overcoming the afflictive emotions is the same for the second concentration as for the first. There are nine levels of afflictive emotions pertaining to the First Concentration, and to overcome them, nine uninterrupted paths and nine paths of release are generated. There are three uninterrupted paths and three paths of release in the mental contemplation of thorough isolation, and there are three uninterrupted paths and three paths of release in the mental contemplation of joy-withdrawal. This is followed by the mental contemplation of analysis, after which the remaining afflictive emotions are overcome in the mental contemplation of final training. With the attainment of the path of release that is the state of having overcome the small of the small afflictive emotions pertaining to the First Concentration, the meditator has attained the second concentration.

Branches of the Second Concentration

The second concentration has four branches—one antidotal branch, two that are benefits, and one that is the basis. The antidotal branch is called internal clarity (*nang rab tu dang ba, adhyātmasamprasāda*). This name is applied to the factors of mindfulness (*dran pa, smṛti*), introspection (*shes bzhin, samprajanya*), and equanimity (*btang snyoms, upekṣā*). Mindfulness here is non-forgetfulness of the objects of observation and the aspects included within the composite called the second concentration. Introspection is a discrimination that analyzes whether the mind is abiding on its object of observation or not. In general, equanimity is a mental factor that causes the mind and its accompanying mental factors to engage equally in its object. The equanimity that exists in the second concentration is that which frees the mind from the fluctuation caused by investigation and analysis during the first concentration; it is a relinquishing of the factors of investigation and analysis and an equalizing of the mind. These three are called internal clarity. It is said that the reason these three are not mentioned openly with regard to the second concentration is that the second concentration still has the fault of joy (*dga' ba, prīti*). Therefore, the antidote that separates one from the faults of the first concentration is called internal clarity.

The benefits and the basis are the same as for the first concentration, and joy and bliss (*bde ba, sukha*) are similarly explained as two ways of positing one factor, mental bliss (*yid bde, saumanasya*), in view of its performing two functions.

Types of Meditative Absorption of the Second Concentration

As with the first concentration, there are two types of meditative absorption of the second concentration—a causal type and a resultant-birth type. These, again, are of three types—pure, uncontaminated, and afflicted—and the way of positing the meaning of all three is the same.

The Third Concentration

Preparations for the Third Concentration

The third concentration, like the first two, is attained by means of the seven preparations. The mental contemplation of individual knowledge of the character views the Second Concentration as gross and the Third Concentration as peaceful, and in dependence upon calm abiding, the meditator engages in this analysis. As before, the meditator overcomes the afflictive emotions pertaining to the Second Concentration by way of the nine uninterrupted paths and the nine paths of release; the ninth path of release is the third concentration.

Branches of the Third Concentration

The third concentration has five branches. There are three antidotal branches, one that is a benefit, and one that is the basis. The three antidotal branches are mindfulness (*dran pa, smṛti*), introspection (*shes bzhin, samprajanya*), and equanimity (*btang snyoms, upekṣā*). These are the path consciousnesses that cause separation from attachment to the second concentration—mainly from the joy and bliss of the second concentration. Thus, since there is a disturbance of the mind due to joy in the second concentration, the equanimity of the third concentration is the factor that relinquishes or pacifies the joy of the second concentration; in this sense, it causes the mind and mental factors to be equal. After giving up attachment to the joy and bliss of the second concentration, the meditator has only the single branch, bliss (*bde ba, sukha*). The feeling of mental bliss that accompanies the mental consciousness of the third concentration is called the branch of bliss. This is the benefit that is produced through the separation brought about by mindfulness, introspection, and equanimity. As before, the basis is meditative stabilization.

Types of Meditative Absorption of the Third Concentration

Like the first two concentrations, the third concentration has a causal and a resultant-birth type of meditative absorption, and these are of three types—pure, uncontaminated, and afflicted.

The Fourth Concentration

Preparations for the Fourth Concentration

The fourth concentration also has the seven preparations. Here the mental contemplation of individual knowledge of the character views the Third Concentration as gross in the sense of having the fluctuation of bliss and the Fourth Concentration as peaceful; again, in dependence upon calm abiding, the meditator engages in analysis. The meditator separates from attachment to the third concentration by way of the nine uninterrupted paths and the nine paths of release, as before.

Branches of the Fourth Concentration

The fourth concentration has four branches. There are two antidotal branches—mindfulness (*dran pa, smṛti*) and equanimity (*btang snyoms, upekṣā*). The benefit branch is neutral feeling (*btang snyoms, upekṣā; sdug bsngal ma yin bde ba yang ma yin, aduḥkhāsukhavedanā*). The basis branch, again, is meditative stabilization. The first three are all called thoroughly pure (*yongs su dag pa, pariśuddha*)—thoroughly pure mindfulness, equanimity, and neutral feeling—because the meditator has separated from eight faults (*skyon, apakṣāla*)—investigation (*rtog pa, vitarka*), analysis (*dpyod pa, vicāra*), inhalation (*dbugs rngub pa, śvāsa*), exhalation (*dbugs 'byung pa, praśvāsa*), the feeling of pleasure (*bde *ba, sukha*), the feeling of pain (*sdug bsngal, duḥkha*), the feeling of mental discomfort (*yid mi bde, daurmanasya*), and the feeling of mental bliss (*yid bde, saumanasya*). The last is not merely mental bliss but the feeling of bliss itself. The equanimity of the fourth concentration is that which causes the relinquishing or pacification of these eight faults and the consequent equalizing of the mind. Because the meditator has separated from these eight faults, the mindfulness, equanimity, and neutral feeling of the fourth concentration are said to be pure.

Although the fourth concentration has introspection, it is not counted as a branch because there is no fluctuation in the fourth concentration. Just as it is not necessary to send out spies when a country has no enemies, similarly there is no need for introspection to analyze whether or not faults are present because there is no fluctuation due to the presence of a fault.

Types of Meditative Absorption of the Fourth Concentration

As in the other concentrations, there are causal and resultant-birth types of meditative absorption of the fourth concentration. The resultant-birth meditative absorptions of the Fourth Concentration are those explained earlier. As before, the causal meditative absorption of the fourth concentration is the ninth path of release, and there are pure, uncontaminated, and afflicted forms of it.

Comparison of the Concentrations

The difference between the first and second concentrations is that there is a non-completion of meditative stabilization in the first; although the meditative stabilization of the first concentration is both clear and stable, its power has not been completed. The reason is that the first concentration has investigation and analysis, which prevent the power of meditative stabilization from reaching its peak. In the second concentration, because investigation and analysis are no longer present, the power of meditative stabilization becomes complete.

The difference between the second and third concentrations is that there is a non-completion of benefit in the second. The reason is that both joy and bliss are present in the second; therefore, the factor of benefit is not complete. Because this fault does not exist in the third concentration, the factor of benefit is complete in the third.

The difference between the third and fourth concentrations is posited from the point of view of non-completion and completion of thorough purity. In the third concentration, the meditator still has some of the eight faults—those of inhalation, exhalation, and the feeling of bliss. Since all eight faults are absent in the fourth concentration, the fourth concentration has the completion of thorough purity (*yongs su dag pa, pariśuddhi*).

6

The Four Formless Absorptions

The four formless absorptions are called limitless space, limitless consciousness, nothingness, and the peak of cyclic existence. They are posited from the point of view of their objects of observation (*dmigs pa, ālambana*) and aspects (*rnam pa, ākāra*). Whereas a practitioner passes into the first concentration or from one concentration to the next by way of the presence or absence of branches, he or she passes beyond the fourth concentration or from one formless absorption to the next by way of the object of observation and subjective aspect; no branches are posited for any of the formless absorptions. In the four concentrations, the main meditative activity is that of analytical meditation; in the formless absorptions, however, the main meditative activity is that of stabilizing meditation.[1] The sign of having attained any of the actual four concentrations is the sense that the body is sinking under the ground, whereas the sign of having attained any of the four formless absorptions is the sense that the body is flying off into space.

Limitless Space

Preparations for Limitless Space

Like the concentrations, the formless absorption of limitless space has the seven preparations; within a mind of calm abiding, the meditator engages in analysis. The mental contemplation of individual knowledge of the character views the Fourth Concentration as gross and the discrimination that space is limitless as peaceful; nevertheless, though the meditator is analyzing, he or she now engages mainly in stabilizing meditation by means of calm abiding. Through viewing the Fourth Concentration as gross and through repeatedly taking to mind the thought, "Space is limitless; space is limitless," the meditator gradually develops the meditative absorption of limitless space and, within focusing on the discrimination that space is limitless, generates the nine uninterrupted paths and the nine paths of release.

The Actual Absorption

With the generation of the actual absorption (*maulasamāpatti, dngos gzhi'i snyoms 'jug*) of limitless space, discrimination (*saṃjñā, 'du shes*) of forms—the appearance of forms to the mind—completely disappears. The meditator loses the perception of obstruction and variety. "Obstruction" refers to such things as walls; a grove is an example of variety, as are colors such as red or white. These disappear. What is cultivated here is the non-appearance of obstructive and various forms to the mind; one is not meditating that they do not exist. The object of observation is the mental aggregates of the meditator; "limitless space" means that for the meditator's mind, space pervades everywhere. Thus, though obstructive and various forms do not exist for the mind of the meditator, the meditator is not meditating that things do not exist at all.

Types of Meditative Absorption of Limitless Space

Like the concentrations, the meditative absorption of limitless space has both the causal and the resultant-birth types. Through cultivating the meditative absorption of limitless space now and achieving it in this lifetime, a practitioner has the causal meditative absorption of limitless space; if, at death, he or she is reborn in the level of Limitless Space, he or she would have a resultant-birth type of meditative absorption of limitless space. Again, there are pure, uncontaminated, and afflicted types.

Limitless Consciousness

To attain the meditative absorption of limitless consciousness, someone who has attained the discrimination of limitless space begins to view that discrimination as gross and to view the discrimination that consciousness is limitless as peaceful. At the beginning, in dependence upon calm abiding, the person engages in some analysis but mainly in stabilizing meditation. There are seven preparations, as before. The meditator must overcome nine cycles of afflictive emotions pertaining to Limitless Space; therefore, there are nine uninterrupted paths and nine paths of release. The ninth path of release is the meditative absorption of limitless consciousness. Its object of observation, again, is the meditator's mental aggregates. Like the other concentrations and formless absorptions, it has causal and resultant-birth types; and again, there are pure, uncontaminated, and afflicted varieties.

Nothingness

To attain the meditative absorption of nothingness, the person who has attained the meditative absorption of limitless consciousness begins to view the discrimination that consciousness is limitless as gross and to view as peaceful the discrimination that there is nothing formed or formless to be apprehended. As before, the person analyzes a little at the beginning in dependence on calm abiding and views the lower absorption as gross and the higher as peaceful but then mainly engages in stabilizing meditation. Again, nine cycles of afflictive emotions pertaining to Limitless Consciousness are posited, as well as nine uninterrupted paths and nine paths of release; with the attainment of the ninth path of release, the meditator attains the meditative absorption of nothingness. In the meditative absorption of nothingness, the meditator engages in the discrimination that there is nothing formed or formless to be apprehended. As before, there are the causal and resultant-birth types, as well as the pure, uncontaminated, and afflicted types.

The Peak of Cyclic Existence

To attain the meditative absorption of the peak of cyclic existence, the person who has attained the meditative absorption of nothingness begins to view as gross the discrimination that there is nothing formed or formless to be apprehended. The meditator then begins to think, "Coarse discrimination does not exist; subtle discrimination is not non-existent." "Coarse discrimination does not exist" means that the gross, or coarse, discrimination called nothingness which the meditator is now viewing does not exist; in other words, the meditator lets it go, and subtle discrimination is left.

The meditator cultivates the meditative absorption of the peak of cyclic existence by way of the seven preparations. Again, there are nine cycles of afflictive emotions pertaining to the level of Nothingness, and there are nine uninterrupted paths and nine paths of release; the ninth path of release is the actual meditative absorption of the peak of cyclic existence.

In general, only pure and afflicted types of the meditative absorption of the peak of cyclic existence are posited. However, there is also a system that posits an uncontaminated type. As before, there are causal and resultant-birth types. The peak of cyclic existence (*srid rtse, bhavāgra*) is so called because it is the highest state within cyclic existence (*srid pa, bhava*).[2] Beings born at this level have the longest lifespan in the three realms.

I have explained the mode of cultivating the four concentrations and the four formless absorptions having the aspect of grossness/peacefulness. These meditative absorptions can be used in many ways; in dependence upon them, a practitioner can achieve various clairvoyances. These absorptions can also be used as the basis for path consciousness. If they are not used for these purposes, the practitioner achieves only the causes for resultant-births in these levels. It is like having a roomful of dollars; we could either use the money or not use it. We could buy a house or an airplane or anything we wanted, but if we did not use the money, it would be only paper. Similarly, if the concentrations and formless absorptions are not used, they lead only to resultant-birth types of meditative absorption in those levels of cyclic existence (*'khor ba, saṃsāra*).

7

Preparations Having the Aspect of the Truths

The mode of achieving the preparations by using the truths (*bden pa, satya*) as one's object of observation is the way out of cyclic existence. "Truths" can refer to either the two truths or the four truths. Though there are cases of achieving the preparations by using the two truths as the object of observation, I will explain the use of the four truths as the object of observation.

The Four Noble Truths

In order to explain how the four truths are used as the object of observation in the achievement of the preparations, it is necessary first to set forth what the four truths (*bden pa bzhi, catvāri satyāni*) are. The four truths are true sufferings (*sdug bsngal bden pa, duḥkhasatya*), true origins (*kun 'byung bden pa, samudayasatya*), true cessations (*'gog pa'i bden pa, nirodhasatya*), and true paths (*lam gyi bden pa, mārgasatya*). These are called the four noble truths (*'phags pa'i bden pa, āryasatya*).

Each of the four noble truths has four attributes (*rnam pa, ākāra*). The four attributes of true sufferings are impermanence (*mi rtag pa, anitya*), misery (*sdug bsngal ba, duḥkha*), emptiness (*stong pa, śūnya*), and selflessness (*bdag med, anātmaka*). The four attributes of true origins are cause (*rgyu, hetu*), origin (*kun 'byung, samudaya*), strong production (*rab skye, prabhava*), and condition (*rkyen, pratyaya*). The four attributes of true cessations are cessation (*'gog pa, nirodha*), pacification (*zhi ba, śānta*), auspiciousness (*gya nom, praṇīta*), and definite emergence (*nges 'byung, niḥsaraṇa*). The four attributes of true paths are path (*lam, mārga*), suitability (*rigs pa, nyāya*), achievement (*sgrub pa, pratipad*), and deliverance (*nges 'byin, nairyāṇika*). Since there are sixteen attributes altogether, they are called the sixteen attributes of the four noble truths.

The four noble truths are called truths because, when Buddha set forth impermanence and so forth, it was clear that these things existed exactly as he said they did. They are called noble (*'phags pa, ārya*), or superior, truths because they are seen as truths by Superiors (*'phags pa, ārya*) but not by common beings (*so so'i skye bo, pṛthagjana*).[1]

The Mode of Cultivation

A practitioner who cultivates the four truths in meditation and seeks to achieve the concentrations begins to analyze within the steadiness of a mind of calm abiding. The practitioner does not analyze the faults of the Desire Realm, and so forth, as in the mode of cultivation having the aspect of grossness/peacefulness but, rather, begins to examine the sixteen attributes—impermanence, and so forth. As in the mode of cultivation set forth earlier, when excitement begins to be generated the meditator engages in stabilizing meditation, and when laxity begins to be generated he or she engages in analytical meditation. Since the ways of eliminating laxity and excitement have already been explained, I will not repeat them.

True Sufferings

Impermanence. There are two bases for meditation on impermanence, one internal and the other external. Among the internal phenomena that can serve as bases for meditation on impermanence are the six sense powers—the eye sense power, ear sense power, nose sense power, tongue sense power, body sense power, and mental sense power. Using these as the basis for meditation, the meditator contemplates the various types of impermanence.

The first type of impermanence is that of changeability. Whether we consider ourselves or others, there are many different states within the continuum from birth to old age, and the earlier and later parts of the continuum are very different. As the earlier entity turns into the later entity, it changes a great deal. We begin as babies; then we become children and adolescents; then we become adults. Later, we become middle-aged and then old. The meditator views the changeability of these states and thinks, "How all compositional phenomena (*'dus byas, saṃskṛta*)—all things that are made—are impermanent!"

Our complexion is also changeable. Sometimes we have a good color; it has brilliance and seems pleasant. At other times, this brilliance diminishes; we have a bad color, and the complexion seems coarse. This is true of our own and others' complexions. Thus, the meditator reflects on the changeability of one's own and others' complexions and thinks, "How all compositional phenomena are impermanent!"

Shape is also changeable. As children, we are small in shape. Later, our shape grows larger, but in old age it shrinks. Furthermore, there is also a relativity of shape. When we go to a place in which others are small in shape, we become large in shape; when we are with others who are large in shape, we become small in shape. In this way, the meditator contemplates the changeability of shape, concluding, "How all compositional phenomena are impermanent!"

There is also the changeability of prosperity and degeneration. Within what we call prosperity, there are different types—prosperity with regard to relatives and friends, resources, proper ethics, and correct view. For all of us, there are times when we have many relatives and friends, when we have sufficient resources, good ethics, and a correct view, but there are times when our friends and relatives disappear, when we have no resources, poor ethics, and bad views. The meditator contemplates such change and reflects on the impermanence of compositional phenomena.

Another form of changeability is the completion and non-completion of limbs. Sometimes we have all our major and minor limbs, but at other times we may meet with bad circumstances and not have all our limbs. The meditator contemplates such change and reflects on the impermanence of compositional phenomena.

Still another form of changeability is that of fatigue and comfort. Sometimes, from jumping or running or working, we become tired, and at other times we experience comfort. Contemplating such change, the meditator reflects on the impermanence of compositional phenomena.

The meditator may also reflect on the changeability of being harmed or not being harmed by others. Sometimes we are harmed by both human and non-human sources. To give one of the smallest examples, sometimes we are harmed by bedbugs and mosquitoes. At other times, we are not harmed. Contemplating such change, the meditator reflects on the impermanence of compositional phenomena.

Another form of changeability is that of cold and heat. Sometimes we are so cold that we lose our physical strength. At other times, we are hot, even burned, and we want coolness. The meditator contemplates such change and reflects on the impermanence of compositional phenomena.

There is also a contemplation of behavior. Behavior, here, is specified as walking, standing, sitting, and lying down. Sometimes these harm ourselves and others, and sometimes they help ourselves and others. The meditator contemplates such change and reflects on the impermanence of compositional phenomena.

Another form of changeability is that of contact. Contact here means coming into contact with pleasurable, painful, or neutral feelings. Again, the meditator reflects on the impermanence of compositional phenomena.

Another type of changeability is that of thorough afflictive emotions. Sometimes our minds are filled with strong desire and hatred, and sometimes desire and hatred are pacified. The meditator contemplates such change and reflects on the impermanence of compositional phenomena.

There is also the contemplation of sickness. Sometimes we are free of sickness and live in comfort, but sometimes the three humors—bile, phlegm, and wind—become imbalanced and we suffer various types of illness. We are in pain and discomfort; our body lacks strength. We have seen and experienced such states. The meditator contemplates this type of change and reflects on the impermanence of compositional phenomena.

Then there is death. Sometimes we are alive and see others alive, but then, for ourselves and others, there is a time of dying. Thus, we contemplate impermanence through reflecting on death. I have talked about the colors of rotting corpses—dull blue, putrid black, pus color, and putrid red. One contemplates decay to the point at which one is reduced to a skeleton. In this case, the meditator reflects on impermanence through contemplating such change.

Finally, there is the contemplation of thorough extinguishment. What is left is the skeleton and after that, only our name. In time, there is no longer even the skeleton, and no one remembers our name. In this way, the meditator contemplates impermanence by reflecting on the changeability of internal compositional phenomena.

We can also meditate on impermanence by reflecting on the changeability of external phenomena. A certain area may sometimes lack houses, stores, and temples, but at another time one may see houses, stores, and temples in that very place. The buildings seem very pleasant when they are new, but in time they become old and dilapidated. Contemplating such change, the meditator reflects on the impermanence of compositional phenomena.

Sometimes, in parks, the grass is well kept and the trees and flowers flourish. At other times, however, those very trees are withered, without leaves, flowers, or fruit. In the autumn, for example, trees lose their leaves; yet only a few months earlier they were green. Contemplating such change, the meditator reflects on the impermanence of compositional phenomena.

Mountains sometimes have many trees and good stones, so that they look like parks, but sometimes they do not. Contemplating such change, the meditator reflects on the impermanence of compositional phenomena.

Lakes and ponds are also changeable. Sometimes they are full, and sometimes they are dry. Contemplating such change, the meditator reflects on the impermanence of compositional phenomena.

There are also many types of work—in stores, in schools, on highways, and so forth. Sometimes these jobs seem good, but sometimes they do not seem good. Contemplating such change, the meditator reflects on the impermanence of compositional phenomena.

There are treasuries in which gold and silver are stored. Sometimes they are full, and sometimes they are empty. Contemplating such change, the meditator reflects on the impermanence of compositional phenomena.

Food and drink are sometimes well prepared and sometimes badly prepared; sometimes they are delicious, and sometimes they are not. Contemplating such change, the meditator reflects on the impermanence of compositional phenomena.

Vehicles such as automobiles work well when they are new. After a while, however, they begin to fall apart and have to be repaired very often. Contemplating such change, the meditator reflects on the impermanence of compositional phenomena.

We can also reflect on clothing. When clothing is new, it looks good, but in time it fades and tears. Contemplating such change, the meditator reflects on the impermanence of compositional phenomena.

Ornaments are also attractive when they are new, and when the wearer is young, they are becoming. In time, however, both ornaments and wearer grow old; the wearer is wrinkled, and the ornaments are no longer becoming. Contemplating such change, the meditator reflects on the impermanence of compositional phenomena.

Songs, dances, and other entertainment sometimes seem very pleasant, but sometimes they do not. Contemplating such change, the meditator reflects on the impermanence of compositional phenomena.

Articles that provide fragrance, such as incense, sometimes seem pleasant, but at other times we have to hold our noses. Contemplating such change, the meditator reflects on the impermanence of compositional phenomena.

Pots and pans are sometimes clean, but at other times they are dirty and need to be washed. Sometimes they are solid; they do not have holes and are useful, but at other times they are worn down; they have holes and are not useful. Contemplating such change, the meditator reflects on the impermanence of compositional phenomena.

Illumination and darkness are also changeable. Sometimes things are brightly lighted, but at other times they are dark, and no one can see them. Contemplating such change, the meditator reflects on the impermanence of compositional phenomena.

There is also the mutual liking of male and female. When they are young, men and women want to stay together, to live together, to sleep together; they walk about holding hands. Sometimes they enjoy each other's company, but at other times they dislike each other. They argue; they refuse to talk to each other, and when one appears, the other wants to run in the opposite direction. Contemplating such change, the meditator reflects on the impermanence of compositional phenomena.

So far, I have talked about the mode of contemplating the impermanence of compositional phenomena through reflecting on the changeability of internal and external phenomena. To reflect on changeability is to contemplate coarse impermanence, the type of impermanence we can see with our own direct perception. The next step is to reflect on the impermanence of disintegration. Disintegration is subtle impermanence; at present, we cannot see it directly. This is because internal and external phenomena are momentary. They are such that, if the causes and conditions have aggregated, they will be produced, and once they have been produced, without depending on any further cause, they naturally, moment by moment, disintegrate. Thus, we contemplate the disintegration of compositional phenomena moment by moment. Common beings cannot perceive this moment-by-moment disintegration directly; only

Superiors can. However, we can meditate on this moment-by-moment disintegration and eventually perceive it directly.

Another type of impermanence is that of separation. Here, the high becomes low, and the low becomes high; the master becomes the servant, and the servant becomes the master. Some people become high officials but later go to prison; they may even have to serve someone else. Other people who begin as servants end up as masters. The former separate from being masters and become servants; the latter separate from being servants and become masters. There are also cases of the rich becoming poor and of the poor becoming rich. Contemplating such change, we reflect on the impermanence of compositional phenomena.

Still another type of impermanence is that of changeability by nature. This means that even if something has not yet changed, it will eventually change.

We can also contemplate the impermanence of the near. This contemplation is reflection on manifest instances of the first three types of impermanence—changeability, disintegration, and separation.

The basis that brings about this impermanence is our own mental and physical aggregates. They are produced only occasionally. The mere fact that they are produced occasionally means that they disintegrate moment by moment. Therefore, we are primarily contemplating that our mind and body change moment by moment. When reflection on impermanence goes well, all the other reflections are easy.

Misery. The second attribute of true sufferings is misery. Contemplation of misery is the reflection that these contaminated mental and physical aggregates disintegrate moment by moment through the power of contaminated actions and afflictive emotions and, therefore, are miserable. They are miserable because, once we have taken rebirth within cyclic existence by the power of contaminated actions, wherever we take rebirth is only a state of suffering. No matter where we are or who our associates may be, there is only suffering. No matter what resources we have, they are resources of suffering. Having taken rebirth in cyclic existence, we continuously undergo the suffering of aging, sickness, and finally, death. In this way, we contemplate the misery of true sufferings.

Emptiness. The basis of designation of a person is just the mind and body, which are called the five aggregates. That is all there is. There is no separate controller of mind and body. If there were, that separate controller would have to be apprehendable apart from mind and body, but it cannot be apprehended so. Thus, we reflect that the aggregates are empty of such a controller.

Selflessness. The mental and physical aggregates are dependent-arisings.

Therefore, they are not independent, and because they are not independent, they lack being an independent self. Thus, we reflect that the mental and physical aggregates do not exist as an independent self, that there is not the slightest independent self.

True Origins

Having meditated on the mental and physical aggregates as impermanent, miserable, empty, and selfless, we develop a lack of desire with respect to them; we develop the wish to abandon them. To abandon the contaminated mental and physical aggregates, we have to abandon their causes; without abandoning contaminated actions and afflictive emotions, we cannot abandon suffering. Thus, the two origins of suffering are contaminated actions and afflictive emotions.

Cause means that contaminated actions and afflictive emotions are the cause of suffering; therefore, we contemplate that contaminated actions and afflictive emotions are the cause, or root, of suffering. We reflect further that because they produce suffering again and again, they are the origin of suffering; because they produce suffering strongly, they are the strong producers, or create strong production, of suffering; and because contaminated actions and afflictive emotions act as the cooperative causes of suffering, they are the condition of suffering.

True Cessations

In order to abandon suffering, it is necessary to abandon the causes of suffering, the origins; thus, in order to overcome contaminated actions, we have to overcome the afflictive emotions. To overcome the afflictive emotions, we have to overcome the root of the afflictive emotions, ignorance. When we analyze whether we have the power to overcome ignorance, we investigate and eventually learn that ignorance engages its object in a perverse way and has no valid foundation. We also learn that ignorance is not in the nature of the mind but is adventitious (*glo bur, ākasmika*). We understand that all phenomena are selfless. In dependence upon these contemplations, we understand that we can abandon ignorance. When we understand that we can abandon the root of actions and afflictive emotions, we also understand that we can abandon actions and afflictive emotions themselves and we develop the wish to actualize true cessations, which are the cessations of true sufferings and of the causes of suffering.

Liberation is called cessation because it is a cessation of suffering; the practitioner has developed the wish to be delivered from suffering and the origins of suffering, and this liberation from true sufferings and true origins is a true cessation. The meditator reflects that because it is a separation from suffering, it is called cessation; from the point of view of its being a separation from the afflictive emotions, it is called pacification; from the point of view of its being helpful or happy, it is called auspiciousness; and because, when we attain liberation, suffering will never again be produced, it is called definite emergence.

True Paths

Then the meditator wonders whether there are any techniques for attaining such a liberation and understands that it can be attained through the wisdom directly realizing that all phenomena are selfless. Therefore, the wisdom directly realizing selflessness is the technique for attaining liberation. Because the wisdom directly realizing selflessness is this technique, it is the path for going to liberation.

The meditator reflects that it is called the path because it is the direct antidote that destroys the afflictive emotions; it is called suitability because the wisdom directly realizing selflessness is the antidote to ignorance; it is called achievement because it is a wisdom consciousness that unmistakenly realizes the mode of being of the mind; and it is called deliverance because it is such that, when we have it, suffering will not be produced again.

As was explained earlier, the meditator engages alternately in analytical and stabilizing meditation with respect to these attributes. With the attainment of the union of calm abiding and special insight observing them, the meditator has attained the mental contemplation arisen from belief.

THE MODE OF PROCEDURE OF HEARERS

Hearers have two modes of procedure, simultaneous (*gcig car, sakṛt*) and gradual (*rim gyis, kramena*).[2] Those who proceed simultaneously cultivate the mental contemplation of individual knowledge of the character at the time of the path of accumulation. When such Hearers attain the mental contemplation arisen from belief, they have attained the path of preparation. When they attain the mental contemplation of thorough isolation, they have attained the path of seeing. The mental contemplation of withdrawal or joy, the mental contemplation of analysis, and the mental contemplation of final training are attained on the path of meditation.

Hearers who proceed gradually, however, achieve the preparations having the aspects of grossness/peacefulness at the time of the path of accumulation and attain an actual concentration. In dependence upon the power of that concentration, they apprehend the truths, achieve the path of seeing, and proceed on up.

THE MODE OF PROCEDURE OF BODHISATTVAS

Bodhisattvas on the path of accumulation engage in the cultivation of the preparations having the aspect of grossness/peacefulness and, having attained an actual concentration, proceed on up. They achieve an actual concentration on the path of accumulation and then take cognizance of emptiness (*stong pa nyid, śūnyatā*). Then, through the alternation of stabilizing and analytical meditation, they eventually achieve a union of calm abiding and special insight observing emptiness and finally, direct perception of emptiness and then proceed on up through the path to Buddhahood.

PART TWO

Denma Lochö Rinbochay's Oral Commentary on Paṇ-chen Sö-nam-drak-ba's "Explanation of the Concentrations and Formless Absorptions" from his *General Meaning of (Maitreya's) "Ornament for Clear Realization"*

Root Text Translated by
Leah Zahler

Oral Commentary Translated by
Jeffrey Hopkins

Please note that Denma Lochö Rinbochay's oral commentary is indented and set in a smaller type size.

1

The Explanation of the Concentrations[1]

The concentrations are very important. As D̄zong-ka-b̄a said, "A concentration is like a king who has control over the mind." Someone who is set in it is unfluctuating (*mi g.yo ba, āniñjya*), like a king of mountains. If we use it, we can engage in all virtuous objects of observation. It induces great physical and mental pliancy. Thus, someone who wishes to engage in the practices of yoga should overcome the enemy, distraction, and abide continuously in meditative stabilization.

Buddhists and non-Buddhists agree on the need to achieve a calm abiding that has one-pointedness of mind (*sems rtse gcig pa, cittaikāgratā*). All the Buddhist systems of tenets also agree on this point, as do the Perfection Vehicle (*phar phyin theg pa, pāramitāyāna*) and Mantra Vehicle (*sngags kyi theg pa, mantrayāna).* As is explained in Ḡön-chok-jik-may-w̄ang-b̄o's (*dkon mchog 'jigs-med dbang po*, 1728–91) *Presentation of the Grounds and Paths,* in order to attain the great path of accumulation of a Hearer, Solitary Realizer, or Bodhisattva, it is necessary to attain an actual concentration. Therefore, the attainment of an actual concentration is essential for a person who is seeking a path of liberation.

The Explanation of the Concentrations That Are Causal Meditative Absorptions [150b.6][2]

In order to be reborn in an upper realm, it is necessary to generate an actual meditative absorption; without it, rebirth there is impossible. Birth in an upper realm is the effect; the meditative absorption is the cause.

The Explanation of the First Concentration That Is a Causal Meditative Absorption [151a]

In general, "first concentration" (*bsam gtan dang po*) refers to the resultant-birth type. However, the term "meditative absorption of the first concentration" (*bsam gtan dang po'i snyoms 'jug*) refers to the preparations and the actual meditative absorption.

The Explanation of the Preparations for the First Concentration

Preparations are the techniques for separating from desires pertaining to the lower level, from which the meditator has not yet separated. When, in dependence upon cultivating the preparations, the meditator separates from desire pertaining to that lower level, he or she has attained the actual meditative absorption.

The definition of a preparation for a concentration (not of a preparation in general) is:

a mental contemplation included within a training for an actual meditative absorption of a concentration, which is its fruit.

The definition of a preparation for the first concentration would be the same except for specifying "first concentration."

[First Debate]

Objection: The mental contemplation of individual knowledge of the character (*mtshan nyid so sor rig pa'i yid byed, lakṣaṇapratisaṃvedīmanaskāra*)[3] that is a preparation for the first concentration is the first of the preparations for the first concentration because Asaṅga says that one enters into meditative absorption with respect to the first concentration by means of seven mental contemplations and he propounds individual knowledge of the character as the first of the seven. Asaṅga's *Grounds of Hearers* says:

> Further, a yogi who makes effort strongly in order to separate from the desires of the Desire Realm attains separation from the desires of the Desire Realm by means of seven mental contemplations. What are those seven? They are individual knowledge of the character, arisen from belief, thorough isolation, joy-withdrawal, the mental contemplation of analysis, final training, and the mental contemplation that is the fruit of final training (*sbyor mtha'i 'bras bu'i yid byed, prayoganiṣṭhaphalamanaskāra*).[4]

Although Asaṅga did indeed say this, the objector is wrong. In our own system, in order to attain the mental contemplation of individual knowledge of the character, it is necessary first to attain the mental contemplation of a beginner—calm abiding. The reason is that the mental contemplation of individual knowledge of the character is a training for the sake of attaining special insight, which is induced by analysis from within a state of calm abiding.

The definition of a mental contemplation of a beginner is:

a calm abiding that is a meditative stabilization which, without striving, spontaneously engages its object of observation from the point of view of being conjoined with pliancy.

It is a calm abiding; it is also a preparation for a concentration. Because the meditator has just attained calm abiding, it is called the mental contemplation of a beginner.

The definition of the next preparation, the mental contemplation of individual knowledge of the character, is:

a mental contemplation that is a mind mainly of hearing and

> *thinking; from within a calm abiding that is of a level of meditative equipoise, it views the Desire Realm and the First Concentration, from the point of view of their faults and [good] qualities, as gross and peaceful, respectively.*

These definitions have been made up for the sake of understanding; they are not intended for debate.

The objector wrongly holds that the mental contemplation of individual knowledge of the character is the initial preparation for the first concentration and has mistakenly cited Asaṅga's *Grounds of Hearers* as his source.

Answer: This is completely unfeasible 1) because a meditative stabilization which is a meditative equipoise conjoined with pliancy in the continuum of a person who has just attained calm abiding is the first of the preparations for the first concentration [151b]; and 2) because, in order to attain the mental contemplation of individual knowledge of the character which is a preparation for the first concentration, one must first attain a beginner at mental contemplation (*yid la byed pa las dang po pa, manaskārādikarmika*)—[that is, calm abiding] which is a preparation for the first concentration.

The first reason [namely, that a meditative stabilization which is a meditative equipoise conjoined with pliancy in the continuum of a person who has just attained calm abiding is the first of the preparations for the first concentration] is established, for Maitreya's *Ornament [for the Mahāyāna Sūtras (mahāyānasūtrālaṃkāra, theg pa chen po'i mdo sde'i rgyan)*, 14:14–15] says:

> Through familiarization with those [nine mental abidings that are included within the level of the Desire Realm]
> One does not engage in application [of the antidotes]
> Then, when one has attained great pliancy of body and mind,
> It should be known that one has a mental contemplation [that is, calm abiding].[5]

"Then, when one has attained great pliancy of body and mind" means that the meditative stabilization of calm abiding is conjoined with great physical and mental pliancy. Thus, when a practitioner attains it, he or she has the first of the preparations for the first concentration.

The second reason [that in order to attain the mental contemplation of individual knowledge of the character which is a preparation for the first concentration, one must first attain a beginner at mental contemplation—that is, calm abiding—which is a preparation for the first concentration] is established, for Asaṅga's *Grounds of Hearers* says:

> A beginner at mental contemplation is a beginner while not having attained a mental contemplation with respect to making one-pointed [that is, while not having attained calm abiding] and until reaching the one-pointedness of mind [that one has with calm abiding]. A beginner at purifying the afflictive emotions (*nyon mongs rnam par sbyong ba'i las dang po pa, kleśaviśuddhyādikarmika*) is undertaken with the mental contemplation of individual knowledge of the character of one who has attained a mental contemplation [that is, calm abiding] and who wishes to purify the mind of the afflictive emotions, and is a familiarization with [that undertaking].[6]

[Second Debate]

Objection: The mental contemplation of individual knowledge of the character that is a preparation for the first concentration is included within the level of the Desire Realm, a state of non-equipoise, because Asaṅga's *Grounds of Hearers* says:

> That individual analysis—by way of mental contemplations of a level of non-equipoise—of the Desire Realm as [having] the character of grossness[7] and of the First Concentration as [having] the character of peacefulness is called the mental contemplation of individual knowledge.[8] [152a]

Answer: This is wrong because [the text of] that passage in the Grounds of Hearers is corrupt.[9] This is because [Yaśomitra's] *Commentary on (Asaṅga's) "Compendium of Manifest Knowledge"* says:

> By means of mental contemplations that are of a level of meditative equipoise, one views the Desire Realm as faulty, and so forth.[10]

> In the Desire Realm, there is manifest suffering of change. There are the sufferings of separation from friends, of meeting the unwanted, and of the unwanted falling upon one. There are many non-virtues in the Desire Realm and many sufferings that are the results of non-virtues.

Thereby, one knows [the Desire Realm] as having the character of grossness. Because that [grossness of the Desire Realm] does not exist [in the First Concentration], one mentally contemplates the First Concentration as having the character of peacefulness. That is to be known as a mixture of hearing and thinking.[11]

> Most debate comes at this point in the discussion of the concentrations and formless absorptions. Yaśomitra says that the mental contemplation of individual knowledge of the character is of the level of meditative

equipoise, which would have to be a state arisen from meditation (*sgom byung, bhāvanāmayī*). He then says that this mental contemplation is to be known as a mixture of hearing and thinking. When this point is debated at length, it must be admitted that the mental contemplation of individual knowledge of the character is included within the Desire Realm because it is a mixture of hearing and thinking. However, it is not necessary to say that it is entirely a mixture of hearing and thinking.

If the mental contemplation of individual knowledge of the character were entirely a mixture of hearing and thinking, it could not very well be a preparation for the first concentration, for if it had to be included within the level of the Desire Realm, the order of first attaining calm abiding would be lost.

Therefore, at the beginning, the meditator settles the Desire Realm as faulty and the First Concentration as peaceful from the point of view of hearing and thinking and reaches the point of the conviction that arises from extended thought. This means that the meditator first thinks about what has been heard and then engages in thinking that is a mental contemplation, not merely reflection on what has been heard. After that, it is no longer necessary to engage intentionally in hearing and thinking; the mind automatically stays on its object. Toward the end of the mental contemplation of individual knowledge of the character, the meditator generates a state arisen from meditation. Although the mind is again one-pointed with respect to its object, this state is not yet a case of special insight.

Another reason [that the passage of *Grounds of Hearers* is corrupt] is that there exists a calm abiding that is associated with the mental contemplation of individual knowledge of the character which is a preparation for the first concentration.

This reason proves that the mental contemplation of individual knowledge of the character which is a preparation for the first concentration is not necessarily a mind of the level of the Desire Realm. It also proves that this mental contemplation is a mind of the Form Realm by showing that it is associated with a mind of calm abiding.

Another reason is that the preparation for the first concentration [called] the not-unable is a level of concentration.

If the mental contemplation of individual knowledge of the character were the first preparation for the first concentration—and it is not—there would be no way of positing the preparation called the not-unable. This preparation is so called because it is able to serve as the mental basis for abandoning any of the afflictive emotions of any of the three realms. Among the preparations for the four concentrations, it is the only one that can serve as a mental basis for an uncontaminated path. It is identified as included within the mental contemplation of a beginner, which, in turn, is a mind of calm abiding, but "not-unable" refers specifically to a preparation that can serve as a mental basis for an uncontaminated path. Therefore, it does not serve as a mental basis for those preparations which have an aspect of grossness/peacefulness, which are not uncontaminated paths, [although calm abiding, in general, can serve as a basis for such preparation].

[Our Own System]

What is a preparation for the first concentration like? The definition[12] of a preparation for the first concentration is:

> *a virtuous knower that is included in the levels of preparation and of concentrations that serve as techniques for attaining an actual meditative absorption of the first concentration, which is its object of attainment.*

When preparations for the first concentration are divided, there are two: a beginner at mental contemplation that is a preparation for the first concentration [152b] and beginners at purifying the afflictive emotions [that are preparations for the first concentration]. An example of the first [a beginner at mental contemplation that is a preparation for the first concentration] is a meditative stabilization that is a meditative equipoise conjoined with pliancy in the continuum of a person who has just attained calm abiding. When the second [beginners at purifying the afflictive emotions] are divided, there are six: the mental contemplation of individual knowledge of the character, [the mental contemplation arisen from belief, the mental contemplation of thorough isolation, the mental contemplation of joy-withdrawal, the mental contemplation of analysis, and the mental contemplation of final training] that are preparations for the first concentration.[13]

A mental contemplation that is the fruit of final training and that is a preparation for the first concentration does not exist because whatever is a mental contemplation that is the fruit of final training for the first concentration is necessarily an actual meditative absorption of the first concentration. This is because whatever is a mental contemplation that is the fruit of final training for the fourth concentration is necessarily an actual meditative absorption of the fourth concentration. This is because Vasubandhu's *Treasury* [*of Manifest Knowledge*, 6.48a–b] says:

> That concentration which has conquered over the three levels
> Or [is] the path of release at the end of the preparations . . . [14]

"That concentration which has conquered over the three levels" is the fourth concentration. It has conquered over the three levels in the sense that it is a state of having removed desire pertaining to the first three concentrations.[15] This concentration is a mental contemplation that is the fruit of final training. Furthermore, "the path of release at the end of the preparations" is also a mental contemplation that is the fruit of final training.

[The *Treasury* also says (8:22a–b):]

With respect to these [four concentrations and four formless absorptions, there are] eight preparations:
[They are] pure [and] neither blissful nor painful.[16]

The preparations for the second concentration and for the concentrations and formless absorptions above it are only pure,[17] and the feeling that is included within a preparation is necessarily neither blissful nor painful, but neutral.

[What I have said] agrees with these statements.

Furthermore, a beginner at mental contemplation that is a preparation for the first concentration is a preparation included within calm abiding, and the remaining six are preparations included within special insight.

Though they are included within special insight, they are not all consciousnesses of special insight; they are cases of training in special insight. The reason is as follows:

The mental contemplation of individual knowledge of the character that is [a preparation] for the first concentration, viewing Desire Realm beings as [having] the aspect of grossness and the First Concentration as [having] the aspect of peacefulness, is a technique for achieving special insight; it analyzes with hearing and thinking. [153a]

The mental contemplation of individual knowledge of the character that is a preparation for the first concentration is not a consciousness of special insight but a technique for achieving it. First, the meditator analyzes with the mind that arises after hearing—that mainly accords with hearing. In the next phase, he or she no longer has to depend intentionally upon hearing but is mainly involved in thinking and, through thinking, analyzes the lower level as gross and the upper as peaceful. Thus, the mental contemplation of individual knowledge of the character that is a preparation for the first concentration is a technique for achieving special insight in that it analyzes by way of hearing and thinking through viewing the various types of Desire Realm beings—gods and humans and those below—as having the aspect of grossness and the First Concentration as having the aspect of peacefulness.

How is this analysis done? In general, analysis is done by way of the six investigations—of meaning (*don, artha*), things (*dngos po, vastu*), character (*mtshan nyid, lakṣaṇa*), class (*phyogs, pakṣa*), time (*dus, kāla*), and reasoning (*rigs pa, yukti*). "Meaning" refers to the meaning of words. To investigate things is to distinguish them as external or internal, matter or consciousness. To investigate the character means, on the one hand, to analyze the specific character of the object—the character that only it has—and, on the other hand, to analyze the general character—the character that it has in common with other things. To investigate the class is to determine whether the object is in the virtuous or non-virtuous class; we determine these by way of their qualities and effects. The investigation of time refers to determination of the occurrence of something in the past, present, or future. The investigation of reasoning has four types: reasoning of dependence (*ltos pa'i rigs pa, apekṣāyukti*) in terms of cause, reasoning of the performance of function (*bya ba byed pa'i rigs pa, kāryakāraṇayukti*), logical reasoning (*'thad sgrub kyi rigs pa, upapattisādhanayukti*), and reasoning of nature (*chos nyid kyi rigs pa, dharmatāyukti*). ("Nature" here refers to the nature of phenomena as it is known in the world.)

The six investigations are applied to viewing the Desire Realm as gross. To investigate the meaning, the practitioner would hear or read ("hearing" also includes reading) scriptures concerning the suffering of birth, aging, sickness, and death, and would think about their meaning, or the practitioner would think about the meaning of statements that we come under the influence of the afflictive emotions without independence, [that is, because of dependent-arising]. For example, it is said in scripture that someone who kills out of anger will experience a fruition of suffering; yet we forget this fact; we do not realize that such actions will harm us in deep ways. Here, the meditator would be thinking that what is said in scripture is true in fact.

With regard to the investigation of things, the meditator considers the impure world of the environment. There are many horrible things in the environment of the Desire Realm. The peoples' bodies consist of impure substances, and there are cases of defective sense powers. The general character of the Desire Realm is that it is under the influence of contaminated actions and afflictive emotions.

With regard to the investigation of class, meritorious actions are included within the virtuous class and non-meritorious actions, within the non-virtuous class. For example, keeping ethics for the sake of being reborn in a happy transmigration would be included in the virtuous class; the activity is good because the person doing it is giving up the bases of harming others. From that person's point of view, there is a happiness that comes from the fruition of rebirth as a god or human. Non-meritorious actions, such as murder, do not accord with either the religious or the worldly way and produce the great suffering of rebirth in a hot or cold hell (*dmyal ba, naraka*). These are faults of the Desire Realm, and they do not exist in the First Concentration

To investigate time, one could reflect that in the Desire Realm it is difficult to live for one hundred years, whereas in the Form and Formless Realms one may live for aeons. Thus, it would probably be suitable in this context to interpret investigation of time as investigation of length of time rather than of past, present, and future.

There are four types of reasoning. With respect to the reasoning of dependence in terms of cause, birth in the First Concentration occurs in dependence upon generating an actual concentration.[18]

In terms of the reasoning of the performance of function, the cultivation of a causal meditative absorption of the first concentration has the function of acting as the cause of rebirth in the First Concentration.[19]

With respect to logical reasoning, the assertions that there are many faults in the Desire Realm and that these faults do not exist in the Form and Formless Realm cannot be damaged by valid cognition.

With regard to the reasoning of nature, there is a natural absorption that occurs when the world system (*'jig rten gyi khams, lokadhātu*) disintegrates. Near the time of disintegration, beings in the bad transmigrations who have heavy karma are reborn in bad transmigrations in other world systems, but those whose bad karma has been consumed are reborn as humans. In this way, the bad transmigrations are emptied. In the mental continua of those humans, a natural equipoise of a concentration is generated effortlessly. In this way, when these humans die, they are reborn as gods in the Desire Realm or higher, so that the human transmigration is emptied. Then those gods are born higher, and in that way the Desire Realm is emptied.

For the most part, the viewing of the Desire Realm as gross and of the First Concentration as peaceful would be included within the investigation of the meaning, but there are also opportunities for the other types of investigation to take place.

The preparation that is the initial attainment of special insight conjoined with a physical and mental pliancy induced by the power of having done analysis in that way is posited as the mental contemplation arisen from belief.

If, at the time of the mental contemplation of a beginner, a meditator viewed the Desire Realm as gross and the First Concentration as peaceful, his or her meditative stabilization would fluctuate; thus, analysis is not used at that time. During the mental contemplation of individual knowledge of the character, the meditator engages first in hearing and thinking and then in analysis; this analysis does not cause the mind to fluctuate, but mental and physical pliancy induced by the power of analysis has not yet been generated. At the time of the mental contemplation arisen from belief, the meditator is able to generate a mental and physical pliancy induced by the power of analysis itself. Because the practitioner then has attained a thorough analysis of phenomena that is conjoined with mental and physical pliancy induced by the power of analyzing from within calm abiding he or she has attained special insight; this initial attainment of special insight is called the mental contemplation arisen from belief.

On the occasion of the mental contemplation arisen from belief, one has not attained a capacity that acts as an antidote to any of the nine [cycles of] afflictive emotions pertaining to the Desire Realm—great, middling, [or small]; therefore, although one has investigation and analysis, they have not become antidotal branches with respect to those [afflictive emotions].

Investigation is a coarse examination of the object, whereas analysis is a subtler examination. Although the meditator has these, they do not serve as branches that are antidotes to any of the afflictive emotions pertaining to the Desire Realm.

After [the mental contemplation arisen from belief], when, through having cultivated such a union of calm abiding and special insight, [one has] the capacity that acts as an actual antidote to the great of the great afflictive emotions pertaining to the Desire Realm, one has attained the mental contemplation of thorough isolation; [the mental contemplation of thorough isolation] is the initial attainment of an antidotal branch [of the first concentration].

Although the mundane path of meditation is not protracted, like the supramundane path, it is possible to posit three mental contemplations of thorough isolation that are the antidotes to the great of the great, middling of the great, and small of the great afflictive emotions.

After that, when, having serially abandoned the manifest [form of the] triple cycle of the great afflictive emotions pertaining to the Desire Realm, one attains the actual antidote to any of the triple cycle of the middling [afflictive emotions pertaining to the Desire Realm, one is] said to have the mental contemplation of joy-withdrawal.

As with the mental contemplation of thorough isolation, it is possible to make internal divisions with respect to the mental contemplation of joy-withdrawal, these being the uninterrupted paths and paths of release—three each—which pertain to the three levels of the middling afflictive emotions.

Although, at this point, not all the afflictive emotions pertaining to the Desire Realm have been overcome, the meditator has overcome most of them; therefore, he or she has joy and bliss. Thus, it is said:

From this [point], one is touched to some extent by joy and bliss, the benefit branches [of the first concentration].

Then, when one has abandoned six of the manifest afflictive emotions pertaining to the Desire Realm, one wonders whether one has abandoned all the afflictive emotions [pertaining to the Desire Realm]. Therefore, one takes to mind a sign that easily generates an afflictive emotion and attains the mental contemplation of analysis, which individually analyzes [whether all the afflictive emotions [pertaining to the Desire Realm] have been abandoned. [153b]

> "Sign" here means an image. The meditator would take to mind, for example, an object that formerly easily caused the generation of hatred, and would see whether hatred is generated This is not called an observed-object condition (*dmigs rkyen, ālambanapratyaya*); it is a matter of taking that image to mind. Although, at that time, desire or hatred would not be generated strongly, nevertheless, because of habit, a slight degree of desire or hatred would be generated. The meditator would then think, "I have not been able to suppress all the afflictive emotions." This is the type of thought of the mental contemplation of analysis.

When one sees, through analyzing in this way, that one has not abandoned the triple cycle of the small manifest afflictive emotions pertaining to the Desire Realm, one cultivates the yoga of the union of calm abiding and special insight as an antidote to those. [This cultivation] is the mental contemplation of final training.

> It is called a training because the practitioner is in training for the sake of attaining an actual first concentration. It is called final because, among the preparations for the first concentration, it is the last. Because the meditator is viewing the upper and lower realms as peaceful and gross, respectively—taking this peacefulness and grossness to mind—it is called a "taking to mind" or mental contemplation (*yid la byed pa, manaskāra*).

In brief, it appears to be the thought of Gyel-tsap's (*rgyal tshab*, 1364–1432) *Explanation* [*of* (*Maitreya's*) "*Ornament for Clear Realization*"] that the attainment of the mental contemplation arisen from belief which is a preparation for the first concentration and the attainment of special insight included within the preparations for the first concentration are simultaneous. With respect to the mental contemplation of thorough isolation, there are the three [that serve as] actual antidotes to the triple cycle of great afflictive emotions pertaining to the Desire Realm. With respect to the mental contemplation of joy-withdrawal, there are the three [that serve as] actual antidotes to the triple cycle of middling afflictive emotions, and with respect to the mental contemplation of final training, there are the three [that serve as] actual antidotes to the triple cycle of small afflictive emotions pertaining to the Desire Realm.

These afflictive emotions pertaining to the Desire Realm, however, must be understood as the afflictive emotions pertaining to the Desire Realm to be abandoned by a mundane path of meditation.

> The reason why these are to be abandoned by a mundane rather than a supramundane path of meditation is that the triple cycle of even the great afflictive emotions pertaining to the Desire Realm cannot be abandoned before the path of seeing. To abandon the afflictive emotions pertaining to the Desire Realm, it is necessary to abandon desire. To abandon desire and other afflictive emotions pertaining to the Desire Realm, it is necessary to begin to abandon their root, the conception of a self of persons in the Desire Realm. The beginning of such an abandonment of the innate (*lhan skyes, sahaja*) conception of a self of persons (*gang zag gi bdag, pudgalātman*) in the Desire Realm does not occur even on the path of seeing, much less before it. However, these six mental contemplations and the seventh, which is their fruit, can be achieved not only before the path of seeing but even before the path of accumulation.
>
> There is none among us who has not achieved an actual concentration in a former lifetime. This is because, in former lifetimes, we have taken rebirth in the Form and Formless Realms up to the Peak of Cyclic Existence. To be reborn in any of the levels of the Form and Formless Realms, it is necessary, as a cause, to have generated its respective meditative absorption. If we make effort, they are easy to attain, but it is also easy to fall from them.
>
> The attainment of any of the actual concentrations and formless absorptions together with the paths that are explained in books on the grounds (*sa, bhūmi*) and paths can serve as causes for the attainment of liberation and omniscience (*rnam pa thams cad mkhyen pa, sarvākārajñāna*). However, through the mere attainment of any of the actual meditative absorptions without the attainment of such paths, it is possible to be born in the Form or Formless Realm and during that time not to have any suffering, but when the impetus of the action that caused rebirth there is exhausted, one will fall. With respect to the paths leading to liberation and omniscience, degeneration from the small path of accumulation is possible, but there is no degeneration from the middling path of accumulation [or any higher path].

For such is established by the fact that Vasubandhu's *Treasury of Manifest Knowledge* explains the mundane path of meditation [at the point of] "a path of meditation has two aspects" [6:1c][20] and explains the path of release and the uninterrupted path of that [mundane path of meditation at the point of] "a mundane path of release and mundane uninterrupted paths, respectively" [6:49a–b].[21]

When paths of meditation are terminologically divided, there are two types, mundane (*'jig rten pa, laukika*) and supramundane (*'jig rten las 'das pa, lokottara*) paths of meditation. The quotation from the *Treasury of Manifest Knowledge* speaks of a mundane path of release and mundane uninterrupted paths. "A mundane path of release" refers to an actual first concentration attained by someone who has not entered the path [that is, who has not attained the path of accumulation]. "Mundane uninterrupted paths" refers to the mental contemplations of thorough isolation, joy-withdrawal, and final training. Although these three have within them uninterrupted paths and paths of release, these mental contemplations in general are here referred to as mundane uninterrupted paths.

Another reason is that, as explained earlier, no matter what afflictive emotions pertaining to the Desire Realm or manifest afflictive emotions pertaining to the Desire Realm have been abandoned, one must have abandoned the conception of a self of persons.[22] [154a]

Even to abandon manifest afflictive emotions it is necessary to abandon the conception of a self of persons, unless such afflictive emotions are qualified as manifest afflictive emotion to be abandoned by a mundane path of meditation. The afflictive emotions pertaining to the Desire Realm to be abandoned by mundane paths of meditation are those afflictive emotions from which a practitioner can be separated by means of an actual meditative absorption. These refer to the strong forms of our usual afflictive emotions [but the subtle forms of our usual afflictive emotions not only cannot be abandoned but cannot even be suppressed by mundane paths of meditation].

According to the explanation concerning the preparations for the first concentration, so, too, [is the explanation of] the remaining preparations until the peak of cyclic existence because Asaṅga's *Compendium of Manifest Knowledge* says, "As with respect to the first concentration, so also until the sphere without discrimination and without non-discrimination (*'du shes med 'du shes med min, naivasaṃjñānāsaṃjñā*)."[23]

This means that just as the mental contemplations of a beginner, of individual knowledge of the character, arisen from belief, and of thorough isolation, joy-withdrawal, analysis, and final training are explained as preparations for the first concentration, so they are explained as preparations for the second, third, and fourth concentrations and for the four formless absorptions.

It is necessary to distinguish [the following] differences: because it is explained in the [Hīnayāna (*theg dman*) and Mahāyāna (*theg chen*)] Manifest Knowledges (*chos mngon pa, abhidharma*)[24] that on the levels of the upper realms [that is, the Form and Formless Realms] there are no states arisen from thinking and, in the Formless Realm, no states arisen from hearing, therefore, in the upper realms [that is, the Form and Formless Realms], when one begins to think, one goes into meditative stabilization without time for thinking.

> In the Formless Realm, there are no states arisen from hearing because there is no form. Beings in the Formless Realm have only four aggregates; they lack the form aggregate. Thus, they have no external form. Where there is no form, there is no sound, and there is no sound to be heard. Hence, there is no mind of hearing. Since there is no hearing of scriptures, there can be no states arisen from hearing.

In accordance with [the explanation from the Manifest Knowledges], when one meditates from within a basis (*rten, āśraya*)[25] of the Formless Realm there is neither hearing nor thinking in the first mental contemplation, and when one meditates from within a basis of the Form Realm, there are no states arisen from thinking.

> "In accordance with [the explanation from the Manifest Knowledges]" implies that according to the Mādhyamika system there is room for analysis whether there could be states arisen from hearing or thinking in the Form and Formless Realms. However, even according to the Mādhyamika system, the mental contemplation of individual knowledge of the character would not be a mixture of hearing and thinking in the Form and Formless Realms. This is because the positing of a mixture of hearing and thinking relates only to the viewing of a lower level as gross and an upper level as peaceful, and in the Form and Formless Realms the mind would naturally flow into meditative stabilization with regard to viewing a lower and an upper level in this way. Still, there would have to be states arisen from hearing and thinking for meditation on the four truths or on any of the profound Mahāyāna doctrines to take place in the Form Realm.
>
> Although there is no hearing of sounds in the Formless Realm, Jam-ȳang-shay-b̄a (*'jam dbyangs-bzhad pa*, 1648–1721) says that before being reborn in the Formless Realm, beings of that realm would have heard teaching about the doctrine, and the sounds of that teaching would establish predispositions which, when activated in the Formless Realm, would cause the beings to remember those doctrines. In that sense they would have states arisen from hearing.

With respect to [states ranging] from the preparations for the fourth concentration to the preparations for the peak of cyclic existence, because there is no feeling of joy [or] bliss, the meaning of "the mental contemplation of joy-withdrawal" is to be taken as just seeing the abandonment [of the afflictive emotions of the level below] as a good quality.

The meditator has separated from the sixth cycle of the afflictive emotions pertaining to the lower level and sees this as an advantage, a good quality.

Question: Are the preparations for the concentrations and formless absorptions meditative absorptions of those [concentrations and formless absorptions]?

Answer: They are thought to be, because whatever is a meditative absorption of a concentration or formless absorption is not necessarily an actual meditative absorption of [either of] those two; this is because whatever is a concentration or formless absorption is not necessarily an actual concentration or formless absorption. [154b]

A preparation for the first concentration is clearly not an actual meditative absorption of the first concentration, and so on for all the others. However, although the preparations for those states are not the *actual* meditative absorptions of those states, they are probably meditative absorptions.

With respect to the preparations for the first concentration, there are both pure [that is, contaminated] and uncontaminated [preparations], but with respect to the remaining seven [the second concentration through the peak of cyclic existence], there are only pure [preparations].

"Pure" here means free of the afflictive emotions of its own level. "Uncontaminated" refers to states of yogic direct perception (*rnal 'byor mngon sum, yogipratyakṣa*) and Superior paths. A pure meditative absorption cannot act as a basis for an uncontaminated consciousness.

There exist uncontaminated preparations for the first concentration because Stream Enterers and so forth actualize the supramundane path that is their object of attainment on the basis of a preparation for the first concentration.

[Hearers, as they overcome the afflictive emotions, become Approachers (*zhugs pa, pratipannaka*) to and Abiders in the Fruit (*'bras gnas, phalasthita*) of Stream Enterer (*rgyun zhugs, śrotāpanna*), Once Returner (*phyir 'ong, sakṛdāgāmin*), Never Returner (*phyir mi 'ong, anāgāmin*), and Foe Destroyer (*sgra bcom pa, arhan*). Thus, there are eight stages in all. It is possible either to overcome the afflictive emotions one by one—that is, gradually—or to overcome the great of the great afflictive emotions of all the levels from the Desire Realm to the Peak of Cyclic Existence simultaneously, and so on for the remaining afflictive emotions. There is also a way of proceeding in a leap-over manner, as explained below.][26]

"And so forth" refers to Once Returners, gradualist Never Returners, and simultaneous Foe Destroyers. They are all persons who have not attained an actual concentration; thus, their mental basis must be a preparation for the first concentration.

Approachers to Stream Enterers and Approachers to Once Returners who have previously separated from desire [by way of a mundane path] attain the fruit of Stream Enterer and the fruit of Once Returner at the time of the path of release of the path of seeing. Once Returners who have previously separated from desire have separated from six of the nine [cycles of] afflictive emotions pertaining to the Desire Realm before the path of seeing and will never attain the fruit of Stream Enterer; therefore, they are called those who leap over the fruit. At the time of the uninterrupted path of the path of seeing, they are Approachers to Once Returner, and at the time of the path of release of the path of seeing, they are Abiders in the Fruit of Once Returner.

Similarly, there are gradualist Never Returners who attain the fruit of Never Returner in dependence upon an uncontaminated preparation. This is because their attainment of the fruit of Never Returner and the attainment of an actual first concentration are simultaneous.

Approachers to Foe Destroyer of the simultaneous variety are special Abiders in the Fruit of Stream Enterer and have not attained an actual first concentration. Therefore, Abiders in the Fruit of Foe Destroyer who have proceeded in a simultaneous manner also have not attained an actual first concentration. They are called Unadorned Foe Destroyers (*dgra bcom rgyan med*). Such Foe Destroyers have been released only from the factor of the afflictive emotions [and not from the obstructions to meditative absorption]. They must have a path by which they attain the fruit, and that which is suitable to serve as such a path can only be a preparation for the first concentration.

There is no purpose in generating a supramundane path on the basis of the remaining [sets of] preparations. Whoever has attained a preparation for the second concentration has necessarily attained an actual meditative absorption of the first concentration because, when an actual meditative absorption of a concentration that is an easier path has been attained, there is no purpose in generating a supramundane path on the basis of a preparation for a concentration that is a more difficult path.

Even someone who had attained an actual second concentration would generate a supramundane path in dependence upon a preparation for the first concentration because it is easier. Someone who has attained an easier path does not discard it for a more difficult path.[27]

In dependence upon this, the reason for not positing an uncontaminated [type of] the seven remaining [sets of] preparations can be known.

There are no afflicted preparations because, in that case, they could not separate from desire for the level below them.

A preparation must be a preparation for attaining its respective actual meditative absorption. If it were afflicted, it could not separate from desire for the level below it and thus could not serve as a preparation.

Calm Abiding

If a beginner preparation—[which is a preparatory] mental contemplation for the first concentration and is included within mere calm abiding—must precede the six preparations included within special insight, what is the way in which that [occurs? What] is the presentation of calm abiding and special insight? [155a]

Without the attainment of calm abiding there is no attainment of special insight.

The attainment of calm abiding must precede the attainment of special insight.

Śāntideva's *Engaging in the Bodhisattva Deeds* (*bodhi[sattva]caryāvatāra, byang chub sems dpa'i spyod pa la 'jug pa*) [8:4] says:

> Having understood that the afflictive emotions
> Are overcome through special insight
> Thoroughly endowed with calm abiding,
> One should first seek calm abiding.[28]

Without calm abiding, the mere thorough analysis of phenomena is not capable of overcoming afflictive emotions. To cut something with a knife, we need a steady hand; without it, we cannot cut anything well. Similarly, although the main cause of overcoming afflictive emotions is wisdom, the mere factor of wisdom without the factor of stability—calm abiding—cannot overcome afflictive emotions. For example, to split a piece of wood we cannot chop here and there; we have to keep chopping in the same place. Similarly, it is not suitable to analyze a little here and there; we need the factor of stability. If we analyze within a very firm factor of stability, we will be able to overcome the afflictive emotions. If the wisdom that penetrates the mode of being is conjoined with an unfluctuating calm abiding, that sharp weapon of the wisdom of the middle way free of the two extremes can destroy every wrong conception. Therefore, we should initially seek calm abiding.

Also, the *Heap of Jewels Sūtra* (*ratnakūṭa, dkon mchog brtsegs pa*) says:

> Abiding in ethics, one attains meditative stabilization; having attained meditative stabilization, one cultivates wisdom as well.

"Ethics" means, at the least, refraining from the ten non-virtues [killing, stealing, sexual misconduct, lying, divisive talk, harsh speech, foolish talk, covetousness, harmfulness, wrong views].[29] Ethics are the basis of all good qualities. Just as all activities such as going, coming, building houses, depend upon the earth, all the higher qualities depend upon ethics. On the basis of ethics, we can cultivate meditative stabilization—a one-pointed mind—for a long time and eventually attain calm abiding. Having attained meditative stabilization, we can [cultivate and] attain special insight that is conjoined with a pliancy induced by the power of reasoned analysis.

With regard to the three trainings (*bslab pa, śikṣā*), one first generates the training in higher ethics (*lhag pa'i tshul khrims, adhiśīla*), then the training in higher meditative stabilization (*lhag pa'i sems, adhicitta*), and then the training in higher wisdom (*lhag pa'i shes rab, adhiprajñā*).

[First Debate]

Objection: That [without the attainment of calm abiding there is no attainment of special insight] contradicts Asaṅga's statement in the *Compendium of Manifest Knowledge:*

> Some have attained special insight but have not attained calm abiding; in dependence upon special insight they make effort at calm abiding.[30]

If this statement is taken literally, then it indeed contradicts our system. It needs to be interpreted.

Answer: It is not contradictory because the thought of this passage is that, in dependence upon the special insight which directly realizes the four truths and is included within the preparations for the first concentration, one achieves the calm abiding, included within an actual first concentration, that directly realizes the four truths.

Although, in general, we must achieve calm abiding first and then achieve special insight, there are cases of achieving a [type of] special insight first and then a [type of] calm abiding. For example, there is a calm abiding, included within the path of seeing, that is an effect of a special insight at the time of the path of preparation.

Preparations and actual concentrations are necessarily in a relationship of cause and effect. The preparations for the first concentration must precede the actual first concentration. What is being referred to here is a special insight directly realizing emptiness or the four truths and included within a preparation for the first concentration. If that special insight serves as the cause, then the effect could be a calm abiding included within an actual first concentration, that calm abiding being a consciousness directly realizing emptiness or the four truths.

Asaṅga's *Actuality of the Grounds* (*bhūmivastu, sa'i dngos gzhi*) says:

> Moreover, one thoroughly knows [the four truths] just as they are, ranging from suffering through to the path, but one has not attained the first concentration, and so forth. Immediately after that, one sets the mind but does not engage in differentiating phenomena. In dependence upon just this special wisdom, that [person] trains in the special mind [an actual first concentration].[31] [155b]

The person described here has directly realized the four truths just as they are but has not attained an actual first concentration. Immediately after [realizing the four truths] the person has to make effort to attain an actual first concentration but does not have to make any effort to realize the four truths newly. Thus, in dependence upon the special insight that directly realizes the four truths, this person makes effort to achieve an actual first concentration.[32]

[Second Debate]

Objection: The nine mental abidings—[namely,] the meditative stabilization of continuous setting, and so forth—are calm abidings because Asaṅga's *Compendium of Manifest Knowledge* says:

> What is calm abiding? It is as follows: setting the mind inside, continuous setting, resetting, close setting, disciplining, pacifying, thorough pacifying, making one-pointed, and setting in equipoise.[33]

Answer: [This passage] does not entail [that the nine mental abidings are calm abidings] because the [nine mental abidings before calm abiding—namely,] the meditative stabilization of continuous setting, and so forth—having been designated by the name "calm abiding," are taught [as such].

When asked, "What is calm abiding?" Asaṅga lists the nine mental abidings because one must achieve them in order to attain calm abiding.

Another reason is that whatever is a calm abiding is necessarily conjoined with pliancy.

The nine mental abidings are not conjoined with pliancy. Therefore, they cannot be actual calm abidings and thus are said to be only called calm abiding.

The *Sūtra Unraveling the Thought* (*saṃdhinirmocana, dgongs pa nges par 'grel pa'i mdo*) says:

"Blessed One (*bcom ldan 'das, bhagavant*), when the Bodhisattva is doing an internal mental contemplation that is the mind observing the mind, what are those mental contemplations called until the attainment of physical and mental pliancy?"

"Maitreya, [they] are not calm abiding; rather, one should say that they are associated with imitations that are similitudes of calm abiding."[34]

Also, Maitreya's *Ornament* [*for the Mahāyāna Sūtras*, 14:14–15] says:

Through familiarization with those [nine mental abidings that are included within the level of the Desire Realm]
One does not engage in application [of the antidotes].
Then, when one has attained great pliancy of body and mind,
It should be known that one has a mental contemplation [that is, calm abiding].[35]

It is explained that whatever is a calm abiding is necessarily meditative stabilization [156a] and that whatever is a special insight is necessarily a wisdom consciousness.

Whatever is a calm abiding must be that which has the function of causing the mind to abide one-pointedly on its object of observation. Therefore, it must be a meditative stabilization.

Whatever is a special insight must be a wisdom consciousness because whatever is a special insight must be a consciousness thoroughly analyzing phenomena. It is a mental factor that has the function of distinguishing the features of an object.

When we talk about attaining meditative stabilization, we are talking about achieving a special meditative stabilization, calm abiding; nevertheless, all of the nine mental abidings are meditative stabilizations in themselves because they are mental factors of meditative stabilization.

There is a stabilization (*ting nge 'dzin, samādhi*) included within the five determining mental factors, but merely being that stabilization is not sufficient for something to be that which is usually designated by the term "meditative stabilization" (*ting nge 'dzin, samādhi*). Context is important. Similarly, if one does something virtuous, one says, "I am achieving religious practice" (*chos, dharma*); yet all phenomena are dharmas.

The *Cloud of Jewels Sūtra* (*ratnamegha, dkon cog sprin gyi mdo*) says:

> Calm abiding is a one-pointed mind. Special insight is an individual analysis.[36]

Also, Maitreya says [in the *Ornament for the Mahāyāna Sūtras,* 14:8]:

> This confining [of the mind] on words of doctrine is also to be known as a path of calm abiding.
> The path of special insight is to be known as analyzing their meanings.[37]

It is said:

> All the important points of the doctrine are included within the four seals (*phyag rgya, mudrā*). Setting the mind on these four mainly to develop the factor of stability is called calm abiding.
>
> [The four seals stamp a doctrine as Buddhist and are held by all Buddhist tenet systems. They are:
>
> All compositional phenomena are impermanent
> All contaminated things are miserable
> All phenomena are selfless
> Nirvāṇa is peace.][38]

If we apply the previous citation to the four seals and [from within calm abiding] analyze their meaning by stating reasons, that analysis is an example of the path of special insight. With respect to the first of the four seals, we may state, "All compositional phenomena are impermanent because of disintegrating moment by moment."

With respect to the second, we may state, "All contaminated things are miserable because of being under the influence of contaminated actions and afflictive emotions."

The third seal, "All phenomena are selfless," will be applied to the selflessness that is the non-existence of the person as a self-sufficient or substantial entity. Since the person cannot be identified unless the aggregates are identified, the person is imputedly existent (*btags yod, prajñaptisat*) and not substantially existent (*rdzas yod, dravyasat*).

With respect to the fourth seal, nirvāṇa is peace because all unpeacefulness is based on the afflictive emotions. When we have eliminated the root of all unpeacefulness, that state is peaceful.

[Maitreya] in the *Ornament for the Mahāyāna Sūtras* also says [18:66]:

> Because one sets the mind on the mind in dependence upon thorough stability

And because one thoroughly differentiates phenomena, [these are respectively] calm abiding and special insight.[39]

"In dependence upon thorough stability" means based on the causes—that is, the nine mental abidings leading to calm abiding. "Because one thoroughly differentiates phenomena"—that is, because the meditator analyzes phenomena with reasoning [from within calm abiding]—refers to special insight.

[Third Debate]

Opinion: Whatever is a calm abiding is necessarily conjoined with the bliss of physical and mental pliancy.

Answer: This is not feasible because, in the Formless Realm, physical pliancy does not exist.

This is because there is no form in the Formless Realm. Thus, it follows that in the Formless Realm there is no physical pliancy.

Another reason is that whatever is a physical pliancy is necessarily a tangible-object sphere (*reg bya'i skye mched, spraṣṭavyāyatana*). The master Sthiramati states that a sūtra says, "When a special physical object of touch is conjoined with joy, [that special physical object of touch] is to be known as physical pliancy, and when the mind is joyous, that is mental pliancy."[40]

Therefore, physical pliancy is a special type of internal object of touch. It is an internal object of touch that arises upon familiarization with steady meditation and affords a physical serviceability such that the body can be directed toward virtuous activity without fatigue for as long as one likes. Therefore, physical pliancy can occur only where there is form; it cannot occur in the Formless Realm.

The opponent is saying, wrongly, that whatever is a calm abiding is necessarily conjoined with the bliss of physical and mental pliancy. [This is wrong because] in the first place, there is no bliss in the Fourth Concentration. In the Fourth Concentration, there is mental pliancy but no bliss of mental pliancy; there is also physical pliancy but no bliss of physical pliancy. Similarly, in the Formless Realm there is mental pliancy but no bliss of mental pliancy. Moreover, in the Formless Realm there is no physical pliancy, much less a bliss of physical pliancy. Therefore, according to our own system, whatever is a consciousness of calm abiding is necessarily conjoined with pliancy but not necessarily conjoined with a bliss of pliancy. We have to know this difference.

Whatever is a physical pliancy must be a tangible object. Whatever is a mental pliancy must be a mental factor. Although there is a pliancy that is included among the eleven virtuous mental factors, it is called a mere pliancy because it accompanies all virtuous minds. It is that which provides a serviceability such that the mind can be directed to a virtuous object; it is merely that. However, in this context, pliancy is a special pliancy because this is a case of a serviceability such that the mind can be directed to any virtuous object as much as one likes. Therefore, the mind is without subtle laxity or excitement, lethargy, or sleep. Pliancy involves a very clear object of observation and a very tight mode of apprehension. Further, the meditator can stay on the object as long as he or she likes, whether for an hour or two hours or three or even longer. The factor that affords this serviceability is [a special] mental pliancy; that is why the phrase "as much as one likes" is used to describe it.

Physical pliancy involves a movement of winds that are concordant with the stabilizing of the mind and a getting rid of winds that are not concordant with a stabilized mind. When the meditation proceeds well, when the mind stays well on its object of observation, there comes about a non-movement of the winds that cause interruption in the mind. Thus, someone who has this can meditate as long as he or she wants without any difficulty. The meditator feels that he or she could fly in the sky and that the body is very healthy and light. In brief, when the meditation is going well, the unfavorable winds no longer move and the favorable ones do.

However, if the mode of meditation is not correct and if one forces the meditation, it is possible to create great discomfort in body and mind and to cause a disease called the life-wind disease. This type of fault occurs when we actually do not have stability but think that we have it and when we actually have not overcome laxity and excitement but think that we have and then [as a result of these wrong discriminations] force the meditation. Therefore, it is extremely important to eliminate laxity and excitement.

[Special Insight]

Also, whatever is a special insight is necessarily conjoined with pliancy.

"Also" means that not only are consciousness of calm abiding conjoined with pliancy but also consciousness of special insight.

The *Sūtra Unraveling the Thought* says:

> "Blessed One, what should one call the mental contemplation that internally takes to mind an image, its object of meditative stabilization, with respect to those phenomena that have been well settled in this way, [this mental contemplation occurring] while a Bodhisattva has not attained physical and mental pliancy?" [156b]
>
> "Maitreya, it is not special insight; rather, one should say that it is associated with an imitation that is a similitude of special insight."[41]

An image which is similar to the object is taken to mind within a meditative stabilization that involves one-pointed concentration on phenomena that have been settled well. At this point, the meditator has not yet attained physical and mental pliancy. This consciousness is not special insight; it is a consciousness engaged in a practice which is a means for attaining special insight and thus is only a similitude of special insight. This passage shows that whatever is a consciousness of special insight is necessarily conjoined with pliancy.

Whoever has attained special insight has necessarily attained a union of calm abiding and special insight. D̄zong-ka-b̄a's *Great Exposition of the Stages of the Path* says:

> With respect to the union [of calm abiding and special insight], it is definitely necessary to attain those two. Moreover, from the initial attainment of special insight one attains [this] union.[42]

Since calm abiding has already been attained, with the attainment of special insight the meditator has calm abiding in a composite of both. Thus, at the very moment of attaining special insight, the meditator attains a union of calm abiding and special insight.

Moreover, [Ge-s̄hay Döl-ba-shay-rap-gya-tso's (*dge bshes dol pa shes rab rgya mtsho*, 1059–1131)] *Blue Small Text* and a [Ḡa-dam (*bka' gdams*)] *Stages of the Path*, and so forth, explain that the meditative stabilization that is a union of calm abiding and special insight is the attainment of a mind that abides non-conceptually on emptiness after special insight is induced through the power of having done analysis by reasoning from within calm abiding observing an object such as emptiness.

It is a common assertion of D̄zong-ka-b̄a's *Great Exposition of the Stages of the Path*, Paṇ-chen s̄ö-nam-drak-b̄a, and other Ge-luk-b̄as that calm abiding is attained first and then, special insight [and, simultaneously with special insight, a union of calm abiding and special insight]. However, the *Blue Small Text* and the Ḡa-dam-b̄a *Stages of the Path* present a slightly different position. They say that when special insight is attained, the meditator does not have a union of calm abiding and special insight but that a union of calm abiding and special insight is attained in the next moment with the attainment of a mind that abides non-conceptually on emptiness. The difference is very slight; it is a difference of only one moment.

With respect to small texts: D̄zong-ka-b̄a said that we need to cause the great texts to appear as instructions for practice. This does not mean that we should have in our hands a small text [setting forth instructions]; rather, it means that all the great texts should appear as instructions to the mind.

In general, it must be asserted that these two, calm abiding and special insight, are only mutually exclusive.

The reason for this is that whatever is calm abiding is necessarily the mental factor of meditative stabilization and whatever is special insight is necessarily the mental factor of wisdom, and those two are mutually exclusive.

Therefore, [once they have been accepted as in all respects mutually exclusive,][43] it is not correct [to say] that, with the attainment of a ground, those two become one entity, and so forth. In any case, if we state, [as our own system does,][44] that whatever is calm abiding is necessarily a stabilizing meditation and whatever is special insight is necessarily analytical meditation, we should know how to posit the two, calm abiding and special insight, that are included within the uninterrupted path of the Mahāyāna path of seeing [that is, the first of the ten Bodhisattva grounds][45] and on up through the uninterrupted path at the end of the continuum [as a sentient being, just before the attainment of Buddhahood].[46]

We must be cautious because there are problems in explaining the higher stages of the path. In the beginning, analytical and stabilizing meditation are different, but later they become as if of one entity. Therefore, some people say that with the attainment of a ground these two become of one entity. Our own system does not say that they become of one entity; moreover, their different functions do not have to become manifest. If there were a different activity, a different type of exertion, with regard to stabilizing meditation and analytical meditation, it would be difficult to posit the uninterrupted path of a Mahāyāna path of seeing as both stabilizing meditation and analytical meditation. Because the uninterrupted path of a Mahāyāna path of seeing is a mind to which, with regard to emptiness, all dualistic appearance has vanished, it cannot have any new analyzing. Therefore, at this point in the path, it is not necessary to have the exertion of newly analyzing the object in order for that consciousness to be called a special insight.

The Explanation of the Actual Meditative Absorptions That Are Concentrations[47] [157a]

The definition of an actual meditative absorption that is a concentration is:

a virtuous knower that is included within the level of a concentration and that has passed beyond the level below it by way of its branches.

"By way of its branches" means that it has not passed beyond the level below it by way of its object of observation.[48]

The definition of an actual concentration that is a causal meditative absorption is:

> *1) an actual meditative absorption that is a concentration and 2) that which is included within cyclic existence and is a producer of a true suffering, its effect.*

> "Suffering" here refers to one's birth in the Form Realm.

The explanation of the actual [first concentration]

The definition of an actual meditative absorption that is a first concentration is:

> *1) an actual meditative absorption that is a concentration and 2) that which abides in the type[49] distinguished by having separated from desire for the Desire Realm.*

When actual meditative absorptions that are first concentrations are divided, there are two: mere actual meditative absorptions that are first concentrations and special [actual meditative absorptions that are first concentrations].

The definition of the first [a mere actual meditative absorption that is a first concentration] is:

> *1) an actual meditative absorption that is a first concentration and 2) that which abides in the type of a feeling of mental bliss.*

> Mere actual meditative absorptions that are first concentrations are called "mere" because they are the usual type. With the attainment of the mental contemplation of joy-withdrawal, the meditator is touched to some extent by bliss. Later, with the attainment of the mental contemplation of final training, the meditator also experiences some bliss, and finally, with the attainment of an actual first concentration, the meditator experiences bliss.
>
> "That which abides in the type of a feeling of mental bliss" means that which either is itself blissful feeling or is accompanied by blissful feeling.

The definition of the second [a special actual meditative absorption that is a first concentration] is:

> *1) [an actual meditative absorption that is a first concentration] and 2) that which abides in the type of the level of neutral feeling.*

> "That which abides in the type of the level of neutral feeling" means that which either is itself neutral feeling or is accompanied by neutral feeling.

The second[50] concentration and above do not have divisions of mere and special because, from there on up, they cannot separate from desire for some of the branches of their own level without separating from their own level.

The explanation of the second, third, and fourth concentrations that are causal meditative absorptions

The definition of an actual meditative absorption that is a second concentration is:

> *1) an actual meditative absorption that is a concentration and 2) that which abides in the type distinguished by having separated from desire for the First Concentration.*

This should be extended through the fourth [concentration]. [157b]

> The same type of definition is applied to actual third and fourth concentrations.

The Explanation of the Concentrations That Are Resultant Births

> A resultant-birth concentration is an effect of having cultivated a concentration in, say, this lifetime; in the next lifetime, such a person would be born in the corresponding concentration in the Form Realm and, there, would have a mind of that concentration, a body, and so forth.

The definition of a concentration that is a resultant birth is:

> *that which is included within either a fruitional effect* (rnam smin gyi 'bras bu, vipākaphala) *or a causally concordant effect* (rgyu mthun gyi 'bras bu, niṣyandaphala) *of having cultivated, in another birth, a concentration that is a causal meditative absorption.*

Examples are inborn phenomena in the continua of sentient beings from the Brahmā Type through the Not Low.

> The Brahmā Type is the lowest level of the First Concentration. The Not Low (or None Higher) is the highest of the Five Pure Places of the Fourth Concentration.
>
> An example of a fruitional effect is the form aggregate that is the body produced by the power of birth in the continuum of a being in any of the seventeen levels of the Form Realm ranging from the Brahmā Type through the Not Low.
>
> Examples of effects that concord with the causes—concordant

effects—are the virtuous consciousnesses that are present from the time of birth in such persons' continua through the power of the persons' being born there. The concentrations that they have by merely being born there are effects concordant with their having cultivated those concentrations in a former life.

2

The Explanation of the Formless Absorptions

The definition of an actual meditative absorption that is a formless absorption is:

> *a virtuous knower that is included within the level of a formless absorption and that has passed beyond the level below it by way of its object of observation.*

> The formless absorptions pass beyond the level below them by way of their objects of observation, whereas the concentrations do so by way of their branches. The concentrations have specific branches associated with them, but the formless absorptions do not have such branches. Thus, it is only by way of the object of observation that each passes beyond the level below it.[1]

The definition of an actual formless meditative absorption which is a causal meditative absorption is:

> *1) an actual meditative absorption which is a formless absorption and 2) that which is included within cyclic existence and is a producer of a true suffering, its effect.*

When actual formless meditative absorptions are divided, there are four, ranging from the actual meditative absorption of limitless space through the actual meditative absorption of the peak of cyclic existence.

The definition of an actual meditative absorption of limitless space is:

> *1) an actual meditative absorption that is a formless absorption and 2) that which abides in the type distinguished by having separated from desire for the fourth concentration. [158a]*

This should be extended to the other three.

> The same type of definition is applied to the actual meditative absorptions of limitless consciousness, nothingness, and the peak of cyclic existence.

The definition of a formless absorption that is a resultant birth is:

> *that which is included within either a fruitional effect or a causally concordant effect of having cultivated, in another birth, a formless absorption*

which is a causal meditative absorption.

> [Fruitional effects are usually associated with the assumption of a new name and form (*ming gzugs, nāmarūpa*).] Since the beings of the Formless Realm have no form aggregate, how can there be a fruitional effect in the Formless Realm? [Such a fruitional effect is possible because, in the twelve links of dependent-arising,] "name" in "name and form" refers to the mental aggregates. This is because the bases of designation of a Formless Realm being are the four mental aggregates—feelings, discriminations, compositional factors, and consciousness. They are called the aggregates that are the basis of name. Through the cultivation, in a former lifetime, of an actual meditative absorption of the Formless Realm, these four aggregates are produced; thus, they are fruitional effects of having cultivated a causal formless absorption in a former lifetime.

Examples are inborn phenomena in the continua of sentient beings who have been born in [any of] the four types of the Formless Realm.

3

Comparisons of the Concentrations and Formless Absorptions

[Pure and Uncontaminated Concentrations and Formless Absorptions]

The four concentrations and the four formless absorptions both have two [types], pure and uncontaminated.

[The Concentrations]

The definition of a pure actual meditative absorption that is a concentration is:

> *1) an actual meditative absorption that is a concentration and 2) that which is included within mundane virtues*[1] *not polluted by the afflictive emotions of their own level.*

A pure actual meditative absorption that is a concentration is a contaminated type. In the definition, "mundane" means that it is in the continuum of a common being—that is, of someone who is not a Superior.

When [pure actual meditative absorptions that are first concentrations] are divided, there are four: actual meditative absorptions that are first concentrations concordant with degeneration (*nyams pa cha mthun, hānabhāgīya*), concordant with abiding (*gnas pa cha mthun, sthitibhāgīya*), concordant with enhancement (*khyad par cha mthun, viśeṣabhāgīya*), and concordant with definite differentiation (*nges 'byed cha mthun, nirvedhabhāgīya*).

The first three varieties probably have only the subjective aspect of viewing the lower level as gross and the upper level as peaceful.

The definition of an actual meditative absorption that is a first concentration concordant with degeneration is:

> *1) a pure actual meditative absorption that is a first concentration and 2) that which is concordant with the generation of afflictive emotions of its own level or of a lower level immediately after itself.*

"Afflictive emotions of its own level or of a lower level" refers to the afflictive emotions to be abandoned by a mundane path of meditation. With reference to the first concentration, "its own level" is the First Concentration; "a lower level" is the Desire Realm. "Immediately after itself" refers to the next moment or period; if it referred to an indefinite future time, any of the pure actual meditative absorptions that are concentrations could be concordant with degeneration. Although an actual meditative absorption concordant with degeneration is necessarily concordant with the generation of afflictive emotions of either its own or a lower level immediately after it, it does not necessarily involve the generation of such afflictive emotions. However, it is proceeding in the direction of generating an afflictive emotion, and if the meditator remains in meditative equipoise as it is proceeding at that point, an afflictive emotion will be generated.

The definition of an actual meditative absorption that is a first concentration concordant with abiding is:

1) [a pure actual meditative absorption that is a first concentration] and 2) that which induces another pure [meditative absorption] of the same level as itself immediately after itself. [158b]

Such a meditative absorption is called concordant with abiding because that very meditative absorption continues to remain. It is not a case of one moment of meditative absorption of the first concentration inducing a second, similar moment. The inducing of a second moment similar to the first is common to compositional phenomena in general and is not what is being referred to here. Rather, a period of meditation comes to a close and induces another pure meditative absorption of the same level.

The definition of an actual meditative absorption that is a first concentration concordant with enhancement is:

1) [a pure actual meditative absorption that is a first concentration] and 2) that which induces another pure [meditative absorption] of a higher level immediately after itself.

Because it induces a meditative absorption higher than itself, this meditative absorption is called concordant with enhancement.

The definition of an actual meditative absorption that is a first concentration concordant with definite differentiation is:

1) [a pure actual meditative absorption that is a first concentration] and 2) that which induces another, supramundane path immediately after itself.

It is called concordant with definite differentiation [because it induces a supramundane path]. The path of preparation is called a partial concordance with definite differentiation because it induces the path of seeing.[2]

It is also [stated] in this way in Vasubandhu's *Treasury of Manifest Knowledge* [8:17]:

> The pure [meditative absorptions] are those concordant with degeneration, and so forth.
> Those four kinds [those concordant with degeneration, abiding, enhancement, and definite differentiation] are [called] respectively,
> Concordant with the generation of afflictive emotions, with [a pure meditative absorption of] its own level,
> With a higher [level], and with the uncontaminated.[3]

[The Formless Absorptions]

One should also understand the four formless absorptions similarly.

> These four—actual meditative absorptions concordant with degeneration, abiding, enhancement, and definite differentiation—also occur in the formless absorptions.

However, there is a difference: the actual meditative absorption of the peak of cyclic existence does not have a type concordant with enhancement because above the peak of cyclic existence there is no other mundane level. According to the upper and lower Manifest Knowledges,[4] there is also no actual meditative absorption of the peak of cyclic existence that is concordant with definite differentiation because there is no uncontaminated actual meditative absorption of the peak of cyclic existence.

> This, in turn, is because, for an actual meditative absorption of the peak of cyclic existence, the movement of the mental factor of discrimination (*'du shes, saṃjñā*) is extremely subtle; therefore, its object of observation and subjective aspect are unclear.

[This is so] because that which is unclear in its object of observation and subjective aspect cannot be a basis of a very clear supramundane path. [This is so] because a Hearer Superior who has attained an actual meditative absorption of the peak of cyclic existence actualizes the supramundane path that is his object of attainment on the basis of a mind of [the level of] nothingness. Vasubandhu's *Treasury of Manifest Knowledge* [8:20a–b] says:

> A Superior in the Peak of Cyclic Existence exhausts contamination
> Having actualized [an absorption of the level of] Nothingness.[5] [159a]

> This means that a Hearer Superior on the path of meditation, to actualize

the fruit of Foe Destroyer, does not use the mind of his or her own level but actualizes the mind of the level just below it, nothingness, and on the basis of that actualizes the supramundane path of a Foe Destroyer.

Also, Asaṅga's *Compendium of Manifest Knowledge* says:

> The sphere without discrimination and without non-discrimination, because of having a very unclear activity of discrimination, is only mundane. Therefore, it is said to be signless (*mtshan med, animitta*).

"Only mundane" means only contaminated. "Signless" here means without the ability to differentiate and discriminate.

> The Blessed One said, "To the extent that one enters into equipoise by means of discrimination, one attains all-knowingness (*kun shes, ājñātāvin*)."[5]

"All-knowingness" refers to consciousness of the paths of seeing, meditation, and no more learning. To actualize these paths discrimination is needed. The new seeing of selflessness on the path of seeing is called the faculty of knowing all that was not known. Since, on the path of meditation, the practitioner again and again becomes accustomed to the direct perception of selflessness previously experienced, it is called the faculty of knowing all. On the path of no more learning the practitioner has the faculty of possessing the knowledge of all; this is because, in dependence upon becoming accustomed again and again to the direct perception of selflessness on the path of meditation, he or she removes all afflictive emotions, and then, on the path of no more learning, has this knowledge.

[Antidotal and Non-antidotal Meditative Absorptions]

It is not necessary for the actual concentrations and formless absorptions to separate from desire for the levels below them because the preparations do the separating. The contaminated actual [meditative absorptions] do not act as antidotes to [the afflictive emotions of] their own and higher levels, but the uncontaminated ones act as antidotes to [the afflictive emotions of] their own and higher levels.

To attain an actual first concentration, it is necessary to separate from the desires associated with the Desire Realm. Therefore, someone who has such a concentration has already separated from those desires; the preparations have done the separating. A contaminated actual meditative absorption of the first concentration does not act as an antidote to the afflictive emotions of its own level because the preparations for the second concentration act as the antidotes to the desires associated with the First Concentration. [The same is true of other contaminated actual meditative absorptions.] Moreover, afflictive emotions in general are overcome only in dependence upon an uncontaminated mind. Thus, in general, a contaminated mind will not act as an antidote to the afflictive emotions. However, although the contaminated actual meditative absorptions do not act as antidotes to the afflictive emotions of their own and higher levels, the uncontaminated actual meditative absorptions act as such antidotes.

For this reason, the preparations for the concentrations and formless absorptions, the contaminated actual [meditative absorptions of the concentrations and formless absorptions], and the uncontaminated [actual meditative absorptions of the concentrations and formless absorptions] are the paths that, respectively, separate from desire, abide blissfully in this lifetime, and thoroughly achieve good qualities.

Because the preparations separate from the desires associated with the lower level, they are called paths that separate from desire.

Because a person who possesses an actual contaminated meditative absorption of the concentrations or formless absorptions in his or her continuum can in this lifetime, without suffering or mental discomfort (*yid mi bde, daurmanasya*), set in meditative equipoise according to his or her wish, it is said that these are paths that abide blissfully in this lifetime. "Blissfully" cannot refer to the feeling of bliss because in the fourth concentration and the formless absorptions there is no feeling of bliss. Thus, it means that such a person can set in meditative equipoise according to his or her wish.

Because, in dependence upon the uncontaminated actual meditative absorptions of the concentrations and formless absorptions, it is possible to achieve true cessations, they are called paths that thoroughly achieve good qualities.

[AFFLICTED MEDITATIVE ABSORPTIONS]

The following discussion is relevant to pure meditative absorptions concordant with degeneration.

What are afflicted meditative absorptions?

An afflicted meditative absorption is not something that is both a meditative absorption and afflicted, as it would appear to be. Rather, in the first period, there is a meditative absorption, but in the second period, it becomes associated with an afflictive emotion, whereby it becomes neutral (*lung du ma bstan pa, avyākṛta*), whereas whatever is a meditative absorption is necessarily virtuous.

Those bases that are made afflicted are the pure actual meditative absorptions that are concentrations and formless absorptions. [159b] Vasubandhu's *Treasury of Manifest Knowledge* [8:6b–c] says:

> The pure [meditative absorptions] are mundane virtues;
> Those [pure meditative absorptions] are tasted by that [associated

with relishing (*ro myang tshungs ldan, āsvādanasaṃprayukta*)].[7]

In the second period of such a meditative absorption, in dependence upon the taste of an afflictive emotion, it becomes afflicted. Thus, the pure actual meditative absorptions that are the concentrations and formless absorptions are what are made afflicted.

The phenomena that make them afflicted are attachment, [bad] view, pride, and ignorance, which are defiled and neutral.

They are defiled by the afflictive emotions and are neither virtuous nor non-virtuous.

Asaṅga's *Compendium of Manifest Knowledge* says:

> In what manner are they afflicted? They are the four neutral roots: attachment, [bad] view, pride, and ignorance.[8]

Vasubandhu's *Treasury of Manifest Knowledge* [5:21] also says:

> The western Vaibhāṣikas say there are four:
> They are attachment, [bad] view, pride, obscuration.[9]

The mode in which they are caused to be afflicted [is as follows]: when one enters into absorption in a pure actual meditative absorption, there arises 1) a predominant attachment that tastes the bliss [of that absorption],[10] 2) a predominant [perverse] view due to generating the bad view of the category of the past (*sngon gyi mtha', pūrvānta*) [as non-existent], and so forth, 3) a predominant pride due to a mind inflated by [the fact that one has achieved] concentration, [or] 4) a predominant obscuration wondering whether or not just that attainment is a path of liberation.

The bad view of the category of the past is the view that former births are non-existent. If the category of the future had been mentioned, it would refer to the view that there is no rebirth after this life. There are many other types of bad view.

Question: Are afflicted actual meditative absorptions that are concentrations and formless absorptions fully qualified meditative absorptions?

Answer: They are not.[11] Vasubandhu's *Autocommentary on the "Treasury of Manifest Knowledge"* [8:1e] says:

> *Question:* How is that which is afflicted a concentration?

This question is based on the thought that an afflicted meditative absorption would have to be a common locus (*gzhi mthun, sāmānādhikaraṇa*) of being a meditative absorption and being afflicted.

Answer: Because of wrong contemplation.

Question: Would there not be the absurd consequence [that there is also wrong contemplation by one thoroughly afflicted by sense desire]?

Answer: There would not be [such a consequence] because [this is a case] of designating that which is only of a type similar to [a concentration] with the name ["concentration"], as is the case, for example, with a rotten seed.[12]

An afflicted meditative absorption is a continuation of a meditative absorption; that continuation is being designated with the name "meditative absorption," even though it no longer is. In the example, a rotten seed is not a seed. It is only given the name "seed."

[They are not fully qualified meditative absorptions] [160a] because whatever is an actual meditative absorption that is a concentration must be virtuous, [whereas] an afflicted meditative absorption is neutral. Furthermore, they are not fully qualified meditative absorptions because they do not possess the branches of a concentration. Vasubandhu's *Treasury of Manifest Knowledge* [8:10a–c] says:

An afflicted [concentration] does not have joy, bliss, internal clarity,
Introspection, mindfulness, neutral feeling, and mindfulness,
And lacks purity [with respect to the afflictive emotions of its own level].[13]

[Mode of Leaving the Lower Level]

With respect to the concentrations, the higher have definitely left the coarser branches of the lower, and there is a difference in the branches [between the higher and the lower]. Therefore, [the concentrations] pass beyond [their respective lower levels] by way of their branches. Because the formless absorptions do not have divisions into various branches and the higher definitely leave the lower by way of their objects of observation, they are said to pass beyond [their respective lower levels] by way of their objects of observation.

In the formless absorptions, the object of observation and subjective aspect get subtler and subtler as the meditator progresses. That is how, in the formless absorptions, the upper levels pass beyond the lower by way of their objects of observation.

In the meditative absorption of limitless space, the meditator thinks that, just as space is a negation of obstructive contact, so all phenomena are just that, and does not take to mind such phenomena as forms.

In the meditative absorption of limitless consciousness, the meditator does not take to mind any external phenomenon, even space, but only his or her own mind. Space is an external phenomenon that is not included in the mental continuum. Thus, the object is one's own consciousness as limitless.

Then the meditator stops taking to mind his or her own consciousness, and it is as though he or she did not take anything to mind. [This is the formless absorption of nothingness.]

In the meditative absorption of the peak of cyclic existence, also called "without discrimination and without non-discrimination," it is as though there were no discrimination. Since, in fact, there is no coarse discrimination at that level, but only subtle discrimination, it is hard to determine that there is any discrimination at all. For example, when we look for the continuation of a very fine thread, we sometimes cannot find it and think that the thread has been cut; however, when we hold the thread up to the light we can see the rest of it even though it is very subtle. Similarly, because the coarse movement of discrimination does not exist at the peak of cyclic existence, the peak of cyclic existence is called "without discrimination"; yet, since discrimination is not totally non-existent, the peak of cyclic existence is called "without non-discrimination."

[The Branches of the Concentrations]

What are the branches of the concentrations? The branches of the first concentration are investigation, analysis, joy, bliss, [and meditative stabilization, which is] one-pointedness of mind. The branches of the second are internal clarity, joy, bliss, [and meditative stabilization, which is] one-pointedness of mind. The branches of the third are mindfulness, introspection, equanimity, bliss, [and meditative stabilization, which is] one-pointedness of mind. The branches of the fourth are mindfulness and completely pure equanimity [that is, a leaving aside of application], neutral feeling, [and meditative stabilization, which is] one-pointedness of mind. [160b] Vasubandhu's *Treasury of Manifest Knowledge* [8:7–8] says:

> The first has five:
> Investigation, analysis, joy, bliss, and meditative stabilization.
> The second has four branches: internal clarity,
> Joy, bliss, and so forth.
>
> The third has five: equanimity, mindfulness,
> Introspection, bliss, and stability [that is, meditative stabilization].

In the last, there are four: mindfulness, equanimity,
No bliss and no pain [that is, neutral feeling], and meditative stabilization.[14]

[The First Concentration]

Furthermore, [with regard to the entry into these] the investigation that is a branch of the first concentration is a mental factor that engages its object in a coarse manner, and analysis is a mental factor that engages its object in a fine manner.

If ground wheat sticks to our fingers, we say that it is coarse, whereas the flour we normally use is finely ground. Similarly, in investigation, the mind investigates its object "in a coarse manner"—not in detail but roughly. This use of the Tibetan word *rtog pa* to mean "investigation" (*vitarka*) is not to be confused with the usual usage of the words *rtog pa* and *rtog med* to mean "conceptual" (*kalpaka*) and "non-conceptual" (*nirvikalpaka*), respectively. Analysis "engages its object in a fine manner"—that is, in detail—because that which is settled in a coarse manner by investigation is gone into more subtly by analysis.

With respect to [identifying] the joy and bliss that are branches of the first concentration, the Vaibhāṣikas assert that joy is the faculty of blissful mental feeling and bliss is the bliss of pliancy. This accords with [the position stated in Vasubandhu's] *Treasury of Manifest Knowledge*: "In the first [concentration] bliss is pliancy" [8:9b] and, "Because of two scriptural passages, joy is mental bliss" [8:9c–d].[15]

According to the Vaibhāṣikas, "the faculty of blissful mental feeling" refers to the feeling of bliss that accompanies the mental consciousness. This is an actual bliss, whereas the bliss of pliancy is not a real bliss; it is called bliss only because of being a condition of serviceability of mind and body such that they can be directed to any virtue at will, and it is free of the discomfort of not having such serviceability. Thus, according to the Vaibhāṣikas, joy is the feeling of bliss that accompanies the mental consciousness, whereas bliss is merely pliancy.

However, [according to] the Mahāyānists' own system [Cittamātra or Mādhyamika], the feeling that is a branch of the first concentration, the single experience of refreshment, is posited as both joy and bliss. [This is so] because it is posited as joy by reason of causing the mind to be serviceable from the point of view of making the consciousness that is associated with it, together with its concomitants, satisfied with joy and bliss, and it is posited as bliss by reason of making the sense powers of the person who possesses it in his or her continuum, together with their bases, to be serviceable. [161a]

In brief, the pleasurable or blissful feeling that accompanies the mental consciousness is posited as both joy and bliss—as joy because it causes the mind to become serviceable and as bliss because it causes the body to be serviceable.

The pleasurable feeling that accompanies the mental consciousness is called blissful mental feeling (*tshor ba yid bde*), whereas the blissful feeling that accompanies a sense consciousness is called blissful feeling (*tshor ba bde ba*). It would be impossible to posit a blissful feeling that accompanies a sense consciousness as a branch of a concentration because whatever is a meditative absorption, be it a preparation or an actual meditative absorption, must be a mental consciousness. In the system of the *Treasury of Manifest Knowledge*, bliss, in this context, is the bliss of pliancy, but in the Mahāyāna it is said that there is no bliss to be posited as separate from joy; they are posited separately—given different names—from the point of view of different functions. The blissful feeling that accompanies the mental consciousness causes the sense powers and the sense consciousness to be able to see and hear far more distant objects than is usual. That is why the text says that mental bliss makes the senses, together with their bases, serviceable. It is from this point of view that the blissful feeling of the mental consciousness is posited as bliss.

Asaṅga's *Grounds of Hearers* says:

> Because the physical body[16] and the mental body, respectively, experience blissful feeling and the bliss of pliancy, bliss is, therefore, called a physical experience.[17]

This sets forth the position of the Vaibhāṣikas. Yaśomitra's *Commentary on (Asaṅga's) "Compendium of Manifest Knowledge"* says:

> With respect to the first two concentrations, because the feeling that accompanies the mental consciousness, the single experience of refreshment, causes the body—that is, the faculties, together with their bases—to be serviceable, it helps the body, and because it causes the mental consciousness in association with it, together with its concomitants, to be satisfied with joy and bliss, it helps the mind. Because it performs [these] two activities, it is posited, respectively, as bliss and joy.[18]

The meditative stabilization that is a branch of the first concentration causes the mind and the mental factors associated with it to come together on one object of observation.

[The Second Concentration]

With respect to the internal clarity that is a branch of the second concentration, according to the author of the *Treasury of Manifest Knowledge* [Vasubandhu], it is asserted as the faith of the conviction that one has emerged from the first concentration, in accordance with the statement, "Internal clarity is faith" [8:9c].[19]

> [From among the three types of faith—the faith of clarity, the faith of conviction, and the faith that is a wish to attain]—this is [the second type,] the faith of conviction. Here, it is the conviction that one has passed beyond the first concentration.

In the Mahāyānists' own system, however, the three—mindfulness, introspection, and equanimity—that are branches of the second concentration are the internal clarity which is a branch of the second concentration. [161b]

> Mindfulness is that which holds on to its object without forgetting it. Introspection is an inspection of the mind to see whether unfavorable conditions have arisen. Equanimity here is that which causes the mind to remain balanced.

Asaṅga's *Compendium of Ascertainments* (*nirṇayasamgrahaṇī; viniścayasaṃgraha, gtan la dbab pa bsdu ba*) says:

> What is the entity of the phenomenon "internal clarity"? It is the entities of mindfulness, introspection, and equanimity.[20]

The joy, bliss, and meditative stabilization that are branches of the second concentration are like those of the first.

[The Third Concentration]

The bliss that is a branch of the third concentration is a faculty of blissful feeling which is devoid of joy. Mindfulness is that which holds on to the object of observation and in which the entanglements of joy have ceased, and introspection watches whether one has or does not have a holding on to the object of observation in which the entanglements of joy have ceased. Equanimity, because of being free of the faults of investigation, analysis, and joy, is an absence of imbalance due to those three.

> Joy is considered a fault because it is coarse.

There are reasons that, although the three—mindfulness, introspection, and equanimity—exist in the first concentration, they are not mentioned as branches; and that, in the second concentration, they are not mentioned by their own names but are indicated by the name "internal clarity"; and that, in the third concentration, they are indicated by their own names. The reasons are explained [as follows]: in the first concentration, [mindfulness, introspection, and equanimity are not mentioned as branches because] they are polluted by investigation and analysis; in the second concentration, [they are not mentioned by their own names but are indicated by the name "internal clarity" because] they possess the entanglements of joy; and in the third [concentration], they have separated from the entanglements of joy [and are, therefore, indicated by their own names]. For these reasons, they are explained in that way. [162a] Asaṅga's *Compendium of Ascertainments* says:

> In the first concentration, because mindfulness, introspection, and equanimity are achieved by way of investigation and analysis, they are not mentioned although they exist. In the second concentration, they are brought about in their own entity, but because they are entangled with the afflictive emotion of mental joy, they are indicated by the name "internal clarity." In the third concentration, because they have separated from that mental secondary afflictive emotion [that is, joy], they are indicated by just their own names.[21]

[The Fourth Concentration]

The mindfulness and equanimity that are branches of the fourth concentration are called completely pure because they have separated from the eight faults of concentration. Vasubandhu's *Treasury of Manifest Knowledge* [8.11a–b] says:

> Because of being released from the eight faults,
> The fourth is unfluctuating.[22]

The eight faults are investigation, analysis, mental bliss, mental discomfort, [the feeling of physical] bliss, [the feeling of physical] pain, exhalation, and inhalation. Vasubandhu's *Treasury of Manifest Knowledge*[23] [8:11c–d] says:

> They are investigation, analysis, the two breaths,
> And the four—[the feeling of physical] bliss, and so forth.[24]

From one point of view, the Fourth Concentration is called unfluctuating because the meditative stabilization in it is unfluctuating. From another point of view, it is so called because the place of the Fourth Concentration is not destroyed when this world-system disintegrates at the end of an aeon. If this world-system is destroyed by fire, the First Concentration and the Desire Realm will disintegrate; if by water, the Second Concentration and everything below it will disintegrate; if by wind, the Third Concentration and everything below it will disintegrate. The

Fourth Concentration will remain no matter what type of destruction occurs.

Investigation, analysis, and so forth, are posited as faults of fluctuation relative to the fourth concentration, but relative to their own levels—the first concentration, and so forth—they are not. [162b]

Relative to the first concentration, investigation and analysis are not faults but good qualities; they are the antidotal branches.

Seeking liberation for our own sake is a similar case. In general, it is good because seeking liberation is good, but from the point of view of the Mahāyāna, seeking liberation for our own sake is a fault because we are doing it only for ourselves and not for the sake of others. Thus, relative to the first concentration, investigation and analysis are not faults, but relative to the fourth concentration, they are.

Asaṅga's *Compendium of Ascertainments* says:

> *Question:* If investigation, analysis, and so forth, which are of the first concentration, and so forth, and which are helpful to meditative stabilization, are engaged in to help and thoroughly purify their own levels of concentration, why has the Blessed One indicated them as having the character of fluctuation?
>
> *Answer:* They are [so] indicated in relation to other levels but not in relation to their own levels.[25]

[Comparison of the Branches]

How do the first, second, third, and fourth concentrations differ? They differ, respectively, in the completion and non-completion of meditative stabilization, in the completion and non-completion of help (*phan 'dogs pa*), and in the completion and non-completion of thorough purity. Asaṅga's *Compendium of Ascertainments* says:

> What is the difference between the first and second concentrations? They differ in the completion[25] of meditative stabilization.
> What is the difference between the second and third concentrations? They differ in the completion of help.
> What is the difference between the third and fourth concentrations? They differ in the completion of thorough purity.[26]

The [eighteen] branches of the concentrations can be condensed into the three [types] [163a] consisting of the antidotal branch, or that which abandons harm; the benefit branch, or that which achieves help; and the basis branch, or one-pointedness. Asaṅga's *Compendium of Manifest Knowledge* says, "... the antidotal branch, the benefit branch, and the branch that is the basis of those two.[28] (See chart below.)

Branches of the Concentrations
Read from bottom to top

Concentration	*Antidote*	*Benefit*	*Basis*
Fourth	Mindfulness Equanimity	Neutral feeling	Meditative stabilization
Third	Mindfulness Introspection Equanimity	Bliss	Meditative stabilization
Second	Internal clarity	Joy Bliss	Meditative stabilization
First	Investigation Analysis	Joy Bliss	Meditative stabilization

There is a way in which those [three types] include [all the branches]. In the first concentration, investigation and analysis are posited in terms of the antidotal branch, the joy and bliss that are generated from isolation are posited in terms of benefit, and meditative stabilization is posited in terms of the basis branch. In the second concentration, internal clarity is posited in terms of the antidotal branch, the joy and bliss that are generated from meditative stabilization are posited in terms of benefit, and meditative stabilization is posited in terms of the basis branch. In the third concentration, the three—mindfulness, introspection, and equanimity—are posited in terms of the antidotal branch, the bliss that is devoid of joy is posited in terms of benefit, and meditative stabilization is posited in terms of basis. In the fourth concentration, thoroughly pure mindfulness and equanimity are posited in terms of the antidotal branch, neutral feeling is posited in terms of benefit, and meditative stabilization is posited in terms of basis. [163b]

[The Number of the Concentrations]

There is a reason for positing the concentrations as four because 1) these concentrations are posited from the point of view of definitely emerging from contaminated feeling and 2) the first concentration is posited from the point of view of definitely emerging from the contaminated feeling of mental discomfort; the second concentration is posited from the point of view of definitely emerging from the contaminated feeling that is the faculty of suffering.

> This does not mean that the first concentration has suffering; both mental discomfort and the faculty of suffering refer to the Desire Realm. The first and second concentrations are only posited from this point of view because the faculty of suffering is slightly more unmanifest.

The third concentration is posited from the point of view of definitely emerging from the contaminated feeling of [mental] bliss; the fourth concentration is posited from the point of view of definitely emerging from the contaminated feeling that is the faculty of bliss.

> The feeling of bliss that accompanies the mental consciousness in the third concentration is called not mental bliss but the faculty of bliss.

There is a reason for not positing a fifth concentration from the point of view of its definitely emerging from contaminated neutral feeling because, since contaminated neutral feeling is a subtle suffering of pervasive[29] conditioning (*'du byed kyi sdug bsngal, saṃskāraduḥkhatā*), a mundane path cannot cause definite emergence from it. This is because non-Buddhists who have attained an actual meditative absorption of the peak of cyclic existence hold the peak of cyclic existence to be a path of liberation and later fall, [whereas] followers of the Teacher [Buddha] realize that even the peak of cyclic existence has a nature of suffering and generate in their continua a supramundane path that is definite emergence from it. This is also indicated in [the following] passage in Aśvaghoṣa's *Praise of the Praiseworthy*: [164a]

> Though beings blinded by ignorance who turn
> From your teaching reach the peak
> Of cyclic existence, they again undergo
> Suffering and achieve cyclic existence.
>
> Those who follow your teaching, though
> They do not attain an actual concentration,
> Overcome cyclic existence
> While demons glare.[30]

> Even if demons glare at them and try to cause them trouble, such meditators can overcome the afflictive emotions.

[The Number of the Formless Absorptions]

There is a reason for positing the formless absorptions as four because the first formless absorption is posited from the point of view of definitely emerging from discrimination of forms and obstructiveness, its objects of abandonment; the second is posited from the point of view of definitely emerging from discrimination of space, the antidote [to discrimination of forms and obstructiveness]; the third is posited from the point of view of definitely emerging from adherence to consciousness, its object of abandonment; the fourth formless absorption is posited from the point of view of definitely emerging from discrimination of nothingness, the antidote [to adherence to consciousness].

[Benefits of Cultivating the Concentrations and Formless Absorptions]

There is a fruit, or benefit, in having cultivated the four concentrations because, from having cultivated the three [types]—lesser, middling, and greater—of the first concentration, one achieves birth in Brahmā Type, In Front of Brahmā, and Great Brahmā, respectively; from having cultivated the three [types]—lesser, middling, and greater—of the second concentration, one achieves birth in Little Light, Limitless Light, and Bright Light, respectively; [164b] from having cultivated the three [types]—lesser, middling, and greater—of the third concentration, one achieves birth in Little Virtue, Limitless Virtue, and Vast Virtue,[31] respectively; from having cultivated the three [types]—lesser, middling, and greater—of the fourth concentration, one achieves birth in Cloudless, Born from Merit, and Great Fruit, respectively; and from having cultivated the five alternating meditations of the concentrations, one achieves birth in Not Great, Without Pain, Auspicious Appearance, Great Perception, and Not Low.

> These are the resultant-birth levels of the Four Concentrations and of the Five Pure Places, which are above the [usual] three levels of the Fourth Concentration.
>
> Only Superiors can be born in the Five Pure Places. To be reborn there, a Superior has to alternate uncontaminated and contaminated meditative equipoises, each being one of the smallest moments (*skad cig, kṣaṇa*) within which an action can be accomplished. There are five types. The first has three moments—uncontaminated, contaminated, and uncontaminated. The second has six moments; the third has nine; the fourth, twelve; and the fifth, fifteen. [Through cultivating one of these five types,] a Superior is born in [the corresponding level of] the Five Pure Places.

There is a fruit, or benefit, in having cultivated the three [types]—lesser, middling, and greater—of the [four] formless absorptions because one achieves various high and low, good and bad rebirths in the Formless Realm.

Though we refer to the Formless Realm as though it were a place, one does not have to go anywhere at death to be reborn there. In the very place of death, the practitioner manifests that meditative equipoise.

How Bodhisattvas Cultivate the Concentrations and Formless Absorptions

Bodhisattvas cultivate all eight of the concentrations and formless absorptions even though all eight are not necessary for the generation of a supramundane path. Moreover, although they take emptiness as their object of observation during the actual meditative absorptions, they use the preparations having the aspect of grossness/peacefulness. Thus, their motivation and mode of procedure need explanation.

Bodhisattvas cultivate the preparations having the aspect of grossness/peacefulness not within the context of meditating on emptiness but within that of the altruistic aspiration to enlightenment. Although Bodhisattvas, like Hearers, view all cyclic existence as full of faults and have no desire to be reborn anywhere in it, even in the Form and Formless Realms, Bodhisattvas wish to attain Buddhahood for the sake of all sentient beings and are willing to be reborn wherever it is possible to help sentient beings—even in a hell. Thus, since it is possible to help sentient beings in the Form Realm, they are willing to be reborn there. There seems to be some question about the Formless Realm, since there are no states arisen from hearing in the Formless Realm and, therefore, no opportunities for others to hear teaching.

Despite the willingness of Bodhisattvas to be reborn in cyclic existence, in doing the preparations having the aspect of grossness/peacefulness Bodhisattvas and those Hearers who use these preparations (Hearers who proceed gradually) would not think of any rebirth state as truly peaceful. They consider all cyclic existence to be like a garbage heap; however, some places in a garbage heap are less dirty than others, and in that sense Bodhisattvas and Hearers view the upper level as peaceful. Moreover, in the concentrations, there is another way of cultivating the preparations having the aspect of grossness/peacefulness. Instead of viewing the lower and upper rebirth states as gross and peaceful, respectively, the meditator views the actual meditative absorptions as gross or peaceful in terms of their branches. Thus, to progress from the first concentration to the second, the meditator would think that the first concentration has many branches, whereas the second concentration has fewer, and that the first concentration has investigation and analysis, whereas the second concentration is free of them. The mode of procedure for the remaining concentrations is similar.[32]

Instead of proceeding directly to the preparations for the first concentration, Bodhisattvas, upon achieving calm abiding, cultivate special insight realizing emptiness. Still, they cultivate all the concentrations by the time of the path of preparation for the sake of enhancing the dexterity of their minds. However, it is not definite when they cultivate the formless absorptions. Thus, although the concentrations and formless absorptions are not necessary for the realization of emptiness, they are essential to progress on the Bodhisattva path.

Glossary

Notes

Bibliography

Index

Glossary

Sanskrit terms that may not occur in Sanskrit but have been constructed on the basis of the Tibetan are preceded by an asterisk.

English	Tibetan	Sanskrit
abandoning religious doctrine	chos spong	
Abider in the Fruit	'bras gnas	phalasthita
absorption	snyoms 'jug	samāpatti
absorption lacking discrimination	'du shes med pa'i snyoms 'jug	asaṃjñisamāpatti
achievement	sgrub pa	pratipad
action	las	karma
actual	dngos gzhi	maula
actual meditative absorption	dngos gzhi'i nyoms 'jug	maulasamāpatti
adamantine posture	rdo rje skyil krung	vajrāsana
adventitious	glo bur	ākasmika
aeon	bskal pa	kalpa
afflicted	nyon mongs can	kliṣṭa
afflictive emotion	nyon mongs	kleśa
aging and death	rga shi	jarāmaraṇa
aggregate	phung po	skandha
all-knowingness	kun shes	ājñātāvin
altruistic mind of enlightenment	byang chub kyi sems	bodhicitta
analysis	dpyod pa	vicāra
analytical image	rnam par rtog pa dang bcas pa'i gzugs brnyan	savikalpaka-pratibimba
analytical meditation	dpyad sgom	
androgynous	mtshan gnyis pa	ubhayavyañjana
anger	khong khro	pratigha
animal	dud 'gro	tiryañc
antidote	gnyen po	pratipakṣa
application	'du byed pa	abhisaṃskāra
Approacher	zhugs pa	pratipannaka

appropriate and the inappropriate, the	gnas dang gnas ma yin pa	sthānāsthāna
arisen from hearing	thos byung	śrutamayī
arisen from meditation	sgom byung	bhāvanāmayī
arisen from thinking	bsam byung	cintāmayī
aspect	rnam pa	ākāra
aspiration	'dun pa	chanda
aspiration to attributes of the Desire Realm	'dod pa la 'dun pa	kāmacchanda
associated compositional factor	ldan pa yin pa'i 'du byed	samprayukta-saṃskāra
associated with relishing	ro myang mtshungs ldan	āsvādanasam-prayukta
attachment	sred pa/'dod chags	tṛṣṇā
attribute	rnam pa	ākāra
Auspicious Appearance	gya nom snang ba	sudṛśa
auspiciousness	gya nom pa	praṇīta
Avalokiteśvara	spyan ras gzigs	avalokiteśvara
basis	āśraya	gnas/rten
beginner at mental contemplation	yid la byed pa las dang po pa	manaskārā-dikarmika
beginner at purifying the afflictive emotions	nyon mongs pa rnam par sbyong ba'i las dang po pa	kleśaviśuddhy-ādikarmika
belligerence	khro ba	krodha
benefit	phan yon	anuśaṃsa
birth	skye ba	jāti
Black Line	thig nag	kālasūtra
blame	smad pa	nindā
Blessed One	bcom ldan 'das	bhagavant
bliss	bde ba	sukha
Blistering	chu bur can	arbuda
Bodhisattva	byang chub sems dpa'	bodhisattva

body	lus	kāya
body consciousness	lus kyi rnam par shes pa	kāyavijñāna
body sense power	lus kyi dbang po	kāyendriya
Born from Merit	bsod nams skyes	puṇyaprasava
Brahmā	tshangs pa	brahmā
Brahmā Type	tshangs ris	brahmakāyika
branch	yan lag	aṅga
Bright Light	'od gsal	ābhāsvara
Buddha	sangs rgyas	buddha
Buddha-field	sangs rgyas kyi zhing	buddhakṣetra
Burning Ashes	me ma mur	kukūla
Bursting Blisters	chu bur rdol pa can	nirarbuda
calm abiding	zhi gnas	śamatha
category of the past	sngon gyi mtha'	pūrvānta
causal absorption	rgyu snyoms 'jug	*kāraṇasamāpatti
causal collection	tshogs bsten pa	
causally concordant effect	rgyu mthun gyi 'bras bu	niṣyandaphala
cause	rgyu	hetu
cessation	'gog pa	nirodha
channel	rtsa	nāḍi
character	mtshan nyid	lakṣaṇa
Chattering	so tham tham pa	aṭaṭa
clairvoyance	mngon par shes pa/mngon shes	abhijñā
class	phyogs	pakṣa
clear	gsal ba	prasanna
close setting	nye bar 'jog pa	upasthāpana
Cloudless	sprin med	anabhraka
coarse	rags pa	audārika
color	kha dog	varṇa
common being	so so'i skye bo	pṛthagjana
common locus	gzhi mthun	sāmānādhikaraṇa
compassion	snying rje	karuṇā
compositional factor	'du byed	saṃskāra
compositional phenomenon	'dus byas	saṃskṛta
concealment	'chab pa	mrakṣa
concentration	bsam gtan	dhyāna

conception of a [bad] view as supreme	lta ba mchog tu 'dzin pa	dṛṣṭiparāmarśa
conception of [bad] ethics and modes of conduct as supreme	tshul khrims dang brtul zhugs mchog tu 'dzin pa	śīlavrata-parāmarśa
conceptual	rtog pa	kalpaka
conceptual consciousness	rtog pa	kalpanā
conceptual determination	zhen pa	adhyavasāna
conceptuality	rnam rtog	vikalpa
concordant effect	rgyu mthun gyi 'bras bu	niṣyandaphala
concordant with abiding	gnas pa cha mthun	sthitibhāgīya
concordant with definite differentiation	nges 'byed cha mthun	nirvedabhāgīya
concordant with degeneration	nyams pa cha mthun	hānabhāgīya
concordant with enhancement	khyad par cha mthun	viśeṣabhāgīya
condition	rkyen	pratyaya
consciousness	shes pa/rnam par shes pa	jñāna/vijñāna
consequence	thal 'gyur	prasaṅga
constituent	khams	dhātu
contact	reg pa	sparśa
contaminated	zag bcas	sāsrava
contaminated action	zag bcas kyi las	sāsravakarma
continent	gling	dvīpa
continuous setting	rgyun du 'jog pa	saṃsthāpana
continuum/mental continuum	rgyud	saṃtāna
contrition	'gyod pa	kaukṛtya
Controlling Others' Emanations	gzhan 'phrul dbang byed	paranirmitta-vaśavartin
conventional truth	kun rdzob bden pa	saṃvṛtisatya

copulation	bsnyen bkur	upacāra
covetousness	brnab sems	abhidhyā
Crushed Together	'dus 'joms	saṃghāta
Crying	ngu 'bod	raurava
cyclic existence	'khor ba	saṃsāra
deceit	sgyu	māyā
definite emergence	nges 'byung	niḥsaraṇa
deliverance	nges 'byin	nairyāṇika
demigod	lha ma yin	asura
demon	bdud	māra
dependent-arising	rten 'brel/rten 'byung/rten cing 'brel bar 'byung ba	pratītya-samutpāda
desire	'dod chags	rāga
Desire Realm	'dod khams	kāmadhātu
determining mental factors	sems byung yul nges	*viśayapratini-yamacaitta
direct perception	mngon sum	pratyakṣa
disciplining	dul bar byed pa	damana
discrimination	'du shes	saṃjñā
discursiveness	rnam rtog	vikalpa
disgrace	ma grags pa	ayaśas
dissimulation	g.yo	śāṭhya
distraction	rnam par g.yeng ba	vikṣepa
divisive talk	phra mar smra ba	paiśunya
Doctrine	chos	dharma
doubt	the tshom	vicikitsā
ear consciousness	rna ba'i rnam par shes pa	śrotravijñāna
ear sense power	rna ba'i dbang po	śrotrendriya
earth	sa	pṛthivī
effect	'bras bu	phala
effort	brtson 'grus	vīrya
emptiness	stong pa nyid	śūnyatā
empty	stong pa	śūnya
Enjoying Emanation	'phrul dga'	nirmāṇarati
enlightenment	byang chub	bodhi
equanimity	btang snyoms	upekṣā
equipoise	mnyam bzhag	samāhita
ethics	tshul khrims	śīla
eunuch	ma ning	paṇḍaka

excitement	rgod pa	auddhatya
exertion	rtsol ba	vyāyāma
exhalation	dbugs 'byung ba	apāna/praśvāsa
existence	srid pa	bhava
extreme	mtha'	anta
Extremely Hot River	chu bo rab med	nadī vaitaraṇī
extreme of annihilation	chad mtha'	ucchedānta
extreme of permanence	rtag mtha'	śaśvatānta
eye consciousness	mig gi rnam par shes pa	cakṣurvijñāna
eye sense power	mig gi dbang po	cakṣurindriya
faculty	dbang po	indriya
fame	snyan grags	yaśas
faith	dad pa	śraddhā
familiarity	yongs su 'dris pa	paricaya
fault	skyon/nyes dmigs	apakṣāla/ādīnava
feeling	tshor ba	vedanā
feeling of mental bliss	yid bde	saumanasya
feeling of mental discomfort	yid mi bde	daurmanasya
feeling of pain	sdug bsngal	duḥkha
feeling of pleasure	bde ba	sukha
female	bud med	strī
fire	me	tejas
first concentration	bsam gtan dang po	prathamadhyāna
Foe Destroyer	dgra bcom pa	arhan
foolish talk	tshig bkyal ba	saṃbhinnapralāpa
forcible engagement	sgrim ste 'jug pa	balavāhana
forgetfulness	brjed nges pa	muṣitasmṛtitā
forgetting the instruction	gdams ngag brjed pa	avavādasammoṣa
form	gzugs	rūpa
form aggregate	gzugs kyi phung po	rūpaskandha
Form Body	gzugs sku	rūpakāya
Form Realm	gzugs khams	rūpadhātu
formless absorption	gzugs med/gzugs med kyi snyoms 'jug	ārūpya/ārūpyasamāpatti
Formless Realm	gzugs med khams	ārūpyadhātu

fortune	'byor ba	sampad
Four Great Royal Lineages	rgyal chen rigs bzhi	cāturmahārāja-kāyika
four immeasurables	tshad med bzhi	catvāryapramāṇāni
fourth concentration	bsam gtan bzhi pa	caturthadhyāna
fruition(al)	rnam smin	vipāka
fruitional effect	rnam smin gyi 'bras bu	vipākaphala
Ḡa-dam-b̄a	dka' gdams pa	
Ḡa-gyu	bka' brgyud	
gain	rnyed pa	lābha
Ge-luk-b̄a	dge lugs pa	
general character	spyi mtshan	sāmānyalakṣaṇa
giving	sbyin pa	dāna
god	lha	deva
god of no discrimination	'du shes med pa'i sems can	asaṃjñisattva
good nature	rnyed bkur	upacāra
gradually	rim gyis	*kramena
grasping	nye bar len pa	upādāna
great aeon	bskal pa chen po	mahākalpa
great	chen po	adhimātra
Great Bliss	bde ba chen	sukhāvatī
Great Body	lus 'phags po	videha
Great Brahmā	tshangs chen	mahābrahmāṇa
Great Crying	ngu 'bod chen po	mahāraurava
Great Fruit	'bras bu che	bṛhatphala
great of the great	chen po'i chen po	adhimātrādhimātra
great of the middling	'bring gi chen po	madhyādhimātra
great of the small	chung ngu'i chen po	mṛdvadhimātra
Great Perception	shin tu mthong ba	sudarśana
Great Seal	phyag rgya chen po	mahāmudrā
Groaning	a chu zer ba	hahava
gross	rags pa	audārika
grossness/peacefulness	zhi rags	*śāntaudārika
ground	sa	bhūmi
Grounds and Paths	sa lam	bhūmimārga
Grove of Swords	ral gri lo ma'i nags tshal	asipattravana
Hahava Hell	a chu zer ba	hahava

happiness	bde ba	sukha
harmfulness	rnam par 'tshe ba/ gnod sems	vihiṃsā/vyāpāda
harsh speech	tshig rtsub smra ba	pāruṣya
hatred	zhe sdang	dveṣa
haughtiness	rgyags pa	mada
Hearer	nyan thos	śrāvaka
hearing	thos pa	śruta
heinous crimes	mtshams med pa	ānantarya
hell	dmyal ba	naraka
hell being	dmyal ba	nāraka
help	phan 'dogs pa	
higher ethics	lhag pa'i tshul khrims	adhiśīla
higher meditative stabilization	lhag pa'i sems	adhicitta
higher wisdom	lhag pa'i shes rab	adhiprajñā
Highest Yoga Tantra	rnal 'byor bla med kyi rgyud	anuttarayogatantra
Hīnayāna	theg dman	hīnayāna
Hot	tsha ba	tāpana
human	mi	manuṣya
hungry ghost	yi dvags	preta
ignorance	ma rig pa	avidyā
immeasurable	tshad med	apramāṇa
impermanence	mi rtag pa	anitya
imputedly existent	btags yod	prajñaptisat
In Front of Brahmā	tshangs mdun	brahmapurohita
incontrovertible	mi slu ba	avisaṃvādin
Indra	dbang po	indra
inestimable mansions	gzhal med khang/ gzhal yas khang	*amātragṛha/ *sumātragṛha
inferential consciousness	rjes dpag	anumāna
inhalation	dbugs rngub pa	āna/śvāsa
inherent existence	rang bzhin gyis grub pa	svabhāvasiddhi
innate	lhan skyes	sahaja
intermediate aeon	bar bskal	antaḥkalpa
internal clarity	nang rab tu dang ba	adhyātma-samprasāda
interrupted engagement	bar du chad cing 'jug pa	sacchidravāhana

introspection	shes bzhin	samprajanya
investigation	rtog pa	vitarka
Iron Grater	lcags kyi shing shal ma li	ayaḥśālmalīvana
Jambu, Land of	'dzam bu gling	Jambudvīpa
jealousy	phrag dog	irṣyā
joy	dga' ba	muditā/prīti
Joyous	dga' ldan	tuṣita
karmic obstruction	las sgrib	karmāvaraṇa
killing	srog gcod pa	prāṇātighāta
knower	rig pa	saṃvedana
lama	bla ma	guru
laxity	bying ba	laya
laziness	le lo	kausīdya
laziness of inferiority (losing compatibility)	sgyid lugs pa'i le lo	
laziness of neutral activities (lack of impulse)	snyoms las kyi le lo	
laziness that is an attachment to bad activities	bya ba ngan zhen gyi le lo	
leisure	dal ba	kṣaṇa
lethargy	rmugs pa	styāna
liberation	thar pa	vimokṣa/mokṣa
life wind	srog 'dzin	
Limitless Bliss/ Limitless Virtue	tshad med bde/ tshad med dge	apramāṇaśubha
Limitless Consciousness	rnam shes mtha' yas	vijñānānantya
Limitless Light	tshad med 'od	apramāṇābhā
Limitless Space	nam mkha' mtha' yas	ākāśānantya
Little Bliss/Little Virtue	bde chung/dge chung	parīttaśubha
Little Light	'od chung	parīttābhā
logical reasoning	'thad sgrub kyi rigs pa	upapatti-sādhanayukti
loss	ma rnyed pa	alābha
love	byams pa	maitrī
lying	rdzun du smra ba	mṛṣāvāda

magical emanation	sprul pa	nirmāṇa
Mahāyāna	theg chen	mahāyāna
making one-pointed	rtse gcig tu byed pa	ekotīkaraṇa
male	skyes pa	puruṣa
Mānasarovara, Lake	yid kyi mtsho	mānasarovara
Manifest Knowledge	chos mngon pa	abhidharma
mantra	sngags	mantra
Mantra Vehicle	sngags kyi theg pa	mantrayāna
meaning	don	artha
meaning commentary	don 'grel	
meditative absorption	snyoms 'jug	samāpatti
meditative equipoise	mnyam bzhag	samāhita
meditative stabilization	ting nge 'dzin	samādhi
mental abidings, nine	sems gnas dgu	navākārā cittasthiti
mental bliss	yid bde	saumanasya
mental consciousness	yid kyi rnam shes	manovijñāna
mental contemplation	yid la byed pa	manaskāra
mental contemplation arisen from belief	mos pa las byung ba'i yid byed	adhimokṣika-manaskāra
mental contemplation of a mere beginner	las dang po pa tsam gyi yid byed	
mental contemplation of analysis	dpyod pa'i yid byed	mīmāṃsāmanaskāra
mental contemplation of final training	sbyor ba mtha'i yid byed	prayoganiṣṭha-manaskāra
mental contemplation of individual knowledge of the character	mtshan nyid so sor rig pa'i yid byed	lakṣaṇaprati-saṃvedīmanaskāra
mental contemplation of thorough isolation	rab tu dben pa'i yid byed	prāvivekyamanaskāra
mental contemplation of withdrawal or joy	dga' ba sdud pa'i yid byed	ratisaṃgrāhaka-manaskāra

mental contemplation that is the fruit of final training	sbyor ba mtha'i 'bras bu yid byed	prayoganiṣṭha-phalamanaskāra
mental discomfort	yid mi bde	daurmanasya
mental engagement	yid la byed pa	manaskāra
mental factor	sems byung	caitta
mental sense power	yid kyi dbang po	mana-indriya
mere actual absorption of a first concentration	bsam gtan dang po'i dngos gzhi'i snyoms 'jug tsam po ba	
merit/meritorious	bsod nams	puṇya
middling	'bring	madhya
middling of the great	chen po'i 'bring	adhimātramadhya
middling of the middling	'bring gi 'bring	madhyamadhya
middling of the small	chung ngu'i 'bring	mṛdumadhya
mind	sems	citta
mind of enlightenment	byang chub kyi sems	bodhicitta
mindfulness	dran pa	smṛti
miserliness	ser sna	mātsarya
misery	sdug bsngal ba	duḥkha
Moaning	kyi hud zer ba	huhuva
mode	ji lta ba	
moment	skad cig	kṣaṇa
monastic discipline	'dul ba	vinaya
Most Torturous	mnar med	avīci
Mud of Corpses	ro myags	kuṇapa
mundane	'jig rten pa	laukika
mundane path	'jig rten pa'i lam	laukikamārga
name and form	ming gzugs	nāmarūpa
neighboring	nye 'khor ba	utsada
neuter	za ma	ṣaṇḍha
neutral	lung du ma bstan pa	avyākṛta
neutral feeling	sdug bsngal ma yin bde ba yang ma	aduḥkhāsukha/upekṣā

	yin/btang snyoms	
Never Returner	phyir mi 'ong	anāgāmin
noble truth	'phags pa'i bden pa	āryasatya
non-analytical image	rnam par mi rtog pa'i gzugs brnyan	nirvikalpaka-pratibimba
non-application	'du mi byed pa	anabhisaṃskāra
non-associated compositional factors	ldan min 'du byed	viprayukta-saṃskāra
non-conceptual	rtog med	nirvikalpaka
non-conscientious-ness	bag med pa	pramāda
non-embarrass-ment	khrel med pa	anapatrāpya
non-faith	ma dad pa	āśraddhya
non-introspection	shes bzhin ma yin ba	asamprajanya
non-meritorious	bsod nams ma yin pa	apuṇya
non-shame	ngo tsha med pa	āhrīkya
non-virtue	mi dge ba	akuśala
nose consciousness	sna'i rnam par shes pa	ghrāṇavijñāna
nose sense power	sna'i dbang po	ghrāṇendriya
Not Great	mi che ba	abṛha
Not Low	'og min	akaniṣṭha
not unable	mi lcog med	anāgamya
Nothingness	ci yang med	ākiṃcanya
object of observation for purifying afflictive emotions	nyon mongs rnam sbyong gi dmigs pa	kleśaviśodhanā-lambana
object of observation for purifying behavior	spyad pa rnam sbyong gi dmigs pa	caritaviśodha-nālambana
object of obser-vation	dmigs yul/dmigs pa	ālambana
obscuration	gti mug	moha
observed-object condition	dmigs rkyen	ālambanapratyaya
observing the limits of phenomena	dngos po'i mtha' la dmigs pa	vastvantālambana
obstruction	sgrib pa	āvaraṇa
odor	dri	gandha

omniscience	rnam pa thams cad mkhyen pa	sarvākārajñāna
Once Returner	phyir 'ong	sakṛdāgāmin
one-pointedness of mind	sems rtse gcig pa	cittaikāgratā
origin	kun 'byung	samudaya
overapplication	'du byed pa	abhisaṃskāra
pacification	zhi ba	śānta
pacifying	zhi bar byed pa	śamana
path	lam	mārga
path of accumulation	tshogs lam	saṃbhāramārga
path of meditation	sgom lam	bhāvanāmārga
path of no more learning	mi slob lam	aśaikṣamārga
path of preparation	sbyor lam	prayogamārga
path of release	rnam grol lam	vimuktimārga
path of seeing	mthong lam	darśanamārga
patience	bzod pa	kṣānti
peaceful, peacefulness	zhi ba	śānta
Peak of Cyclic Existence	srid rtse	bhavāgra
perfection	pha rol tu phyin pa/phar phyin	pāramitā
perfection of wisdom	shes rab kyi pha rol tu phyin pa	prajñāpāramitā
Perfection Vehicle	phar phyin gyi theg pa	pāramitāyāna
permanent	rtag pa	nitya
person	gang zag	pudgala
pervasion	khyab pa	vyāpti
pervasive object of observation	khyab pa'i dmigs pa	vyāpyālambana
perverse view	log par lta ba	mithyādṛṣṭi
phenomenon	chos	dharma
physical basis	lus rten	
Plain of Razors	spu gri gtams pa'i lam po che	kṣuramārga
pliancy	shin tu sbyangs pa/ shin sbyangs	prasrabdhi/ praśrabdhi
power	stobs	bala
praise	bstod pa	praśaṃsā
predisposition	bag chags	vāsanā
preparation	nyer bsdogs	sāmantaka

prerequisite	tshogs bsten pa	
pride	nga rgyal	māna
pure	dag pa	śuddha
Pure Place	gnas gtsang ma'i sa	śuddhāvāsakāyika
realms, three	khams gsum	tridhātu
reasoning	rigs pa	yukti
reasoning of dependence	ltos pa'i rigs pa	apekṣāyukti
reasoning of nature	chos nyid kyi rigs pa	dharmatāyukti
reasoning of the performance of function	bya ba byed pa'i rigs pa	kāryakāraṇayukti
religion/religious practice	chos	dharma
resentment	'khon du 'dzin pa	upanāha
resetting	slan te 'jog pa	avasthāpana
resultant-birth absorption	'bras bu skye ba'i snyoms 'jug	*kāryasamāpatti
Reviving	yang sros	saṃjīva
root afflictive emotion	rtsa nyon	mūlakleśa
Sa-gya	sa skya	
scattering	'phro ba	
seal	phyag rgya	mudrā
second concentration	bsam gtan gnyis pa	dvitīyadhyāna
secondary afflictive emotion	nye ba'i nyon mongs	upakleśa
self	bdag	ātman
self of persons	gang zag gi bdag	pudgalātman
selflessness	bdag med pa	nairātmya, anātmaka
selflessness of persons	gang zag gi bdag med	pudgalanairātmya
sense power	dbang po	indriya
sentient being	sems can	sattva
setting in equipoise	mnyam par 'jog pa	samādhāna
setting the mind	sems 'jog pa	cittasthāpana
sexual misconduct	'dod pas log par g.yem pa	kāmamithyācāra
shape	dbyibs	saṃstāna
sign	rtags	liṅga
signless	mtshan med	animitta

simultaneously	gcig car	sakṛt
skillful object of observation	mkhas pa'i dmigs pa/mkhas par byed pa'i dmigs pa	kauśalyālambana
sleep	gnyid	middha
small	chung ngu	mṛdu
small of the great	chen po'i chung ngu	adhimātramṛdu
small of the middling	'bring gi chung ngu	madhyamṛdu
small of the small	chung ngu'i chung ngu	mṛdumṛdu
Solitary Realizer	rang sangs rgyas	pratyekabuddha
sound	sgra	śabda
space	nam mkha'	ākāśa
special actual absorption of a first concentration	bsam gtan dang po'i dngos gzhi'i snyoms 'jug khyad par can	
special insight	lhag mthong	vipaśyanā
specific character	rang mtshan	svalakṣaṇa
sphere	skye mched	āyatana
sphere without discrimination and without non-discrimination	'du shes med 'du shes med min skye mched	naivasaṃjñānāsaṃjñāyatana
spheres, six	skye mched drug	ṣaḍāyatana
Spiritual Community	dge 'dun	saṃgha
spite	'tshig pa	pradāśa
Split like a Great Lotus	padma chen po ltar gas pa	mahāpadma
Split Like a Lotus	padma ltar gas pa	padma
Split like an Utpala	utpala ltar gas pa	utpala
spontaneous engagement	lhun grub tu 'jug pa	anābhogavāhana
stabilization	ting nge 'dzin	samādhi
stabilizing meditation	'jog sgom	
stage of completion	rdzogs rim	niṣpannakrama
stealing	ma byin par len pa	adattādāna
Stream Enterer	rgyun zhugs	śrotāpanna
strong production	rab tu skye ba	prabhava
subcontinent	gling phran	

subject	chos can	dharmin
substantial existence	rdzas su yod pa	dravyasat
subtle	'phra ba	sūkṣma
suffering	sdug bsngal	duḥkha
suffering of conditioning	'du byed kyi sdug bsngal	saṃskāraduḥkhatā
suitability	rigs pa	nyāya
Superior	'phags pa	ārya
supramundane	'jig rten las 'das pa	lokottara
supramundane path	'jig rten las 'das pa'i lam	lokottaramārga
sūtra	mdo	sūtra
syllogism	sbyor ba	prayoga
tangible object	reg bya	spraṣṭavya
tangible-object sphere	reg bya'i skye mched	spraṣṭavyāyatana
taste	ro	rasa
textual [lineage]	gzhung pa pa	
textual commentary	gzhung khrid	
thing	dngos po	vastu/bhāva
thinking	bsam pa	cintā
third concentration	bsam gtan gsum pa	tritīyadhyāna
Thirty-three	sum cu rtsa gsum	trāyastriṃśa
thorough achievement of the purpose	dgos pa yongs su grub pa	kṛtyānuṣṭāna
thorough pacifying	nye bar zhi bar byed pa	vyupaśamana
thorough purity	yongs su dag pa	pariśuddhi
thoroughly pure	yongs su dag pa	pariśuddha
Three Jewels	dkon mchog gsum	triratna
time	dus	kāla
to abide in a favorable area	mthun pa'i yul na gnas pa	
to forsake commotion	bya ba mang po'i 'du 'dzi yongs su spang ba	
to forsake desire/ to forsake [thoughts of] desire	'dod pa la sogs pa'i rnam rtog yongs su spang ba	
to have few desires	'dod pa chung ba	

to have pure ethics	tshul khrims dag pa	
to know satisfaction	chog shes pa	
tongue consciousness	lce'i rnam par shes pa	jihvāvijñāna
tongue sense power	lce'i dbang po	jihvendriya
training	bslab pa	śikṣā
transmigration	'gro ba	gati
transmigration, bad	ngan 'gro	durgati
transmigration, happy	bde 'gro	sugati
trifling	nyi tshe ba	prādeśika
true cessations	'gog pa'i bden pa	nirodhasatya
true origins	kun 'byung bden pa	samudayasatya
true paths	lam gyi bden pa	mārgasatya
true sufferings	sdug bsngal bden pa	duḥkhasatya
truth	bden pa	satya
ugliness	mi sdug pa	aśubha
ultimate truth	don dam bden pa	paramārthasatya
Unadorned Foe Destroyer	dgra bcom rgyan med	
uncontaminated	zag med	anāsrava
unfluctuating	mi g.yo ba	āniñjya
uninterrupted engagement	chad pa med par 'jug pa	niśchidravāhana
uninterrupted path	bar chad med lam	ānantaryamārga
union of calm abiding and special insight	zhi lhag zung 'brel	śamathavipaśyanāyuganaddha
Unpleasant Sound	sgra mi nyan	kuru
Using Oxen	ba lang spyod	godānīya
vajra	rdo rje	vajra
varieties	ji snyed pa	
Vast Bliss/Vast Virtue	bde rgyas/dge rgyas	śubhakṛtsna
Very Hot	rab tu tsha ba	pratāpana
view	lta ba	dṛṣṭi
view holding to an extreme	mthar 'dzin par lta ba	antagrāhadṛṣṭi
view of the transi-	'jig tshogs la lta	satkāyadṛṣṭi

tory collection	ba	
virtue	dge ba	kuśala
virtuous mental factor	sems byung dge ba	kuśalacaitta
water	chu	āp
welfare	don	artha
wind (constituent)	rlung	vāyu
wind/current of energy	rlung	prāṇa
wisdom	shes rab/ye shes	prajñā/jñāna
Without Combat	'thab bral	yāma
without discrimination and without non-discrimination	'du shes med 'du shes med min	naivasaṃjñānāsaṃjñā
Without Pain	mi gdung ba	atapas
world system	'jig rten gyi khams	lokadhātu
worldly concerns, eight	'jig rten gyi chos brgyad	aṣṭalokadharma
wrong view	log par lta ba	mithyādṛṣṭi
yogi	rnal 'byor pa	yogi
yogic direct perception	rnal 'byor mngon sum	yogipratyakṣa

Notes

Introduction

1. An edited version of his lectures has been published as Gedün Lodrö, *Walking Through Walls: A Presentation of Tibetan Meditation*, trans. and ed. by Jeffrey Hopkins, co-edited by Anne C. Klein and Leah Zahler (Ithaca, NY: Snow Lion, 1992).
2. Ibid., pp. 22–23. The list has been divided here into those sources quoted by Paṇ-chen Sö-nam-drak-ba and those not quoted by him.
3. Jeffrey Hopkins, *Meditation on Emptiness* (London: Wisdom Publications, 1983), p. 864 n. 527, citing the oral commentary of Kensur Lekden.
4. Anne Carolyn Klein, trans. and ed., *Path to the Middle: Oral Mādhyamika Philosophy in Tibet: The Oral Scholarship of Kensur Yeshey Tupden* (Albany, NY: State University of New York Press, 1994), p. 5.
5. Ibid., pp. 2–3, and electronic mail communication, July 24, 1995.
6. In Geshe Lhundup Sopa and Jeffrey Hopkins, *Cutting through Appearances: The Practice and Theory of Tibetan Buddhism* (Ithaca, NY: Snow Lion, 1989), p. 66. (First pub. as *Practice and Theory of Tibetan Buddhism* [New York: Grove Press, 1976].)
7. Ibid., p. 67.
8. See pages 85–92 for a full explanation.
9. Pur-bu-jok (*phur bu cog byams pa rgya mtsho,* 1825–1901), "Explanation of the Presentation of Objects and Object-Possessors as well as Awareness and Knowledge," translation edited by Elizabeth Napper (unpublished), p. 88; *Yul yul can dang blo rig gi rnam par bshad pa,* 25b.2.

Part One: Lati Rinbochay's Oral Presentation of the Concentrations and Formless Absorptions

1. Opening Remarks

1. The Tibetan term for sentient being (*sattva*) is *sems can*—literally, "having a mind," but referring to someone who has a mind with obstructions yet to be abandoned. Thus, the term excludes Buddhas.
2. Cyclic existence (*saṃsāra, 'khor ba*) is the round of deaths and rebirths in which sentient beings wander powerlessly through the force of past actions and afflictive emotions, the chief afflictive emotion being ignorance (*ma rig pa, avidyā*).
3. Lati Rinbochay here lists the eight worldly concerns (*'jig rten chos brgyad,*

aṣṭalokadharma)—happiness (*bde ba, sukha*), suffering (*sdug bsngal, duḥkha*), gain (*rnyed pa, lābha*), loss (*ma rnyed pa, alābha*), praise (*bstod pa, praśaṃsā*), blame (*smad pa, nindā*), fame (*snyan grags, yaśas*), disgrace (*ma grags pa, ayaśas*).

4. In this paragraph, Lati Rinbochay gives a brief outline of the Mahāyāna path.
5. Those who are able to achieve enlightenment in one short lifetime are the special disciples of Highest Yoga Tantra (*rnal 'byor bla med kyi rgyud, anuttarayogatantra*), a division of the Mantra Vehicle.
6. The paths for achieving enlightenment in one very long lifetime are also paths of the Mantra Vehicle (*sngags kyi theg pa, mantrayāna*). The achievement of enlightenment over many aeons is accomplished through the Perfection Vehicle (*phar phyin theg pa, pāramitāyāna*). The Perfection and Mantra Vehicles are the two divisions of the Mahāyāna.
7. Solitary Realizers (*rang sangs rgyas, pratyekabuddha*) in their last lifetime achieve liberation from cyclic existence without the aid of a teacher. Hearers (*nyan thos, śrāvaka*) hear the doctrine, either from a Buddha or from other teachers, and cause others to hear it. The Solitary Realizer and Hearer Vehicles are the two divisions of the Hīnayāna.
8. A pure place, or so-called pure land, is a pure Buddha-field (*sangs rgyas kyi zhing, buddhakṣetra*). The Buddha-field of Amitābha, Great Bliss (*bde ba chen, sukhāvatī*), is one of the best known.
9. See pages 31, 36, and 38 in Lati Rinbochay's discussion of cyclic existence for specific examples.

2. Cyclic Existence

1. The usual order of the cold hells, from the third chapter of Vasubandhu's *Treasury of Manifest Knowledge* (*abhidharmakośa, chos mngon pa'i mdzod*), is Blistering (*chu bur can, arbuda*), Bursting Blisters (*chu bur rdol ba can, nirarbuda*), Chattering (*so tham tham pa, aṭaṭa*), Groaning (*a chu zer ba, hahava*), Moaning (*kyi hud zer ba, huhuva*), Split like an Utpala (*utpala ltar gas pa, utpala*), Split like a Lotus (*padma ltar gas pa, padma*), and Split like a Great Lotus (*padma chen po ltar gas pa, mahāpadma*).
2. In addition to males (*skyes pa, puruṣa*) and females (*bud med, strī*), Gedün Lodrö lists so-called eunuchs (*ma ning, paṇḍaka*), the neuter (*za ma, ṣaṇḍha*), and the androgynous (*mtshan gnyis pa, ubhayavyañjana*). He does not mention the impotent (Gedün Lodrö, *Walking through Walls,* p. 48).

   Although "eunuch," the usual translation of *paṇḍaka,* has been retained here, it has been disputed by Leonard Zwilling, who argues that the word *eunuch* "implies intentional castration as opposed to accidental castration," whereas eunuchs were "virtually unknown in pre-Muslim India." He suggests that *paṇḍakas* were probably "a socially stigmatized class of passive, probably transvestite, homosexuals" (Leonard Zwilling, "Homosexuality as Seen in Indian

Buddhist Texts," *Buddhism, Sexuality, and Gender*, ed. José Ignacio Cabezón [Albany, NY: State University of New York Press, 1992], pp. 208, 204, 209).

3. The source of Lati Rinbochay's list of the lands of the demigods is not known. *Asuras* are not part of the cosmological system of the *Treasury of Manifest Knowledge*, although Vasubandhu mentions that they occur in the systems of other schools. Nga-w̄ang-b̄el-den's *Annotations for (Jam-ȳang-shay-b̄a's) "Great Exposition of Tenets"* gives a different list from Lati Rinbochay's (section on beings and realms, 87b.6).

4. Maitreya's place in the Joyous Land is called the Pleasant Doctrine-bearing Joyous Place (*dga' ldan yid dga' chos 'dzin*). It is not part of cyclic existence. According to Gedün Lodrö, "it is in the Joyous Land but away from it, just as monasteries are within cities but at a distance from them" (Gedün Lodrö, *Walking through Walls*, p. 262). Ganden Tri Rinbochay uses the same simile (oral communication, 1981).

5. Paṇ-chen S̄ö-nam-drak-b̄a gives these three as Little Virtue (*dge chung*), Limitless Virtue (*tshad med dge*), and Vast Virtue (*dge rgyas*; see page 174). Nga-w̄ang-b̄el-den's *Annotations* (section on beings and realms, 88a.4) explains that the Sanskrit *kuśala* can be translated as either "bliss" (*bde ba*) or "virtue" (*dge ba*). The Sanskrit word *śubha*, in the usual form of these three names, is a synonym of *kuśala*.

6. A Superior (*'phags pa, ārya*) has directly realized emptiness; one becomes a Superior at the time of the path of seeing. Sentient beings who have not yet attained such a realization are called common beings (*so so'i skye bo, pṛthagjana*).

7. Uncontaminated (*zag med, anāsrava*) meditative absorptions are those of a supramundane path leading out of cyclic existence. Contaminated (*zag bcas, sāsrava*) absorptions, such as those of the preparations having the aspect of grossness/peacefulness, do not lead out of cyclic existence.

3. Background to the Concentrations and Formless Absorptions

1. This section gives a brief overview of the topic of the physical bases (*lus rten*) of the concentrations and formless absorptions. "Basis" (*rten, āśraya*) in this context refers to the collection of aggregates (*phung po, skandha*) in dependence upon which the person is designated. In discussions of this topic, the term "physical basis" is used loosely to refer to beings of all three realms even though beings of the Formless Realm do not have a form aggregate (*gzugs kyi phung po, rūpaskandha*) and, therefore, do not have bodies.

2. Gedün Lodrö gives a somewhat different opinion. According to him, the six types of gods of the Desire Realm are divided into those who depend on the earth and those who are in the sky. Those who depend on the earth—those of the Four Great Royal Lineages and the Thirty-three (see page 41)—can generate the concentrations and formless absorptions, but those who are in the sky cannot, since they cannot see the faults of the Desire Realm (Gedün Lodrö,

Walking through Walls, p. 54).

3. Gedün Lodrö states that although the neuter, eunuchs, and the androgynous cannot newly attain calm abiding, someone who had previously attained calm abiding or any of the concentrations or formless absorptions and later fell into one of these categories through accident or illness would not necessarily lose his or her previous attainment. Some people would be able to use their previous understanding to hold on to their attainment, but if the accident were strong, the attainment could be lost (ibid., p. 54).

4. To the list of humans who cannot generate calm abiding, Gedün Lodrö adds the insane and those whose minds are overcome by poison (ibid., pp. 47, 52).

5. This section summarizes topics concerning the relationship between calm abiding and special insight: the benefits of cultivating each, the need for cultivating both, and the order in which they are cultivated.

6. Śāntideva, *Engaging in the Bodhisattva Deeds* (*bodhi*[*sattva*]*caryāvatāra*), 9:1, Vidhushekara Bhattacharya, ed., *Bodhicaryāvatāra*, Bibliotheca Indica, vol. 280 (Calcutta: The Asiatic Society, 1960), p. 185.

7. Āryadeva, *Four Hundred* (*catuḥśataka, bstan bcos bzhi brgya*), 6:10 (P5246, vol. 95); cited in Gedün Lodrö, *Walking through Walls*, p. 207.

4. Calm Abiding

1. According to Gedün Lodrö, the Ge-luk-b̄as' way of presenting the cultivation of calm abiding combines the two major presentations of their Indian sources. One is that of the abandonment of the five faults by means of the eight antidotes, from Maitreya's *Differentiation of the Middle and the Extremes* (*madhyāntavibhaṅga, dbus dang mtha' rnam par 'byed pa*). The other is that of the nine mental abidings from Asaṅga's *Grounds of Hearers* (*śrāvakabhūmi, nyan sa*) and *Compendium of Manifest Knowledge* (*abhidharmasamuccaya, mngon pa kun btus*) and Maitreya's *Ornament for the Mahāyāna Sūtras* (*mahāyānasūtrālaṃkāra, theg pa chen po'i mdo sde'i rgyan*). Along with the nine mental abidings, Asaṅga sets forth the six powers and the four mental engagements. The two systems were combined by the textual (*gzhung pa pa*) lineage of the Ḡa-dam-b̄a (*dka' gdams pa*) school, which derives from Atīśa (Gedün Lodrö, *Walking through Walls*, pp. 93–94, 360).

2. The second way of reflecting on the faults of distraction appears to be a paraphrase of Śāntideva, *Engaging in the Bodhisattva Deeds*, 5:15–17 (Vidhushekara Bhattacharya, ed., *Bodhicaryāvatāra*, Bibliotheca Indica, vol. 280, p. 56).

3. Gedün Lodrö lists the three types of laziness as the laziness of neutral activities (*snyoms las kyi le lo*), the laziness that is an attachment to bad activities (*bya ba ngan zhen gyi le lo*), and the laziness of losing affinity (*sgyid lugs pa'i le lo*). The third is the laziness of inferiority. According to Gedün Lodrö, the first type of laziness is the worst because, since the activities involved are not non-virtuous, it is the hardest to identify (Gedün Lodrö, *Walking through Walls*, pp. 165–67).

4. According to Gedün Lodrö, it is better at the beginning to see the whole object of observation in a coarse way than to see part of it in great detail and the rest not at all (ibid., pp. 142–43).

5. According to Gedün Lodrö, the meditator is not so much keeping the mind on the object as putting it there (ibid., p. 191).

6. Gedün Lodrö explains the five faults and the eight antidotes in a different order. Instead of presenting all of them in relation to the first mental abiding, as Lati Rinbochay does, he presents them at the point at which they become overriding faults. In the first three mental abidings, the overriding faults are laziness and forgetting the instruction, although laxity and excitement also occur. In the fourth, fifth, and sixth mental abidings, the meditator deals primarily with laxity and excitement. The mind goes from one to the other, with the changes gradually becoming less extreme. In the last three mental abidings, the meditator gradually approaches equilibrium (ibid., pp. 165, 169, 173–74, 180, 186, 191–93).

   According to Denma Lochö Rinbochay, the meditator gauges progress through the appearance and correction of these faults (meditation classes, 1978).

7. Asaṅga, *Compendium of Manifest Knowledge* (*abhidharmasamuccaya, mngon pa kun btus*). Walpola Rahula, trans., *Le Compendium de la super-doctrine (philosophie) (Abhidharmasamuccaya) d'Asaṅga* (Paris: École française d'extrême-orient, 1971), p. 8; P5550, vol. 112, 238.3.8.

8. According to Gedün Lodrö, lethargy accompanies all non-virtuous minds, even excitement, whereas laxity results from the mind's turning inward too much and, therefore, occurs only during the cultivation of meditative stabilization. Thus, it is necessary for a meditator to study beforehand to learn its characteristics (Gedün Lodrö, *Walking through Walls*, pp. 179–80, 175).

9. Gedün Lodrö distinguishes among four relevant terms: 1) the factor of stability (*gnas cha*); 2) the factor of subjective clarity (*dvang cha*); 3) the factor of clarity (*gsal cha*), in which both the subject and object have to be clear; and 4) intensity (*ngar*); (ibid., p. 177).

10. D̄zong-ka-b̄a explains the Great Seal as "the indivisibility of wisdom and method" (Tsong-ka-pa, *Tantra in Tibet: The Great Exposition of Secret Mantra*, trans. and ed. by Jeffrey Hopkins [London: George Allen & Unwin, 1977], pp. 146, 240). The term is most familiar as the name of a meditation technique taught especially in the S̄a-ḡya (*sa skya*) and Ḡa-gyu (*bka' brgyud*) traditions of Tibetan Buddhism. S̄a-ḡya Paṇḍita, and Lati Rinbochay, warn emphatically against the misuse of this technique.

    It is difficult to see how the position that mistaking subtle laxity for meditative stabilization during cultivation of the Great Seal will cause rebirth as an animal can be taken literally, since laxity is neutral at worst but not non-virtuous, whereas the cause of being reborn in a bad transmigration (including that of animals) is a non-virtuous action. The argument seems to be based on analogy, since mistaking subtle laxity for meditative stabilization can produce, in this lifetime, an animal-like mental condition of forgetfulness and lack of clarity. The implication seems to be that, even if subtle laxity is not non-virtuous and does not *directly* cause rebirth as an animal, the animal-like mental condition produced by it will eventually lead to the type of non-virtuous action that causes such rebirth.

11. Discursiveness (*rnam rtog, vikalpa*) can also be translated as "coarse conceptuality." Although Asaṅga also uses the term *vitarka* in this connection (Asaṅga, *Grounds of Hearers* [*śrāvakabhūmi, nyan* sa], Tibetan Sanskrit Works Series, vol. 14: *Śrāvakabhūmi,* ed. by Karunesha Shukla [Patna: K. P. Jayaswal Research Institute, 1973], p. 364), *vitarka* in this sense is to be distinguished from the investigation (*rtog pa, vitarka*) that is a branch of the first concentration.

12. Gedün Lodrö explains that giving up the object of observation means loosening the mode of apprehension of the original object of observation, considering the new object of observation until laxity has been overcome, and then again tightening the mode of apprehension of the original object of observation (Gedün Lodrö, *Walking through Walls,* pp. 186–87).

13. Jeffrey Hopkins (in conversation) reports that some Tibetan scholars equate Pa-dam-b̄a-sang-gyay with Bodhidharma.

14. A Stream Enterer is one of the eight Approachers and Abiders. For a discussion of these, see pages 143–44.

15. *Oṃ maṇi padme hūṃ* is the mantra of the Bodhisattva Avalokiteśvara (*spyan ras gzigs*), who embodies the compassion of all the Buddhas.

16. Gedün Lodrö holds the contrary opinion but says that there is no clear explanation of this point. According to him, laziness would not exist in the seventh mental abiding because the meditator has the power of effort and because the powers of mindfulness and introspection have already matured: "if one were to generate laziness, this would mean that one could not notice it with mindfulness" (Gedün Lodrö, *Walking through Walls,* p. 189).

17. Nāgārjuna, *The Precious Garland of Advice for the King* (*Rājaparikathā-ratnāvalī*), stanzas 240–54, in Nāgārjuna and Kaysang Gyatso, Seventh Dalai Lama, *The Precious Garland and The Song of the Four Mindfulnesses,* trans. and ed. by Jeffrey Hopkins and Lati Rinpoche (New York: Harper and Row, 1975), pp. 53–55. Michael Hahn, ed. *Nāgārjuna's Ratnāvalī. Vol. 1, The Basic Texts* (Bonn: Indica et Tibetica Verlag, 1982), 3:50–64, pp. 81–84.

18. Lati Rinbochay gave these lectures in the fall of 1976, when the social programs of President Franklin D. Roosevelt's New Deal and President Lyndon B. Johnson's Great Society were still in effect.

19. According to Harvey Aronson (oral communication), Ge-luk-b̄a practice is strikingly different in this respect from Theravāda insight (Pāli, *vipassanā*) meditation, in which long sessions in retreats lasting at least ten days are suggested for beginners in order to establish a pattern of mindfulness (Pāli, *sati*).

20. In his introduction to *Tantra in Tibet* (p. 22), His Holiness Tenzin Gyatso, the Fourteenth Dalai Lama, explains "vajra" as follows:

A 'vajra' is the best of stones, a diamond; there are external symbolic vajras, as in the case of the vajra and bell used in ritual, and there are vajras that are the meanings symbolised. With respect to the latter, a vajra common to all four sets of tantras is an undifferentiability in one entity of method and wisdom.

21. The swastika (*svāstika*) is an ancient Indian symbol of auspiciousness. It should in no way be misunderstood as signifying the swastika used by the Nazi regime.

22. The vajra posture is commonly known in the West as the lotus posture.

23. Mar-b̄a (*mar pa*) was the teacher of the eleventh-century Tibetan yogi Mi-la-re-b̄a (*mi la ras pa*).

24. Tārā (*sgrol ma*) is a female Bodhisattva associated with the Bodhisattva Avalokiteśvara.

25. Although Lati Rinbochay warns against using one's own mind as the object of observation because of errors likely to be incurred in this type of practice, the meditator's own mind is the main object of observation mentioned in the *Sūtra Unraveling the Thought* (*saṃdhinirmocana, dgongs pa nges par 'grel pa'i mdo*); it is mentioned in one of Paṇ-chen S̄ö-nam-drak-b̄a's citations from that text (see pages 148 and 151). For a more favorable description of this type of meditation, with brief instructions for practice, see the His Holiness Tenzin Gyatso, the Fourteenth Dalai Lama, "Meditation," in *Kindness, Clarity, and Insight,* trans. and ed. by Jeffrey Hopkins (Ithaca, NY: Snow Lion, 1984), pp. 68–70. A Tibetan Lhaso Apso is a species of dog.

26. In the terms "analytical image" (*rnam par rtog pa dang bcas pa'i gzugs brnyan, savikalpakapratibimba*) and "non-analytical image" (*rnam par mi rtog pa'i gzugs brnyan, nirvikalpakapratibimba*), *savikalpaka* (*rnam par rtog pa dang bcas pa*) literally means "conceptual" and *nirvikalpaka* (*rnam par mi rtog pa*), "non-conceptual." In this context, "conceptual" means "analytical"; the Tibetan word *rnam par rtog pa* has both meanings, and "analytical" is the sense of *vikalpaka* in both terms. *Pratibimba* (*gzugs brnyan*) literally means "reflection"—a reflection in a mirror. In this context, it is the likeness of the object appearing to the mind.

    According to Gedün Lodrö, a non-analytical image is posited according to the way in which calm abiding observes its object and an analytical image, according to the way in which special insight observes its object. "Calm abiding is non-analytical in the sense that it does not analyze the mode (or final nature) of phenomena"—that is, their emptiness. An analytical image "involves special insight analyzing the mode" (Gedün Lodrö, *Walking through Walls,* p. 83).

27. Gedün Lodrö distinguishes among various ways in which meditators recognize a predominant afflictive emotion. Some people can recognize their predominant afflictive emotion as soon as they hear the list. For others, it appears clearly during the course of meditation. In still other cases, the meditator experiences only an inability to progress but cannot recognize the predominant afflictive emotion and has to ask his or her teacher. Usually, problems relating to a predominant afflictive emotion occur during the third mental abiding, and the meditator finds it impossible to progress to the fourth. Occasionally, however, a practitioner can progress

through all nine mental abidings without being able to attain calm abiding (ibid., pp. 71–75, 151, 170–73).

28. According to Gedün Lodrö, "There is another interpretation of the fourth type of desire." It can also be understood as "the desire for another's 'good nature.'" He explains:

> This is a broad term: it refers to a person's favorable disposition or good mind but may also include the fact that [the person] is served and respected by others. Even though another person may lack those qualities which would lead us to favor [his or her] color or shape, or to desire physical contact…, [he or she] may still have a good nature which we covet. While the first three types of desire are for external objects, the last is for an internal one.

The antidote is still meditation on an unmoving corpse, since a corpse has neither good nature not bad.

Gedün Lodrö adds that in texts on monastic discipline (*'dul ba, vinaya*) the fourth type of desire is to be understood as copulation, whereas, in the First Dalai Lama's *Path of Liberation*, "it should be understood as good nature." Harvey B. Aronson notes further that the Sanskrit word *upacāra* is translated as *bsnyen bkur* ('copulation') in Vasubandhu's *Autocommentary on the "Treasury of Manifest Knowledge"* but as *rnyed bkur* ('good nature') in the First Dalai Lama's *Path of Liberation* (Harvey B. Aronson, trans. and ed., "The Buddhist Path: A Translation of the Sixth Chapter of the First Dalai Lama's *Path of Liberation*," *Tibet Journal* 5:4 [1980], 35, 47).

A general antidote to all forms of desire is meditation on the skeleton; according Gedün Lodrö, it is the best antidote. It is set forth in Vasubandhu's *Treasury of Manifest Knowledge*, 6:9–11 and Vasubandhu's autocommentary on those verses (ibid., pp. 34–36, and Gedün Lodrö, *Walking through Walls*, pp. 98–99).

29. Gedün Lodrö points out that "When love is used as a means for developing calm abiding, there is no definiteness that the meditator will generate love . . . in his or her continuum," since the purpose of using love as an object of observation for purifying behavior is not to generate love but, rather, to reduce the predominant afflictive emotion of hatred. Thus, it is possible that, when hatred has been sufficiently diminished, the meditator may return to the original object of observation—for instance, the body of a Buddha (Gedün Lodrö, *Walking through Walls*, p. 107).

30. Nāgārjuna, *Precious Garland*, trans. Hopkins, stanza 283, p. 59; ed. Hahn, 3:83, p. 88.

31. Ibid., trans. Hopkins, stanzas 284–85, p. 59l; ed. Hahn, 3:84–85, p. 88. The division into eight is not clear, either from the text or, according to Hopkins, from Gyel-tsap's (*rgyal tshab*, 1364–1432) commentary on it. Hopkins suggests (1) the friendliness of gods; (2) the friendliness of humans; (3) protection by non-humans; (4) pleasures of the mind; (5) pleasures of the body; (6) non-harming by poisons and weapons; (7) effortless attainment of one's aims; (8) rebirth in the world of Brahmā (oral communication).

32. The twelve-membered dependent-arising is not an object for purifying behavior but, rather, one of the skillful objects of observation (see pages 80–82).

33. Gedün Lodrö suggests another way in which this meditation overcomes pride: it not only generates a sense of unpleasantness with respect to the body, as Lati Rinbochay states; it also shows us how little we know about it, since, "if we look at the way the body is formed and divide it into smaller and smaller parts, it is impossible to identify everything that is there" (Gedün Lodrö, *Walking through Walls,* p. 112).

    This meditation may be hard for Westerners to understand because the categories are unfamiliar; yet if we think about our bodies in Western biological terms, we also develop a sense of unpleasantness—with regard to our digestive secretions, for example—and find out how little we know.

5. *The Four Concentrations*

1. According to Gedün Lodrö (Gedün Lodrö, *Walking through Walls,* p. 304), this preparation "is not explicitly mentioned in Asaṅga's *Grounds of Hearers*...but it can be established by reasoning." Asaṅga's *Grounds of Hearers* refers, however, to a beginner at mental contemplation (*yid la byed pa las dang po pa, manaskārādikarmika*). The passage is cited by Paṇ-chen S̄ö-nam-drak-b̄a (see page 132).

2. The translation of *zhi rags*—"grossness/peacefulness" rather than "grossness and peacefulness"—reflects Jam-ȳang-shay-b̄a's position that *zhi rags* cannot mean "grossness *and* peacefulness" because the two aspects cannot occur simultaneously in the same consciousness (Jam-ȳang-shay-b̄a, *Great Exposition of the Concentrations and Formless Absorptions,* 231.3–6). The literal translation of *zhi rags* is "peacefulness/grossness." As in the Sanskrit and Tibetan of "joy-withdrawal," the order is reversed for reasons of euphony (see page 100 and note 5 below).

3. For Paṇ-chen S̄ö-nam-drak-b̄a's and Denma Lochö Rinbochay's discussion of the degree to which reflection on the grossness of the Desire Realm and the peacefulness of the First Concentration is a mixture of hearing and thinking, see pages 132–34.

4. The six investigations are: meaning (*don, artha*), things (*dngos po, vastu*), character (*mtshan nyid, lakṣaṇa*), class (*phyogs, pakṣa*), time (*dus, kāla*), and reasoning (*rigs pa, yukti*). They are explained by Denma Lochö Rinbochay, pages 136–37

5. The Tibetan *dga' ba sdud pa* is a translation of the Sanskrit *ratisaṃgrāhaka,* in which the order is also "joy-withdrawal." According to Jam-ȳang-shay-b̄a's explanation, "withdrawal/joy," like "grossness/peacefulness," reflects the order of cultivation. However, the literal translation is retained here to make it clear that Jam-ȳang-shay-b̄a's Tibetan gloss (see note 6 below) is an interpretation and not the term itself.

6. Like Lati Rinbochay, Jam-ȳang-shay-b̄a explains "withdrawal" as referring to the uninterrupted paths and "joy," to the paths of release. Arguing that these two

are mutually exclusive and cannot occur in a single consciousness at the same time, he glosses the name of this mental contemplation as "the mental contemplation of *either* joy or withdrawal" (*dga' sdud* ci rigs *kyi yid byed*—emphasis added); (Jam-ȳang-shay-b̄a, *Great Exposition of the Concentrations and Formless Absorptions,* 217.2–219.2, 229.1, 232.1–2).

7. These etymologies are given by Jam-ȳang-shay-b̄a (*Great Exposition of the Concentrations and Formless Absorptions,* 319.1–320.3). According to him, *samāpatti* is derived from *sama* ("equal") and *pad,* meaning "go"—that is, "to enter into that" (Tibetan, *der 'jug pa*) or "to go into that" (Tibetan, *der 'gro ba*). According to Jeffrey Hopkins (oral communication), *'jug* is causative here and is the equivalent of *'jug par byed pa*—"to cause them to enter [into equality]." Jam-ȳang-shay-b̄a does not explain how the two are combined and does not account for the long *ā.*

   Monier-Williams (*Sanskrit-English Dictionary,* p. 1161) gives the basic sense of *samāpatti* as "coming together, meeting, . . . falling into any state or condition," from *sam-ā-pad,* "to fall upon,...to fall into any state or condition, attain to..."

8. This contextual etymology of *dhyāna,* formed by adding letters to the original word, is given by Jam-ȳang-shay-b̄a (*Great Exposition of the Concentrations and Formless Absorptions,* 318.4–319.4), who cites Maitreya's *Ornament for the Mahāyāna Sūtras* and Sthiramati's commentary on it as his Indian sources. He traces *dhyāna* to the verbal root *dhyai,* "to contemplate"; this derivation agrees with that of Monier Williams (*Sanskrit-English Dictionary,* p. 521).

9. Gedün Lodrö holds that resultant-birth meditative absorptions would not have an uncontaminated type (Gedün Lodrö, *Walking through Walls,* p. 353).

10. In this section and throughout the book, the form realm resultant-birth is indicated by capital letters, e.g., First Concentration, and the corresponding meditative state is indicated by lower case letters, i.e., first concentration.

11. According to Ganden Tri Rinbochay, the first concentration is not the first preparation for the second concentration (oral communication, 1981).

6. The Four Formless Absorptions

1. Although Lati Rinbochay here identifies "the main meditative activity" of the concentrations as analytical meditation, Vasubandhu's *Autocommentary on the "Treasury of Manifest Knowledge"* asserts merely that they are a balance of calm abiding and special insight (Vasubandhu, *Autocommentary on the "Treasury of Manifest Knowledge,"* 8.1e [P5591, vol. 115, 270.4.3; Shastri, part 4, p. 1126; La Vallée Poussin, 16:5, p. 131; Pruden, vol. 4, p. 1218]). In the Theravāda commentarial tradition, however, the concentrations (Pāli, *jhāna;* usually translated "absorption" in Theravāda contexts) are not considered to involve analysis. Rather, they are a development of what is translated here as "meditative stabilization" and in Theravāda contexts as "concentration" (*samādhi;* Buddhaghosa, *The Path of Purification,* trans. by Bikkhu Ñyāṇamoli [Berkeley and London:

Shambhala, 1976], vol. 1, p. 85) and are equated with calm abiding (*śamatha;* Pāli, *samatha;* ibid., p. 88). According to Harvey B. Aronson (oral communication), what is here called calm abiding appears to correspond to access concentration (Pāli, *upacāra*), and absorption (Pāli, *jhāna*) is seen as a deepening of that state.

2. "Existence" (*srid pa, bhava*) here refers to cyclic existence (*'khor ba, saṃsāra*).

7. Preparations Having the Aspect of the Truths

1. Here Lati Rinbochay follows the explanation of Vasubandhu's *Autocommentary on the "Treasury of Manifest Knowledge,"* 6:2 (P5591, vol. 115, 241.3.7–8; Shastri, part 3, p. 874–75; La Vallée Poussin 16:3, pp. 123–24; Pruden, vol. 3, p. 898). For an etymology of "noble truth" (*'phags pa'i bden pa, āryasatya*) according to the Prāsangika-Mādhyamika school of tenets, see Hopkins, *Meditation on Emptiness,* pp. 291–92.
2. See pages 143–44.

Part Two: Denma Lochö Rinbochay's Oral Commentary on Paṇ-chen Sö'-nam-drak-ba's "Explanation of the Concentrations and Formless Absorptions" From his *General meaning of (Maitreya's) "Ornament for Clear Realization"*

1. The Explanation of the Concentrations

1. At this point, the text gives a partial outline of the contents; this outline has been used to supply the headings. Headings in brackets have been supplied by the translator.
2. Numbers in brackets refer to the page numbers of Paṇ-chen Sö-nam-drak-ba's text.
3. See Lati Rinbochay's discussion of the mental contemplation of individual knowledge of the character on pages 85-92 and Denma Lochö Rinbochay's definition on page 130.
4. Asaṅga, *Grounds of Hearers,* Tibetan Sanskrit Works Series, vol. 14, p. 439; P5537, vol. 110, 115.3.5–7.
5. Maitreya, *Ornament for the Mahāyāna Sūtras,* 14:14–15: P5521, vol. 108, 10.5.5–6; *Mahāyāna-sūtrālaṅkāra of Asaṅga,* ed. S. Bagchi, Buddhist Sanskrit Texts, no. 13 (Dharbhanga: Mithila Institute), pp. 89–90.
6. Asaṅga, *Grounds of Hearers,* Tibetan Sanskrit Works Series, p. 284. P5537, vol. 110, 88.1.4 6.
7. "Grossness," 151b.6, reading *rags pa* for *rogs pa.*

8. Asaṅga, *Grounds of Hearers.* P5537, vol. 110, 116.3.3–7 has *mnyam par bshag pa'i sa pa'i yid la byed pa,* "a mental contemplation of a level of equipoise," as well as other, less significant differences from the text quoted by Paṇ-chen Sö-nam-drak-ba. The only extant Sanskrit manuscript lacks the crucial phrase altogether (Tibetan Sanskrit Works Series, vol. 14, p. 439).

9. Paṇ-chen Sö-nam-drak-ba considers the "non-" of "non-equipoise," in the version of the text cited by the other party in the debate, to be a textual corruption.

10. Yaśomitra (also known as Jinaputra [*rgyal ba'i sras*]), *Commentary on (Asaṅga's) "Compendium of Manifest Knowledge,"* P5554, vol. 113, 113.1.6–7, reads *mnyam par bzhag pa'i sa pa'i yid la byed pa gang gi 'dod pa rnams la nyes dmigs la sogs par lta bas rags pa'i mtshan nyid rab tu rig pa ste/ de med pa'i phyir bsam gtan dang po la zhi ba'i mtshan nyid do // 'di ni mtshan nyid rab tu rig pa'i yid la byed pa zhes bya ste/ de ni thos pa dang sems pa dang 'dres par rig par bya'o /* whereas the text quoted by Paṇ-chen Sö-nam-drak-ba reads *mnyam par bzhag pa'i sa pa'i yid la byed pa dag gis 'dod pa rnams la nyes dmigs la sogs par lta bas/ rags pa'i mtshan nyid du rig par byed pa de med pa'i phyir bsam gtan dang po la zhi ba'i mtshan nyid de yid la byed pa zhes bya ste/ de ni thos pa dang bsam pa 'dres mar rig par bya'o.*

11. Ibid. The last sentence also occurs in Asaṅga's *Grounds of Hearers,* P5537, vol. 110, 116.3.7.

12. Here and throughout most of this text, the word "definition" has been used to translate *'jog byed* (literally "positor") rather than the more usual *mtshan nyid* ("definition"). The two terms are mutually inclusive (*don gcig*).

13. According to Jam-yang-shay-ba's *Great Exposition of the Concentrations and Formless Absorptions* (227.2), although there are six preparations for the first concentration which are purifiers of the afflictive emotions, only the first, the mental contemplation of individual knowledge of the character, is a beginner at purifying the afflictive emotions. See also Gedün Lodrö, *Walking through Walls,* pp. 305, 308.

14. Vasubandhu, *Treasury of Manifest Knowledge,* 6:48a–b (P5591, vol. 115, 253.2.4, 6; Shastri, part 3, p. 976; La Vallée Poussin 16:3, pp. 237–38; Pruden, vol. 3, pp. 988–89).

15. According to Jam-yang-shay-ba's understanding of the Vaibhāṣika position, "that concentration which has conquered over the three levels" is the third concentration rather than the fourth, as Paṇ-chen Sö-nam-drak-ba and Denma Lochö Rinbochay say; the three levels over which it has conquered are the first three of the nine levels—that is, the Desire Realm and the First and Second Concentrations. To support his position that "that concentration which has conquered over the three levels" is the third concentration, Jam-yang-shay-ba (*Great Exposition of the Concentrations and Formless Absorptions,* 252.7) cites Vasubandhu's *Autocommentary on the "Treasury of Manifest Knowledge"* [6:48a–b]:

> The levels of birth are nine in all: the Desire Realm and the eight concentrations and formless absorptions. That which has conquered over three

levels by freedom from attachment to [levels] up to the second concentration is generated as the last path of release as either a preparation or an actual [absorption] (P5591, vol. 115, 253.2.4; Shastri, part 3, p. 976; La Vallée Poussin 16:3, p. 237; Pruden, vol. 3, pp. 988–89).

16. Vasubandhu, *Treasury of Manifest Knowledge,* 8:22a–b (P5591, vol. 115, 274.5.2; Shastri, part 4, p. 1161; La Vallée Poussin, 16:5, p. 178; Pruden, vol. 4, p. 1253).

17. For discussions of pure concentrations and absorptions, see pages 106–107 and 159–161.

18. Denma Lochö Rinbochay also gives as an example of reasoning of dependence in terms of cause the consideration that the achievement of calm abiding depends upon the achievement of its prerequisites.

19. Other examples of reasoning of the performance of function given by Denma Lochö Rinbochay are that calm abiding performs the activity of placing the mind one-pointedly on an object and that special insight performs the function of analyzing phenomena.

20. Vasubandhu, *Treasury of Manifest Knowledge,* 6:1c (P5591, vol. 115, 241.1.2; Shastri, part 3, p. 871; La Vallée Poussin, 16:3, p. 119; Pruden, vol. 3, p. 895).

21. Ibid., 6:49a–b (P5591, vol. 115, 253.3.33; Shastri, part 3, p. 977; La Vallée Poussin, 16:4, pp. 238–391; Pruden, vol. 3, pp. 990).

22. This point is explained in a section of Paṇ-chen S̄ö-nam-drak-b̄a's *General Meaning of (Maitreya's) "Ornament for Clear Realization"* not translated here and in Denma Lochö Rinbochay's oral commentary, page140.

23. Asaṅga, *Compendium of Manifest Knowledge,* P5550, vol. 112, 261.2.3; Rahula, trans., *Le Compendium de la super-doctrine,* p. 112.

24. The Hīnayāna Manifest Knowledge (*chos mngon pa, abhidharma*) is Vasubandhu's *Treasury of Manifest Knowledge* (*abhidharmakośa, chos mngon pa'i mdzod*). The Mahāyāna Knowledge is Asaṅga's *Compendium of Manifest Knowledge* (*abhidharmasamuccaya, mngon pa kun btus*).

25. The basis, or support, of a sentient being consists of the aggregates that are its basis of designation. For Desire and Form Realm beings, these are physical and mental aggregates (or, loosely, body and mind). For a Formless Realm being, however, the basis consists entirely of the mental aggregates, since Formless Realm beings do not have bodies.

26. See page 124. For a fuller presentation, see Sopa and Hopkins, *Cutting through Appearances: The Practice and Theory of Tibetan Buddhism,* pp. 212–14.

27. Gedün Lodrö holds a different opinion. According to him,

> most persons attain the path of seeing using the fourth concentration as their mental basis... Because this must serve as the mental basis for the consciousness that is realizing emptiness for the first time—and thus is for the first time acting as an actual antidote—it must be the best of mental bases. The fourth concentration is the best of mental bases. (Gedün Lodrö, Walking through Walls, p. 324).

The fourth concentration is the best of mental bases because it "is free from the eight faults, such as the fluctuations of bliss."

Gedün Lodrö adds that it is also possible to attain the path of seeing on the basis of the not-unable preparation for the first concentration and that there are Hīnayānists—notably, Stream Enterers who proceed in a simultaneous manner—who do so. However, although it is possible to abandon the afflictive obstructions on the basis of the not-unable preparation, it is not possible to abandon even the artificial obstructions to omniscience, which are abandoned on the Mahāyāna path of seeing, on that basis; to abandon the latter, an actual concentration is necessary. All four concentrations will be attained at the time of the Mahāyāna path of preparation, and the Mahāyāna path of seeing is attained on the basis of the fourth concentration (ibid., pp. 377–81).

28. Śāntideva, *Engaging in the Bodhisattva Deeds,* 8:4, Vidhushekara Bhattacharya, ed., *Bodhicaryāvatāra,* Bibliotheca Indica, vol. 280, p. 136.

29. Sopa and Hopkins, *Cutting through Appearances: The Practice and Theory of Tibetan Buddhism,* pp. 26–27.

30. Asaṅga, *Compendium of Manifest Knowledge,* P5550, vol. 113, 263.3.3–4; Rahula, trans., *Le Compendium de la super-doctrine,* p. 126.

31. Asaṅga, *Actuality of the Grounds,* P5536, vol. 109, 283.4.2–3. Asaṅga's *Actuality of the Grounds* is also known as *Grounds of Yogic Practice* (*yogacaryābhūmi, rnal 'jbyor spyod pa'i sa).*

32. See page 51 for Lati Rinbochay's explanation of how special insight can precede calm abiding.

33. Asaṅga, *Compendium of Manifest Knowledge,* P5550, vol. 112, 263.2.8–263.3.1; Rahula, trans., *Le Compendium de la super-doctrine,* p. 126.

34. Étienne Lamotte, trans. and ed., *Saṃdhinirmocanasūtra: L'Explication des mystères* (Louvain: Bibliothèque de l'université, 1935), pp. 90, 211.

35. Maitreya, *Ornament for the Mahāyāna Sūtras,* 14:14–15: P5521, vol. 108, 10.5.5–6; Buddhist Sanskrit Texts, no. 13, pp. 89–90.

36. "Individual analysis," 156a.1, reading *rtog pa* for *rtogs pa.*

37. Maitreya, *Ornament for the Mahāyāna Sūtras,* 14:8: P5521, vol. 108, 10.5.1; Buddhist Sanskrit Texts, no. 13, p. 81.

38. Sopa and Hopkins, *Cutting through Appearances: The Practice and Theory of Tibetan Buddhism,* pp. 176–78.

39. Maitreya, *Ornament for the Mahāyāna Sūtras,* 18:66: P5521, vol. 108, 16.1.6–7; Buddhist Sanskrit Texts, no. 13, p. 140.

40. This appears to be a paraphrase of the discussions of physical and mental pliancy in Sthiramati, *Explanation of (Vasubandhu's) "Commentary on (Maitreya's) 'Ornament for the Mahāyāna Sūtras'"* (*sūtrālaṃkāravṛttibhāṣya, mdo dse'i rgyan gyi 'grel bshad*), P5531, vol. 108, 319.5.1–7 and 320.3.1–6.

41. Lamotte, *Saṃdhinirmocanasūtra,* pp. 90, 211.

42. Dzong-ka-ba, *Great Exposition of the Stages of the Path* (Dharmsala: shes rig par khang, no date), 1059.3.
43. Material in brackets from Denma Lochö Rinbochay's oral commentary.
44. Material in brackets from Denma Lochö Rinbochay's oral commentary.
45. Material in brackets added by the editor.
46. Material in brackets added by the editor.
47. The topic head given in the text at this point is inconsistent with that given on p. 151a.2, "the explanation of the actual [meditative absorption that is a first concentration]." That heading is a division of "the explanation of the first concentration that is a causal meditative absorption."
48. See pages 113, 157, and 165-66.
49. "Abides in the type" (*rigs su gnas pa*) can be used interchangeably with "posited from the point of view of" (*cha nas bzhag pa*)—more loosely, "with qualification"; both mean that there are exceptions.
50. "Second," 157a.6, reading *gnyis pa* for *gsum pa.*

2. The Explanation of the Formless Absorptions

1. See pages 113, and 165-66.

3. Comparisons of the Concentrations and Formless Absorptions

1. "Included within mundane virtues," 158a.4, eading *'jig rten pa'i dge bas bsdus pa* for *'jig rten pa'i dge ba'i bsdus pa.*
2. According to Vasubandhu's *Autocommentary on the "Treasury of Manifest Knowledge"* (6:20a), the path of seeing is called that of definite differentiation (*nges 'byed, nirvedha*) because "by means of it there is abandonment of doubt through differentiating the truths, ranging from 'This is suffering' through 'This is the path'" (P5591, vol. 115, 246.5.3; Shastri, part 3, p. 914; La Vallée Poussin, 16:4, p. 169; Pruden, vol. 3, p. 935). In oral commentary on the First Dalai Lama's commentary on this passage, Kensur Yeshey Tupden says:

   > Among all the objects to be abandoned by the path of seeing, doubt is the most important, for when it is given up, the truths become definite; that is, one has certainty with regard to them. (Harvey B. Aronson, trans. and ed., "The Buddhist Path," [Part Three, unpublished], p. 121.)
3. Vasubandhu, *Treasury of Manifest Knowledge*, 8:17 (P5591, vol. 115, 274.1.4–5; Shastri, part 4, p.1156; La Vallée Poussin, 16:5, p.172; Pruden. vol. 4, p.1247).
4. As Denma Lochö Rinbochay has explained (page 142), the implication of "according to the upper and lower Knowledges" is that "according to the Mādhyamika system there is room for analysis." Lati Rinbochay, following Jam-ȳang-shay-ba, indicates the existence of another system that posits an

uncontaminated form of the actual meditative absorption of the peak of cyclic existence. (See page 115.)

5. Vasubandhu, *Treasury of Manifest Knowledge,* 8:20a–b (P5591, vol. 115, 274.3.8; Shastri, part 4, pp. 1158–59; La Vallée Poussin, 16:5, p. 175; Pruden, vol. 4, p. 1251).

6. Asaṅga, *Compendium of Manifest Knowledge,* P5550, vol. 112, 261.3.5–7; Rahula, trans., *Le Compendium de la super-doctrine,* p. 113.

7. Vasubandhu, *Treasury of Manifest Knowledge* and *Autocommentary on the "Treasury of Manifest Knowledge,"* 8:6b–c (P5591, vol. 115, 271.5.1–4; Shastri, part 4, pp. 1169; La Vallée Poussin, 16:5, pp. 144–46; Pruden, vol. 4, p. 1228). The bracketed material is from Vasubandhu's *Autocommentary* and from the First Dalai Lama's commentary (Varanasi, 1973), 371.1.

8. Asaṅga, *Compendium of Manifest Knowledge,* P5550, vol. 112, 261.1.1–2; Rahula, trans., *Le Compendium de la super-doctrine,* p. 110.

9. Vasubandhu, *Treasury of Manifest Knowledge,* 5.21 (P5591, vol. 115, 227.1.1–2; Shastri, part 3, p. 795–96; La Vallée Poussin, 16:4, p. 43; Pruden, vol. 3, p. 799). The term *nyi 'og ma* (*aparāntika*) is translated here as "western Vaibhāṣikas," an adaptation of Pruden's "Vaibhāṣikas of the West" in volume 4 of *Abhidharmakośabhāṣyam* (see, for example, page p. 1136. See also Das, *Tibetan-English Dictionary,* p. 481.

10. See Denma Lochö Rinbochay's commentary, page 163, concerning the meaning of "bliss" with respect to the fourth concentration and the four formless absorptions.

11. "They are not," 159.b.6, reading *min* for *yin.*

12. Vasubandhu, *Autocommentary on the "Treasury of Manifest Knowledge"* 8:1e (P5591, vol. 115, 270.4.3; Shastri, part 4, p. 1126–28; La Vallée Poussin, 16:5, p. 131; Pruden, vol. 4, p. 1218). The bracketed material is from Yaśomitra's commentary on Vasubandhu's *Autocommentary,* Shastri, part 4, p. 1128.

13. Vasubandhu, *Treasury of Manifest Knowledge,* 8:10a–c (P5591, vol. 115, 273.1.1; Shastri, part 4, p. 1045; La Vallée Poussin, 16:5, p. 160; Pruden, vol. 4, p. 1238).

14. Ibid., 8:7–8 (P5591, vol. 115, 271.5.6–272.1.5; Shastri, part 4, p. 1140; La Vallée Poussin, 16:5, p. 147; Pruden, vol. 4, pp. 1229–30).

15. Ibid., 8:9b–d (P5591, vol. 115, 272.2.2, 272.5.6; Shastri, part 4, 1151–58; La Vallée Poussin, 16:5, pp. 150, 158–60; Pruden, vol. 4, pp. 1231, 1237).

16. "Body," 161a.2, reading *lus* for *las.*

17. Asaṅga, *Grounds of Hearers,* Tibetan Sanskrit Works Series, vol. 14, p. 453; P5537, vol. 110, 118.4.2–3.

18. This may be a paraphrase of Yaśomitra's *Commentary on (Asaṅga's) "Compendium of Manifest Knowledge"* P5554, vol. 113, 106.1.6–106.2.4. Gön-chok-jik-may-wang-bo, *Condensed Statement of (Jam-yang-shay-ba's) "Great*

Exposition of the Concentrations and Formless Absorptions," 598.5–599.1, cites a similar passage from D̄zong-ka-b̄a's *Golden Rosary of Good Explanation* in which D̄zong-ka-b̄a explicitly paraphrases the same passage in Yaśomitra's *Commentary on (Asaṅga's) "Compendium of Manifest Knowledge"* and also points out the agreement between Yaśomitra's explanation and the passage in Asaṅga's *Grounds of Hearers* which Paṇ-chen S̄ö-nam-drak-b̄a cites immediately before the Yaśomitra passage. It is possible that Paṇ-chen S̄ö-nam-drak-b̄a's reference to Yaśomitra is derived from D̄zong-ka-b̄a's even though D̄zong-ka-b̄a is not cited here.

19. Vasubandhu, *Treasury of Manifest Knowledge,* 8:9c (P5591, vol. 115, 272.2.2, 272.5.6; Shastri, part 4, 1151–58; La Vallée Poussin, 16:5, pp. 150, 158–60; Pruden, vol. 4, p. 1236).

20. Asaṅga, *Compendium of Ascertainments,* P5539, vol. 111, 14.2.1.

21. Ibid., P5539, vol. 111, 14.2.3–4.

22. Vasubandhu, *Treasury of Manifest Knowledge,* 8:11a–b (P5591, vol. 115, 273.1.5–6; Shastri, part 4, p. 1150; La Vallée Poussin, 16:5, p. 161; Pruden, vol. 4, p. 1239).

23. "*Treasury of Manifest Knowledge,*" 162a.6, reading *mdzod las* for *brjod de.*

24. Vasubandhu, *Treasury of Manifest Knowledge,* 8.11c–d (P5591, vol. 115, 273.1.6–7; Shastri, part 4, p. 1150; La Vallée Poussin, 16:5, p. 161; Pruden, vol. 4, p. 1239). "The two breaths" are inhalation and exhalation. "The four" are the feeling of pleasure, the feeling of pain, the feeling of feeling of mental discomfort, and the feeling of mental bliss (Vasubandhu, *Autocommentary on the "Treasury of Manifest Knowledge,"* 8:11c–d).

25. Asaṅga, *Compendium of Ascertainments,* P5539, vol. 111, 14.4.8–14.5.1.

26. "Completion," 162b.5, reading *yongs su rdzogs pa* for *yangs su rdzogs pa.*

27. Asaṅga, *Compendium of Ascertainments,* P5539, vol. 111, 14.4.8–14.5.1.

28. Asaṅga, *Compendium of Manifest Knowledge,* P5550, vol. 112, 261.2.1–2; Rahula, trans., *Le Compendium de la super-doctrine,* p. 111. P5550, vol. 112, 261.2.2 reads *de gnyi kyi'* [for *gnyis kyi*] *gnas kyi rang bzhin gyi yan lag,* "the branch that is the nature of the basis of those two," whereas Paṇ-chen S̄ö-nam-drak-b̄a, "Concentrations," 163a.2 reads *de gnyis kyi'* [for *kyi*] *gnas kyi yan lag.*

29. "Pervasive," 163b.5, reading *khyab pa* for *khyad pa.*

30. This work is not indexed in any printed edition of the Tibetan Tripiṭaka.

31. See Part One, Chapter Two, note 5.

32. In the Theravāda tradition, too—although the term "grossness/peacefulness" is not used—the meditator's present level of concentration and the next level to be attained are compared in terms of the branches, so that the inferior branches of the lower level can be relinquished. This mode of progress from one concentration (Pāli, *jhāna*) to the next is given under the heading "mastery in reviewing" (Pāli, *paccavekkhaṇavasī;* Buddhaghosa, *Path of Purification,* vol. 1, pp. 161, 165, 171).

BIBLIOGRAPHY

P = *Tibetan Tripiṭaka,* Peking edition (Tokyo-Kyoto: Tibetan Tripiṭaka Research Foundation, 1956).

1. WORKS IN TIBETAN AND SANSKRIT

Āryadeva (*'phags pa lha,* second–third century C.E.)

Four Hundred

catuḥśataka

bstan bcos bzhi brgya

P5246, vol. 95

Edited Tibetan and Sanskrit fragments along with English translation: Karen Lang. *Āryadeva's Catuḥśataka: On the Bodhisattva's Cultivation of Merit and Knowledge.* Indiske Studier VII. Copenhagen: Akademisk Forlag, 1986.

Asaṅga (*thogs med,* fourth century C.E.)

Actuality of the Grounds/Grounds of Yogic Practice

bhūmivastu/yogacaryābhūmi

sa'i dngos gzhi/rnal 'jor spyod pa'i sa

P5536–8, vol.109–110

Compendium of Ascertainments

nirṇayasamgrahaṇī/viniścayasamgraha

gtan la dbab pa bsdu ba

P5539, vol. 110–111

Compendium of Manifest Knowledge

abhidharmasamuccaya

mngon pa kun btus

P5550, vol. 112

Sanskrit text: *Abhidharma Samuccaya of Asaṅga.* Pralhad Pradhan, ed. Visva-Bharati Series, vol. 12. Santiniketan: Visva-Bharati, 1950.

French translation: Walpola Rahula, trans. *Le Compendium de la super-doctrine (philosophie) (Abhidharmasamuccaya) d'Asaṅga.* Paris: École française d'extrême-orient, 1971.

Grounds of Hearers

śrāvakabhūmi

nyan sa

P5537, vol. 110

Sanskrit text: *Śrāvakabhūmi.* Karunesha Shukla, ed. Tibetan Sanskrit Works Series, vol. 14. Patna: K. P. Jayaswal Research Institute, 1973.

Also: Wayman, Alex. *Analysis of the Śrāvakabhūmi Manuscript.* University of California Publications in Classical Philology, vol. 17. Berkeley and Los Angeles: University of California Press, 1961.

Dzong-ka-ba Lo-sang-drak-ba (*tsong kha pa blo bzang grags pa*, 1357–1419)

Golden Rosary of Good Explanation/Extensive Explanation of (Maitreya's) "Ornament for Clear Realization, Treatise of Quintessential Instructions on the Perfection of Wisdom," As Well As Its Commentaries

legs bshad gser gyi phreng ba/shes rab kyi pha rol tu phyin pa'i man ngag gi bstan bcos mngon par rtogs pa'i rgyan 'grel pa dang bcas pa'i rgya cher bshad pa

P6150, vol. 154

Also: The Collected Works of Rje Tsoṅ-kha-pa Blo-bzaṅ-grags-pa, vol. 25. New Delhi: Ngawang Gelek Demo, 1975ff.

Also: Collected Works, vol. 17. New Delhi: Guru Deva, 1979.

Great Exposition of Secret Mantra

snags rim chen mo/rgyal ba khyab bdag rdo rje 'chang chen po'i lam gyi rim pa gsang ba kun gyi gnad rnam par phye ba

P6210, vol. 161

English translation (chap. 1): By Jeffrey Hopkins. In *Tantra in Tibet: The Great Exposition of Secret Mantra.* The Wisdom of Tibet Series, 3. London: George Allen & Unwin, 1977

Notes on the Concentrations and Formless Absorptions

bsam gzugs zin bris

P6148, vol. 154

Also: modern block print, n.p., n.d.

Also: The Collected Works of Rje Tsoṅ-kha-pa Blo-bzaṅ-grags-pa, vol. 27. New Delhi: Ngawang Gelek Demo, 1975ff.

Also: Collected Works, vol. *tsha.* New Delhi: Guru Deva, 1979.

Fourth Paṇ-chen Lama, Lo-sang-bel-den-den-bay-nyi-ma (*blo bzang dpal ldan bstan pa'i nyi ma,* 1781–1852/4)

Instructions on [Dzong-ka-ba's] "Three Principal Aspects of the Path": Essence of All the Scriptures, Quintessence of Helping Others

lam gyi gtso bo rnam gsum gyi khrid yig/gsung rab kun gyi snying po lam gyi gtso bo rnam pa gsum gyi khrid yig gzhan phan snying po

n.d.

English translation: Sopa, Geshe Lhundup, and Hopkins, Jeffrey. *Cutting through Appearances: The Practice and Theory of Tibetan Buddhism.* Ithaca, NY: Snow Lion, 1989, pp. 41–107.

Also: Geshe Wangyal, trans. *The Door of Liberation: Essential Teachings of the Tibetan Buddhist Tradition.* Boston: Wisdom Publications, 1995, pp. 135–72. First pub. 1973. Republished 1978.

Gön-chok-jik-may-wang-bo (*dkon mchog 'jigs med dbang po,* 1728–91)

Condensed Statement of (Jam-yang-shay-ba's) "Great Exposition of the Concentrations and Formless Absorptions"/An Excellent Vase of Good Explanation Presenting the Concentrations and Formless Absorptions

bsam gzugs chen mo las mdor bsdus te bkod pa bsam gzugs kyi rnam bzhag legs bshad bum bzang

The Collected Works of Dkon-mchog-'jigs-med-dbaṅ-po, the Second 'Jam-dbyans-bzad-pa of La-braṅ Bkra-sis-'khyil; Reproduced from Prints from the Bkra-sis-'khyil Blocks, vol. 6. New Delhi: Ngawang Gelek Demo, 1972.

Presentation of the Grounds and Paths, Beautiful Ornament of the Three Vehicles

sa lam gyi rnam bzhag theg gsum mdzes rgyan

The Collected Works of Dkon-mchog-jigs-med-dbaṅ-po, vol. 7. New Delhi: Ngawang Gelek Demo, 1972.

Also: Buxaduor: Gomang, 1965.

Jam-ȳang-shay-b̄a (*'jam dbyangs bzhad pa*, 1648–1721)

Great Exposition of the Concentrations and Formless Absorptions/Treatise on the Presentations of the Concentrative and Formless Absorptions, Adornment Beautifying the Subduer's Teaching, Ocean of Scripture and Reasoning, Delighting the Fortunate

bsam gzugs chen mo/bsam gzugs kyi snyoms 'jug rnams gyi rnam par bzhag pa'i bstan bcos thub bstan mdzes rgyan lung dang rigs pa'i rgya mtsho skal bzang dga' byed).

Folio printing in India; no publication data.

Also: The Collected Works of 'Jam-dbyans-bzad-pa'i-rdo-rje: Reproduced from Prints from the Bkra-sis-'khyil Blocks, vol. 12. New Delhi: Ngawang Gelek Demo, 1974.

Jinaputra. *See* Yaśomitra

Maitreya (*byams pa*)

Ornament for the Mahāyāna Sūtras

mahāyānasūtrālaṃkārakārikā

theg pa chen po'i mdo sde'i rgyan gyi tshig le'ur byas pa

P5521, vol. 108

Sanskrit text: *Mahāyāna-sūtrālaṅkāra of Asaṅga.* S. Bagchi, ed. Buddhist Sanskrit Texts, no. 13. Dharbhanga: Mithila Institute.

English translation: Maitreyanātha's "Ornament of the Scriptures of the Universal Vehicle." Translation edited by Robert A. F. Thurman. Unpublished.

Nāgārjuna (*glu sgrub*, first–second century C.E.)

The Precious Garland of Advice for the King

rājaparikathāratnāvalī

rgyal po la gtam bya ba rin po che'i phreng ba

P5658, vol. 129

Edited Sanskrit, Tibetan, and Chinese: *Nāgārjuna's Ratnāvalī. Vol. 1, The Basic Texts (Sanskrit, Tibetan, and Chinese)*. Michael Hahn, ed. Bonn: Indica et Tibetica Verlag, 1982

English translation: Jeffrey Hopkins and Lati Rinbochay in Nāgārjuna and Kaysang Gyatso, Seventh Dalai Lama, *The Precious Garland and The Song of the Four Mindfulnesses.* New York: Harper and Row, 1975.

Nga-w̄ang-b̄el-den (*ngag dbang dpal ldan*, b. 1797)
Annotations for (Jam-ȳang-shay-b̄a's) "Great Exposition of Tenets," Freeing the Knots of the Difficult Points, Precious Jewel of Clear Thought
grub mtha' chen mo'i mchan 'grel dka' gnad mdud grol blo gsal gces nor
Sarnath: Pleasure of Elegant Sayings Press, 1964.

Paṇ-chen S̄ö-nam-drak-b̄a (*paṇ chen bsod nams grags pa*, 1478–1554)
General Meaning of (Maitreya's) "Ornament for Clear Realization"/A Good Explanation of the Meaning of (Gyel-tsap's) "Explanation Illuminating the Meaning of (Maitreya's) 'Treatise of Quintessential Instructions on the Perfection of Wisdom, Ornament for Clear Realization,' Together with Its Commentaries, Ornament for the Essence," A Lamp Illuminating the Meaning of the Mother [Perfection of Wisdom Sūtras]
phar phyin spyi don/shes rab kyi pha rol tu phyin pa'i man ngag gi bstan bcos mngon par rtogs pa'i rgyan 'grel pa dang bcas pa'i rnam bshad snying po rgyan gyi don legs par bshad pa yum don gsal ba'i sgron me
Buxaduor: Nang bstan shes rig 'dzin skyong slob gnyer khang, 1963.

Pur-bu-jok (*phur bu lcog byams pa rgya mtsho*, 1825–1901)
Explanation of the Presentation of Objects and Object Possessors as well as Awareness and Knowledge in The Magical Key to the Path of Reasoning, Presentation of the Collected Topics Revealing the Meaning of the Treatises on Prime Cognition
yul yul can dang blo rig gi rnam par bshad pa [located in] tshad ma'i gzhung don 'byed pa'i bsdus grva'i rnam bshag rigs lam 'phrul gyi sde mig
Buxa: n.p., 1965
English translation: Elizabeth Napper. Unpublished

Rājaputra Yaśomitra (*rgyal po'i sras grags pa'i bshes gnyen*)
Explanation of (Vasubandhu's) "Treasury of Manifest Knowledge"
abhidharmakośaṭikā
chos mngon pa'i mdzod 'grel bshad
P5593, vol. 116
Sanskrit text: In *Abhidharmakośa & Bhāṣya of Ācārya Vasubandhu with Sphuṭārtha Commentary of Ācārya Yaśomitra.* Dwarikadas Shastri, ed. Bauddha Bharati Series, no. 5. Varanasi: Bauddha Bharati, 1971.

Śāntideva (*zhi ba lha*, eighth century C.E.)
Engaging in the Bodhisattva Deeds
bodhi[sattva]caryāvatāra
byang chub sems dpa'i spyod pa la 'jug pa
P5272, vol. 99
Sanskrit and Tibetan edition: *Bodhicaryāvatāra.* Vidhushekara Bhattacharya, ed. Bibliotheca Indica, vol. 280. Calcutta: The Asiatic Society, 1960.
English translation: Stephen Batchelor. *A Guide to the Bodhisattva's Way of Life.* Dharamsala: LTWA, 1979. Also: Marion Matics. *Entering the Path of Enlightenment.* New York: Macmillan, 1970.

Contemporary commentary: Geshe Kelsang Gyatso. *Meaningful to Behold.* London: Wisdom, 1980.

Sūtra Unraveling the Thought
saṃdhinirmocanasūtra
dgongs pa nges par 'grel pa'i mdo
P774, vol. 29
Edited Tibetan text (transliterated) and French translation: Étienne Lamotte, trans. and ed. *Saṃdhinirmocanasūtra: L'Explication des mystères.* Louvain: Bibliothèque de l'université, 1935.
English translation: John Powers, *Wisdom of Buddha: The Saṃdhinirmocaṇa Mahāyāna Sūtra.* Berkeley: Dharma Publishing, 1995.

Vasubandhu (*dbyig gnyen*, fl. 360 C.E.)
Treasury of Manifest Knowledge
abhidharmakośakārikā
chos mngon pa'i mdzod kyi tshig le'ur byas pa
P5590, vol. 115
Explanation of the "Treasury of Manifest Knowledge"
abhidharmakośabhāṣya
chos mngon pa'i mdzod kyi bshad pa
P5591, vol. 115
Sanskrit text: *Abhidharmakośa & Bhāṣya of Ācārya Vasubandhu with Sphuṭārtha Commentary of Ācārya Yaśomitra.* Dwarikadas Shastri, ed. Bauddha Bharati Series, no. 5. Varanasi: Bauddha Bharati, 1971.
French translation: Louis de La Vallée Poussin. *L'abhidharmakośa de Vasubandhu.* First pub. Paris: Geuthner, 1923–31. *Mélanges Chinois et Bouddhiques* 16 (reprinted 1971).
English translation: Leo M. Pruden. *Abhidharmakośabhāṣyam by Louis de La Vallée Poussin.* 4 vols. Berkeley: Asian Humanities Press, 1988–90.

Yaśomitra (*grags pa'i bshes gnyen*; indexed in P as Jinaputra [*rgyal ba'i sras*])
Commentary on (Asaṅga's) "Compendium of Manifest Knowledge"
abhidarmakośaṭīkā
chos mngon pa'i 'grel bshad
P5554, vol. 113
See also Rājaputra Yaśomitra

2. Other Works

Aronson, Harvey B., trans., ed., and annotator. "The Buddhist Path: A Translation of the Sixth Chapter of the First Dalai Lama's *Path of Liberation*; The Path of Preparation and The Path Directly Seeing the Truths." Oral commentary by Lati Rinbochay, Ge-shay Gedun Lodrö, and Kensur Yeshay Tupden. Parts 1 and 2, *Tibet Journal*, 5:3 and 5:4 (1980); part 3, unpublished.

Buddhaghosa. *The Visuddhi-Magga of Buddhaghosa.* Rhys Davids, C. A. F., ed. First pub. 1920. London: Pali Text Society: Routledge & Kegan Paul, 1975. English translation: Buddhaghosa, *The Path of Purification (visuddhimagga).* Ñyāṇamoli, trans. 2 vols. Berkeley and London: Shambhala, 1976.

Gyatso, Tenzin, Fourteenth Dalai Lama. *Kindness, Clarity, and Insight.* Ithaca, NY: Snow Lion, 1984.

Hopkins, Jeffrey. *Meditation on Emptiness.* London: Wisdom Publications, 1983.

Klein, Anne Carolyn, trans. and ed. *Path to the Middle: Oral Mādhyamika Philosophy in Tibet; The Oral Scholarship of Kensur Yeshey Tupden.* Albany, NY: State University of New York Press, 1994.

Lodrö, Gedün. *Walking Through Walls: A Presentation of Tibetan Meditation.* Jeffrey Hopkins, trans. and ed. Anne C. Klein and Leah Zahler, co-editors. Ithaca, NY: Snow Lion, 1992.

Sopa, Geshe Lhundup, and Hopkins, Jeffrey. *Cutting through Appearances: The Practice and Theory of Tibetan Buddhism.* Ithaca, NY: Snow Lion, 1989. First pub. as *Practice and Theory of Tibetan Buddhism,* 1976.

Wylie, Turrell. "A Standard System of Tibetan Transcription." *HJAS* 22 (1959), 261–76.

Zwilling, Leonard. "Homosexuality as Seen in Indian Buddhist Texts." *Buddhism, Sexuality, and Gender.* José Ignacio Cabezón, ed. Albany, NY: State University of New York Press, 1992.

INDEX

Tibetan words are indexed under the root letter.

About the Contributors

Lati Rinbochay, a recognized incarnate lama, was Abbot of the S̄har-d̄zay College of the reestablished Gan-den Monastery in Mungod, South India. He was born in 1922 in Kham, the southeastern region of Tibet. At an early age he entered Gan-den Monastery, located in the vicinity of Lhasa, the capital of Tibet. After many years of intensive study, he attained his Ge-s̄hay degree, after which he went on to study at the Tantric College of Upper Lhasa. He presently resides in exile in Dharamsala, India.

Denma Lochö Rinbochay is a recognized incarnate lama of the L̄o-s̄el-l̄ing College of Dre-pung Monastery. Upon receiving the Ge-s̄hay degree from L̄o-s̄el-l̄ing, he entered the Tantric College of Upper Lhasa. A former abbot of the Dalai Lama's Namgyal Monastery, he now resides in exile in Dharamsala, India.

Leah Zahler, editor and annotator of this book, was a poet and scholar who received an M.A. in English literature from Yale University and a Ph.D. in Buddhist Studies from the University of Virginia. She also translated the root text by the second Paṇ-chen Lama in Part Two of this book.

Jeffrey Hopkins, translator of much of this book, is Professor of Tibetan Studies at the University of Virginia. He has acted as the oral interpreter for His Holiness the Dalai Lama on numerous occasions, and his expertise in this area is again demonstrated in the present work. Author or translator of numerous books on Buddhist theory and practice, including *Meditation on Emptiness* and *The Meaning of Life,* Dr. Hopkins is one of the foremost scholars of Tibetan Buddhism in the world today.

Wisdom Publications

Wisdom Publications, a not-for-profit publisher, is dedicated to making available authentic Buddhist works for the benefit of all. We publish translations of the sutras and tantras, commentaries and teachings of past and contemporary Buddhist masters, and original works by the world's leading Buddhist scholars. We publish our titles with the appreciation of Buddhism as a living philosophy and with the special commitment to preserve and transmit important works from all the major Buddhist traditions.

To learn more about Wisdom, or to browse books online, visit our website at wisdompubs.org. You may request a copy of our mail-order catalog online or by writing to:

Wisdom Publications
199 Elm Street
Somerville, Massachusetts 02144 USA
Telephone: (617) 776-7416
Fax: (617) 776-7841
Email: info@wisdompubs.org
www.wisdompubs.org

The Wisdom Trust

As a not-for-profit publisher, Wisdom is dedicated to the publication of fine Dharma books for the benefit of all sentient beings and dependent upon the kindness and generosity of sponsors in order to do so. If you would like to make a donation to Wisdom, please do so through our Somerville office. If you would like to sponsor the publication of a book, please write or email us at the address above.

Thank you.

Wisdom is a nonprofit, charitable 501(c)(3) organization affiliated with the Foundation for the Preservation of the Mahayana Tradition (FPMT).